Roman Catholicism & the Coming One World Religion

FIRST PRINTING

Billy Crone

Cover Design:
CHRIS TAYLOR

To Robert & Mary Tozier.

It only made sense
to dedicate this book
to the both of you.

You know firsthand
the lies, deceit, and errors
of the Roman Catholic religion.

You were there,
saw it all,
tried to reform,
but to no avail.

The so-called Mother Church
will always remain the Harlot.

And so God did
what only God can do.
He saved you
from its horrible clutches
into a real relationship with Him
through our Lord and Savior Jesus Christ.

Thank you for being great friends
to me and my family
and champions of God's truth
working to set the captives free.

Great is your reward in Heaven.
I love you both.

Contents

Preface

If there's one thing in life I think we can all agree upon, it would have to be our universal dislike for "false advertisements." You know, those ads or commercials that say one thing but deliver another, or even promise a certain outcome but turns out to be a big bold-faced lie designed to get you to buy their product just to rip you off of your cash. Now, even though this type of behavior is clearly illegal and we have actual government entities out there that are supposed to prosecute the offenders and protect us consumers from this type of fraud, somehow, someway, these deceptive entities keep getting away with their dishonest tactics every single year. Believe it or not, I can't think of a better way to describe Roman Catholicism. It's pure religious fraud. Not only is it not true Biblical Christianity, but it never has been, nor will it ever be. Yet, this is the constant daily lie foisted upon mankind all around the world. Their "false advertisement" is even played out in the media. You've seen the trickery. Over and over again, no matter what news station, by and large, if the news broadcast or broadcaster wants to bring in a so-called "Christian" perspective to a story, who do they call upon? A Christian Pastor? A strong Evangelical voice? No. Who does the camera pan to next? Invariably it's a Roman Catholic priest or bishop. That's not only an obvious "false advertisement" but it's just as deceptive as if someone said they were going to bring in Jesus but then brought in Buddha. What a scam. What a sham. And so it is with Roman Catholicism. They say they are Christian, they say they have the same means of salvation, they say they have the same Bible, they say they worship the same God, and are just like us, but it's a lie. It appears Roman Catholicism is unfortunately relying upon the age old chicanery of, "If you repeat a lie loud enough, long enough, and often enough, people will believe it. Especially if it's a big lie." Therefore, this book seeks to sound the alarm, provide the real evidence, and unmask one of the biggest ongoing shams and scams in all of history, Roman Catholicism. Here you will discover the long hidden truth of their antithetical teachings to the Bible, their false beliefs, and heretical practices that are so unlike real deal, Biblical Christianity. It's worse than oil and water, and the two cannot, and never will, mix. Oh, one last piece of advice. When you are through reading this book, will you please READ YOUR BIBLE? I mean that in the nicest possible way. Enjoy, and I'm looking forward to seeing you someday!

Billy Crone
Las Vegas, Nevada
2019

Chapter One

Christianity or Cult?

As you've no doubt noticed these days when you watch the news and other shows seeking expert opinions and perspective on religious or moral issues, they interview all the secular people, including secular scientists and university professors. Then they'll say they want to be fair and balanced, so they go to what they label as the Christian perspective. However, nine times out of ten, who is it that they pull in? It's most often a Catholic priest and then oftentimes you'll even hear Christians verbalize that Catholicism is the same as Christianity, even though it is not. So, we're going to begin that journey to discover the difference. We'll look at their own writings, their teachings, their Catechism, their Bible, and their own belief system. As you'll discover, it is not Christianity. This is something we need to get equipped on because we are talking about a huge number of people around our planet who are being duped by this entity called Roman Catholicism.

Christians are wrongly said to be the largest population of the larger religions on the planet. Islam is said to be number two and Hinduism, number three. But when we break down the statistics, we see that their total number of Christians lumps in the Catholics, Mormons, Jehovah's Witnesses, and others. So really, Christianity is not the number one religion on the planet. Roman Catholicism is. However, Roman Catholicism is not Biblical Christianity. That means a lot of people around the world are being duped by this pseudo-Christian cult.

When you look at Judaism, Islam, Eastern religions like Hinduism and Buddhism, along with the U.S. variant of the latter, which is the New Age Movement that is spreading quickly now throughout the entire planet's population, these religions all have one thing in common. We can definitively say they are non-Christian. When you really began to take a look at all these different faiths, there's no way in the world you can make the completely false statement that: *"All religions are basically the same thing."*

When you've done your homework, there is simply no way you can say that all religions have the same core beliefs and that their followers will get to Heaven. If anyone, even in the Church, says that all religions are basically the same, what they just told you is they don't know anything about world religions and they certainly don't know anything about Biblical Christianity. The statement that all religions are basically the same is impossible and one of the craziest things anyone could put forward. So why is it such a popular phrase these days even though it has been proven to be disastrously wrong? We should be able to at least agree that those above are not Christian religions. Now I want to move into an examination of the major pseudo-Christian ("pseudo" meaning fake and false) religions commonly termed as Christian cults.

First, we'll talk about how Roman Catholicism is a cult just like Mormonism, Jehovah's Witnesses, Seventh Day Adventists, and others of that nature. The category of a cult definitely includes Roman Catholicism. As you will discover, Roman Catholicism is a pseudo fake Christian cult. You'll see that as we just deal with the facts. It is easy to demonstrate. I want to give you some evidence but keep in mind that you'll hear statements like:

"That's what they used to believe. Catholics don't follow that anymore. Haven't you heard of the Second Vatican Council? They changed their belief system. You guys are just wacky conspiracy theorists."

No, the Roman Catholic Church did not alter their belief system. What they did change was how inclusive they are. They now want all religions to come together under their umbrella, which means under the Vatican. Even recently I saw this headline:

"Is Roman Catholicism the same thing as Biblical Christianity?"

The answer is that it is not even close. In this chapter alone, we're going to get to seven strikes concerning that comparison. And again, I'm just dealing with current facts. Number one is from a recent headline in a CNN article:

"Pope Francis extends Catholic priests the power to forgive abortion."

Is that Christianity? Is that Biblical? Is that what we as Christians believe? Then how in the world can anyone sit there and make the statement that Roman Catholicism is the same thing as Biblical Christianity? You can't! And this is not a subset or secondary issue like differing versions of the Rapture or something like the spiritual gifts, this is a core issue about how sins get forgiven. This is salvation! You can't get this one wrong! If you sit there and say the Pope has the ability to extend authority and power to other men to forgive sins, I've got a problem with that! Again, I'm just dealing with current facts pointing out that Roman Catholicism is not Biblical Christianity. How can anyone call it that? This part of an article mentions what the Catholic Church is doing:

"A special dispensation was granted for the year of mercy, which gave all priests, rather than just bishops and specially designated confessors, the power to absolve the sin of abortion."

Now what do they mean by absolve? That means this: The Pope is saying these church officials, who are just your average men or women like you and I, now have the power, according to Roman Catholicism, to declare sinners free from blame, free from guilt, and free from responsibility for the sin of murdering a child. Is that Biblical? No! Well, what's going on here then? And why would television and radio interview those guys and say it's the Christian perspective? This is major stuff!

Why did the Pope do that? Because doing so makes it easier to achieve their larger goal. What is that goal? It is one global religion. They want everybody to come under their umbrella just like it was before the Protestant Reformation. Before that time, the Catholic Church controlled both the ecclesiastical and the governmental systems. The same is going to be repeated in the Seven Year Tribulation. As Revelation tells us, the Woman rides the Antichrist Beast. The Woman is a religious harlot. She is Babylon, The Harlot, riding the Antichrist, which has the reigns of the global government. So, who is working together there? It's religion and government. It's going to be repeated.

But even as Christians whose ancestors fought and died to give us freedom of worship, we don't know our history. This domination and the practices they used to oppress populations around the world was what Rome did for many centuries prior to the Protestant Reformation. What were the Protestants protesting? They were protesting the Catholic practices we are about to get into.

Back in those earlier days, Rome had power over the governments. It wasn't just ecclesiastical control, the Catholic Church would hold power over the heads of the governments by decreeing that if those countries would not do what the Catholic Church says, the church would take away their salvation. The church would not allow them to do the sacraments anymore, which according to the Catholic Church would mean those people are then doomed. So Roman Catholicism literally made them grovel. The Catholic Church had control of it all and they've never given up that desire. They want it back.

I'll never forget what I heard on the radio one day when I was pastoring in New York state in a heavily Catholic area. It was an AM Catholic channel and I was curious to listen to what they would talk about. Even though the Protestant Reformation was in the 1500's, guess how the Roman Catholics on that radio program, here in modern days, described you and I. They are still calling us the "Protestant experiment!" And by the way, they're claiming our "experiment" will be ending soon. Actually, we can see signs of that because the Christian Church is, in many ways, turning back to Rome. They call us the Protestant experiment like we are just a small aberration of history and they teach that we'll come back to the mother church. Those are not my words, that's their words.

Have you seen the verbiage they put out in banners, billboards, and literature enticing Christians to, "Come Home?!" Some of it says, "Welcome Home." According to Roman Catholicism, you and I just need to come back to them because we're just rebels involved in an irrational little experiment. However, we Protestants rightly rebelled for good reason! We'll get to that in a minute.

But back to the pope; why is he now allowing these average flawed sinning people to forgive sin? That is full-blown blasphemy! The reason Catholicism is now allowing this is because the new directive makes it easier for women who have had abortions to be absolved for their actions and rejoin the Catholic Church. It's all about getting more in and under the Catholic roof.

That's what it's all about. They now want everyone to be a part their church. Here is the report from CNN:

"Since the first century, the Catholic Church has held that any Catholic, who procures an abortion [who kills a child in an abortion] incurs automatic excommunication and the penalty that only a bishop could lift."

Though it is wrong no matter what man might do, it used to be just the bishops, but now the Pope is going to spread the practice even more by allowing it from priests. That's in case the bishops are busy, right? And lest you think forgiveness of sin by an average man is not really what they mean, Kate D'Annunzio of Rachel's Vineyard said:

"Pope Francis has clarified that now priests have the power to do both; forgive and welcome women back into the church."

So, this is exactly what they mean. The Catholic Church is now saying they're giving authority to even more men to forgive sin. Is that Christianity? It absolutely is not!

"The year of mercy is a long-standing Catholic tradition during which believers may receive indulgences."

Indulgences are something we will spend more time on later but basically, they are special alleviation of Catholic follower's sins. During this season, the Catholic leadership comes up with these new ways that you can get out of the punishment for your sins. Uhmmm, okay! It's all because Roman Catholicism has a different view of sin. Again, we can definitely say that sin is not a secondary issue. It's not like discussing differing views on something like eschatology, which involves Bible prophecy interpretations. It's not debating views on the gifts of the Spirit where Christians disagree about whether all the gifts are functioning today or whether just some are. This idea of forgiving sin is dealing with the core issues of what we believe in. If you get sin wrong, you get eternity wrong!

Part of the reason Catholicism gets it wrong is because they randomly decided to break sin into two categories. The first one is what they call "Mortal Sins" and the other they label "Venial Sins." But first of all, who gave you that authority? Of course, we have all sinned, but who told you that a sinful man like yourself can determine what is sin and put different levels to it? So, we're talking about something that is not at all a secondary issue. This is a core belief. Again, remember that they break sin into mortal versus venial sin.

"The consequence though, of not having a Biblical understanding of sin and thus not responding to sin accordingly to the Bible, is devastating beyond words. An incorrect understanding of sin can result in eternity separated from God in Hell."

Would you say it's a big issue? Yes! Of all things we must get right, what we do with sin is crucial. How do we have our sins forgiven? Who forgives sin? If you claim forgiveness isn't only from Jesus, you're in a heap of trouble!

"The Catholic Catechism states: 'Mortal sin is an intentional violation of the Ten Commandments in thought, word, or deed committed in full knowledge of the gravity of the matter and results in the loss of salvation."

That's from their church catechism, which is an extensive summary of their church principles! The simple question which that excerpt brings up is: Can we lose our salvation? The simple answer is: No, we certainly cannot!

So, there is strike two. And how can the media sit there and say that they're interviewing a Catholic priest on television to get the "Christian perspective?" How can you say that? Number one, man does not forgive sin. You don't have that power. It's only God Who does. You got it wrong on number two as well. A Christian can't lose their salvation! Is the Catholic Church implying that Christ's work on the cross is insufficient? Yes, they are because that is what they believe. The result of that view allows Catholicism to dictate what you must "do" to get right with God, and it supposedly needs to be done through the Catholic Church.

That brings up the third strike. They say you'll need to do certain things to get your salvation back. You must perform works outlined by the Roman Catholic Church. Let's get deeper into that. Supposedly if you commit what they get to define as one of their mortal sins, then you lose your salvation. That's not Biblical!

They say: *"Salvation may be regained through repentance and God's forgiveness."*

But you've got to do their works to get there.

"Venial sin may be a violation of the Ten Commandments or a sin of lesser nature..."

Well, who gets to decide that God's list of sins in His Ten Commandments are somehow "lesser" sins?

"...but it is committed unintentionally and/or without full consent. Although damaging one's relationship to God, venial sin does not result in loss of eternal life."

Let's examine that claim: First of all, the concept of mortal sin versus venial sin presents an unbiblical picture of how God views sin. The Bible states that God will be just and fair in his punishment of sin. God will punish all sin because He is a just God. He is not only loving, He is a just God as well. The Bible does not state that some sins are worthy of eternal death whereas others are not. Here's the issue and it shows exactly what the Bible teaches: All sins including only one sin, no matter what the severity, causes guilt by the offender and that person is deserving to go to Hell. It's very simple, right? Yes, that's it! That's what the Bible says. All sins are mortal sins. Even one sin makes the offender worthy of eternal separation from God.

James 2:10 says, *"Whoever keeps the whole law and yet stumbles in one point, becomes guilty of the whole thing."*

Let me give you a simple analogy. They want to say one type of sin is in the bad category and another sin is not so bad. They further tell us that unfortunately, if your sin is in the bad category you have lost your salvation, which is unbiblical, but luckily for you, either way, we have some things you can "do" to get yourself out of the mess. Coincidentally, a lot of it involves money. We'll get to that church wealth machine in a little bit. So, here's a Biblical analogy to give you a clear picture of sin: It doesn't matter if a person throws a very small pebble through a window or several large boulders. What's the result? The window is broken.

"In the same way, it doesn't matter if a person commits one small sin or several huge sins..."

And by the way, how does Catholicism choose the fallen sinful men who decide the category for each sin?

"...one small sin or several huge sins, the result is the same. The person is guilty of breaking God's law and the Lord declares He will not leave the guilty unpunished."

But that's what the Catholic doctrines say. They'll tell you that one sin is a boulder-size sin, but another might be just a pebble-size sin. Unfortunately though, sin is sin as far as the punishment qualifying you for eternal damnation in Hell.

"Second, the concepts present an unbiblical view of not just God's view of sin, but the 'payment' of sin. In both cases, mortal and venial sin, forgiveness of the given transgression is dependent upon the offender making some type of restitution."

Can I translate that for you? You have to "work" your way out of your mess, that is, your sin. Is that what Biblical Christianity teaches? No. So strike three is that Roman Catholicism is a works-based salvation system where you must do something to keep receiving your salvation back after repeatedly losing it. You need to get it back. However, that false teaching represents an attack on the atonement work that Jesus Christ did for us on the cross. And again, notice we're talking about sin and how to get rid of sin, eternity, how to get to Heaven, and other serious salvific issues. You can't get those wrong! They are the core of what we believe! Again, these are not secondary issues. It's not like a debate between Christian groups on what the robe color should be or whether robes should even be worn. We're not talking about minor disagreements. The issue we're looking at defines what is Christian and what is not.

Roman Catholicism already has three strikes. It's not looking good. Of course, it only takes one strike if you're teaching the wrong Jesus and how to deal with sin. If you get that wrong, you're in a heap of trouble and you are headed to Hell. With anyone propagating a lie that sends people to Hell, should you and I work or partner with that? No way!

"In both cases, mortal and venial sin, you have to do some type of restitution. In Roman Catholicism this restitution may take on the form of going to confession..."

There is nothing wrong with confessing sin, but they turn it into a work needing to be performed toward salvation.

"...praying certain prayers."

Is there anything wrong with prayer? No, we pray through our relationship with God. But the Roman Catholic Church also turns that into a work for salvation. In fact, in many cases you have to pray a specific type of prayer and in the specific verbiage they say, in order to supposedly get that sin absolved. Excuse me?! And they require it over and over again. We'll get more into their prayer practices later.

Receiving the Eucharist is their perverted version of Communion. It's not the same thing as Christian communion. They believe the food and drink is the *actual body and blood* of Jesus after being transformed by a ceremony, even though it literally remains the exact same substances.

"The basic thought is that in order for Christ's forgiveness to be applied to the offender, the offender must perform some work for forgiveness to be granted. The payment and forgiveness of the transgression is [Listen!] *dependent upon the offender's action."*

How is that any different from what an Islamist, a Muslim does, who has to keep the five pillars? He has to pray every day, give alms, fast at Ramadan, hopefully make that pilgrimage, and on and on. How is it any different from what Catholicism is prescribing? We would call those Islamist practices out in a heartbeat. We'd say it's a works-based system. And how are these Catholic teachings any different from those in Mormonism or Jehovah's Witnesses where you try to be a good person, stay away from caffeine, go on your bike tour as a missionary, and so many other ways in which you have to work your way into the kingdom. How is that any different? Well then, why would people hesitate to call false teaching out when it comes to this? It's all blatantly false! And again, it's not a secondary issue. This is salvation we're talking about. Don't mess with that! Don't get that one wrong.

"The Bible clearly teaches that payment for sin is not found in or based upon the actions of the sinner. Consider the words of 1 Peter 3:18: 'For Christ also died for sins once for all, the just for the unjust, so that He [Christ Jesus] might bring us to God...'"

Jesus paid it all!

"...the person who is believing in Jesus Christ, all of his or her sins have been taken care of on the cross. Christ died for all of them. This includes the sins the believer committed before salvation and the ones that he committed and will commit after salvation."

Also, dare I say, even more wonderful news is that this also includes sins you're clueless of. It covers sins you're not aware that you've committed. Christ has taken care of all sins! He doesn't divide them into different categories and then prescribe what you have to do to get yourself free of each type of sin. That's why Christ's love compels us. It does so because it's complete. He did it all. In fact, just think about it: The Catholic idea is logically impossible. How can you or I know of every individual sin we've ever committed? I don't know that! And the Bible confirms the heart cannot know. The heart is also deceitfully wicked. Who is the only one who can know every sin? Only God can! But man cannot, so even if works did actually take care of the problem, and of course it doesn't, how can I ever get rid of them all? I don't even know them all. So, under their scenario, not matter what you do, you are doomed! But praise God that is not the case and they are teaching false doctrine. Christ did it all! That's the good news but it's not what they teach, which means they are leading people to where? They are leading God's children to Hell. It's a serious issue!

"Colossians 2:13 and 14 confirms this fact: '*...Christ having forgiven us of all our transgressions...*'"

Not just transgressions in the past, but all of them!

"They have been nailed to the cross and taken out of the way. When Jesus, on the cross, stated, 'It is finished' (John 19:30), he was stating that He had fulfilled all that was necessary to grant all total forgiveness and eternal life."

"Paul states this fact in Romans 8:1: *"Therefore there is now no condemnation for those who are in Christ Jesus."*

In fact, it's a double negative in the Greek, which is really cool. It means no, not one bit, nada, zilcho. There is not one smidgen, not one smell, and not one vapor of sin remaining with a Christian. There is nothing at all of condemnation for those who are in Christ. Why? Because He did it all! And that's good news! Then Paul goes on in Romans 8 to say that nothing can now separate us from the love of God; neither death, nor life, nor angels, nor demons. It's called "eternal security." Praise Jesus, He did it all! But if you sit there and say, "Yes Jesus did it, but we ourselves still need to..." That's not the Gospel and it's not Christianity.

This again brings up a tried and true rule. Anytime you hear something like, "It's Jesus, or...", "It's Jesus, and...", or "It's Jesus, but...", *that's not the Gospel.* Still, that's what Catholicism does. They start with a statement to suck you in like, "Oh yes, it is Jesus!" But that's just how they snooker you. The rest comes after you start to follow them. It's no different than the Mormons or Jehovah's Witnesses. When you've been talking with them and professing your belief in Jesus, what do they say almost every time? It's normally some form of: "We believe in him too!" But you need to get them to go beyond that. Get them to tell you about their Jesus. When you do, the Mormons should confess that they teach how Jesus is the "spirit brother" of Lucifer. Uhmmm, nope! That's not my Jesus! Of course, that claim is so opposed to Biblical Christianity, they won't tell you it. What about the Jesus of the Jehovah's Witnesses? They say he is the Archangel Michael. Nope! That's not my Jesus!

How about with Roman Catholicism? Who's their Jesus? They'll say, "Oh, He's good and He's God's son." Here's what they won't tell you, but it is what they teach: You have to keep your salvation by doing the things that Catholicism prescribes for you to do and you have to go through us, man, in order to be forgiven for your sins. Whoa! Nope! That's not my Jesus! But yet, because we haven't done our homework, people still stumble along thinking and professing that Roman Catholicism is the same thing as Christianity. They think Catholics are Christian. Nope! They're not!

"Third, these concepts present an unbiblical picture of God's dealings with his children."

Catholic teachings mess up the view God has towards sin, the payment of sin, and how God deals with all his children concerning sin. Does the Bible teach that a person who is fully saved by God through Christ can lose their salvation or even somehow regain it again after supposedly losing it? The answer is: No and double no!

"Once a person has placed his faith in Christ for forgiveness of sins and eternal life, the Bible teaches that that person is eternally secure--he cannot be lost."

Let me give you just one of the verses on that. Jesus is speaking in John 10:27-28:

"My sheep hear My voice, and I know them, and they follow me; I [Jesus] give eternal life to them and they shall never perish, and no one will snatch them out of My hand."

So, He says we who choose to be saved through the work of Jesus alone, on the cross, will never perish. How long is never? It is infinity, which means guaranteed to be forever. So that's number one, but then He followed it up with another emphatic statement:

"...no one will snatch them out of my hands."

So, does that include you, me, and anyone else who chooses to follow Christ? Yes! Paul continues in Romans 8:

"Neither death, nor life, nor angels, nor demons..."

Nothing and no one can take you out of the hand of Jesus Christ because, praise God, He paid it all! That's the good news! But it's not what Roman Catholicism teaches. They say you can lose it, which means you're saying Christ's work on the cross is not sufficient, and because of Christ's failure to secure our lives, it's up to us to pull ourselves up by our bootstraps to finish the job for Him.

You may have heard me say this before but it's an effective visual to illustrate what someone is really saying when they tell you to work off your sins. I would point this out to them: Okay, so basically, you're telling me to climb up there on the cross, slap Jesus, and ask Him to please finish the job. You're literally accusing Him of not finishing the work. When you profess that you have to maintain your salvation because you can lose your salvation, you are attacking the cross of Christ. You are claiming it is up to you to finish it. That's what you're doing. You're attacking Christ on the cross!

So, with the question of eternal security and people teaching that you can lose your salvation, how far can you push that? Is it really a secondary issue? Because if you think people can repeatedly have salvation and lose it, then what are you trusting in? Is it the all sufficiency of Christ on the cross or is it really professing that you yourself can make your way back to salvation? That's a very scary thing! Again, in Romans 8, Paul says:

"...Neither death, nor life, nor angels, nor principalities, nor things present, nor things to come, nor power, nor height, nor depth, nor any other created thing, will be able to separate us from the love of God, which is in [In what? In your own works? No!] *Christ Jesus our Lord."*

Continuing with what one author wrote: *"...the concepts of mortal and venial sin are not Biblical and should be rejected."*

That's another example of where they get it wrong because they mess up salvation after also getting sin wrong. As I've said, we're just dealing with their own teachings they promote, unfortunately. According to their false view of sin, where they break it into these categories of mortal and venial, they then say there are works you can perform to get salvation back. I want to list some of those works. They use all kinds of interesting verbiage to describe these works. It's a whole system of things you can supposedly do to get rid of part or all of your punishment. We'll get more into the specific different parts in a minute.

Catholicism's supposed alleviations of punishment are called "indulgences." According to their false teachings, indulgences are the actions you can supposedly take to rid yourself of your debt for committing either of the two types of sin; mortal and venial sin. None of it is Biblical but this is what they teach:

"An indulgence is a way in the Roman Catholic Church to reduce the amount of punishment one has to undergo for sins."

What?! Who absolves us from the punishment of our sins? It's Jesus Christ, so that's strike four and we're just getting started. Who actually absolves and forgives us? How do we escape the punishment? Who saves us and rescues us? According to Romans 5, 1 Thessalonians 1, and 1 Thessalonians 5, who saves and rescues us from God's wrath? It is only Jesus Christ! Who releases us from the punishment? Again, it's Jesus Christ alone! There is nothing you can do yourself! Yet this is what Catholicism's indulgences mean.

You see, it's a very appealing concept for those who are into religion. This practice of indulgences will really fit that kind of personality. I'm convinced a lot of people want to be religious. Man inherently wants to be religious. Here's the reason why: Religion makes you feel good. When you become a Christian, you have to humble yourself and acknowledge that God is holy, and you are not. When you really understand Jesus' sacrifice, you may think of yourself as a wretch and may even beat your chest saying, "Oh God, save me and have mercy on me!" That is just an example of someone humbling themselves, but it shows how deep the level is of diminishing ourselves in comparison to God. You bow before Christ in acknowledgment of what the Bible tells us: That He is God. We know that He is holy, and we certainly are not. We deserve to go straight to Hell, but we humble our broken selves before Jesus and ask the Lord to please have mercy on us.

That's where man has the huge dilemma. We have something inside us called pride, which was what caused the fall of Satan, so with the free will God created us to have, if man can escape from that humiliating situation of bowing a knee before Christ and instead prescribe or be given these religious ethereal things to do, then he still gets to feel good about himself, right? Even though we've got the quandary of sin where you know you've blown it, you're rotten, and you've done bad stuff, something inside us does not want to bow a knee before Christ so maybe I can throw out some things you can do to feel better about yourself. It's a simple false solution but effective to gain followers because man is very susceptible. Man loves religion! And this Roman Catholic system is all about that. It teaches that you can feel better about yourself through your own action and they've got the top-shelf step-by-step plan on how to do it. Again, they bust sin into the two mythical categories; mortal and venial. Then in order to fix those mythical categories, you've got to do all these actions called indulgences. Let's get more into those:

"They also teach that these indulgences can reduce the temporal punishment after death in a state or process of purification called Purgatory."

Is that what the Bible teaches? Does Scripture say that when you die you go to some Purgatory, which is supposedly some kind of "purge-atory?" Is there really a mythical limbo sort of place where you in your own pain and suffering, over who knows how long of a period, can buy your way out of more suffering and in that way purge your own sins to finally then maybe make it to Heaven later? Is that what Biblical Christians believe? No, no, no, and no!

So that's strike five because; what is it the Bible says in 2 Corinthians 5? Scripture tells us that to be absent from the body is to be where? Praise God, you go straight to be with the Lord! You don't go to some mythical place. Purgatory is not at all Biblical. These false teachings say you can get indulgences to remove the punishment for all or part of your sins either now or in the afterlife. Oh, and by the way, Catholicism even has works you can do to help your loved ones who've already passed away and are supposedly now suffering in Purgatory. This is no joke! I'm telling you, if you're looking to practice some serious religion, this one is it. Here is more:

"The catechism of the Catholic Church describes an indulgence as a remission before God of punishment due to sin."

Again, who deals with our sin? It not you or a certain work, and certainly not the Catholic Church. It's not something they can prescribe. It has only been done through the work on the cross of Jesus Christ.

"And under certain conditions prescribed by the church, the recipients of an indulgence must perform an action to receive it."

So, what is that? It is works and not at all what Biblical Christians believe.

Catholicism also breaks indulgences down into a nightmare of categories. If you thought it was already getting confusing, we are actually just starting. They have categories with sub-categories, and you have to do x, y, and z with it. It's all very complex so it's no wonder their catechisms are extensive, and you've got to study long and hard to know what is expected of you. That struggle is probably why most followers throw their hands up and say, "I don't know, let's just go to the priest and have him tell us what to do."

Indulgences are first split into categories of either a "partial" indulgence or what is called a "plenary" indulgence. The latter is full remission, or full pardon of punishment. Then there are four general categories of indulgences. But as mentioned, first they split them into partial or plenary (full).

With indulgences that are partial, it depends on the fervor with which the person performs the recommended actions, so you better be careful when you do these works. You can't just go through the motions. You've got to do really well and if you're not exceptionally serious about it, it doesn't count. But do they have some sort of police available to watch people and make that judgment?

Breaking it down further, according to Catholicism, if you want to get partial removal of the punishment for your sin, first you must be:

"Raising the mind to God with humble trust while performing one's duties and bearing life's difficulties and adding at least mentally, some pious invocation."

So, as you go about your day, you probably should verbalize it but at least think about something pious. And that's just for partial forgiveness, it's not full forgiveness but at least you get part of it.

Number two: *"Devoting oneself or one's goods compassionately in service of one's brothers and sisters in need."*

Is it good to help people in need? Absolutely! But why do we do it? Is it supposed to be for some sort of gain for ourselves? No, we are to do so because Christ loves us, because of what Christ has done for us, and that's what Christ wants us to do so our love for Him compels us. We want to share Christ and His love with other people. But that's not the motivation with this indulgence stuff. Your thinking is that somehow you need to get rid of your punishment for your own sins. That's what Catholicism teaches.

Number three: *"Freely abstaining..."*

Note that they claim it must not be done because the Catholic Church wants you to. They're saying to do it because you need to or because they are watching you! Contradicting that, they'll also tell you to do it out of your own free choice.

Three continued: *"...from something pleasant."*

Number four: *"Freely giving open witness to one's faith."*

Whose faith are they talking about? Is it Biblical faith? No, it's not. They want you to give witness in favor of the Catholic faith so according to their doctrine of indulgences, those were in the subcategory, about four different ways you can get partial removal of punishment for your sins. Crazy, right?!

Now let's go to the plenary ones, which are supposedly full pardon of punishment for a particular sin. However, there is a caveat! Again, I'll remind you that these are their teachings. I'm not making these false teachings up. A plenary indulgence can be gained on any day, though it can only be accumulated at one per day so don't get too excited. If you're religious and eager enough to take the actions needed for achieving more than one per day [who's going to know anyway, right?], then I'm sorry but you'll only get credit for one. Folks, it's all laid out for maximum control and it's crazy!

Here is their list of ways to supposedly get a sin fully absolved.

Number one: *"Piously reading or listening to sacred scripture for at least a half an hour."*

Dude…be careful though! If your watch is messed up and it turns out your Bible study was only twenty-nine minutes, you just wasted your time. That is unless God's watch hopefully shows you at thirty. Twenty eight has no chance of working, right? Do you get extra credit if you keep going to thirty-two? I'm not sure of all that, but they say it's got to be a half hour.

Number two: *"Adoration of Jesus in the Eucharist for at least a half an hour."*

On this one, you apparently need to sit during their version of communion and really get into it for at least a good half hour. Hopefully your priest is not too quick in getting past communion. But either way through your thirty minutes, you really need to mean it. Maybe it works to just stare intensely at the wafer or cup. I don't know but if you do it: Woo hoo! That takes care of one full sin! Remember though, your adoration session can't be even one second under a half hour. It appears there is no word on whether time can be banked against another present or future sin.

Number three: *"The pious exercise of the Stations of the Cross."*

Here is an explanation for the Stations of the Cross: *"The Stations of the Cross is a fourteen step Catholic devotion that's supposed to commemorate Jesus' last day here on Earth."*

Catholicism says there are fourteen different events Jesus went through on His last day so in your mind, you are supposed to conduct something like a mini pilgrimage where you mentally walk through these events as if moving from station to station. You must think about where He was at a certain part of the day and then what he does after and then after that:

"At each station the individual recalls and meditates on a specific event from Christ's last day and specific prayers are to be recited. Then the individual moves to the next station until all fourteen are completed."

So, if you do that one, it supposedly eliminates all of *one* sin. But remember, it's only available at one per day, per sinner.

Number four: *"Recitation of the Rosary..."*

You have probably seen people flipping through beads that are connected together on a necklace-type chain or string. The Catholic Church actually has a specific formula for moving through the beads because they're split up into five different sections. You'll notice a few are bigger beads than the rest. The larger beads are for when you get to a more major milestone in your Rosary work. Basically, the different size beads are so that you can more easily recite correctly as it becomes a mindless procedure. You are supposed to run them through your fingers keeping track of where you're at because you have a lot to do to be rid of all your punishment.

Let's take a look at the Rosary: The Rosary can't be done just anywhere. For example, you can't do it while driving, from a buddy's house, or at a restaurant. It must be performed:

"...in a church or oratory [which is a small chapel], or in a family, or religious community, an association of the faithful and, in general, when several people come together for an honorable purpose."

So, number one, it has to be in the right setting. You've got to have the right environment while doing your work with the Rosary or it doesn't count.

The Rosary comes from Latin meaning, "the garland of roses." They say the rose is supposed to be one of the flowers that symbolize the Virgin Mary. The Rosary is a devotion in honor of the Virgin Mary and consists of a set number of specific prayers in succession.

Wait a second! Do you smell that? I smell another strike! Do we pray to the Virgin Mary? Do we pray to dead people? No! We're up to six strikes now and still only getting started. Yet, when they want the Christian perspective on CNN or Fox News, who do they go to? They pull in a Catholic priest. And again, with every one of these issues, we're talking about salvific matters (salvation/redemption). And now we're seeing that Catholicism teaches their followers to pray to dead people. These are not secondary issues. It's not traditional hymns versus modern Christian music. It's not robes or suits versus jeans and a three-button pullover. It's not about having chairs versus pews, pianos instead of guitars, or drums or no drums. We're not talking about those kinds of secondary issues. This is salvation! This is how you get to Heaven!

Why would we shy away from confronting this as Christians? Listen; it's not just something to debate in order to get a win. Catholicism is the largest religious group on the planet with even more followers than Islam. If what they teach in fact leads people to Hell, how can we not get involved? Hey, if a Mormon comes to your door, you don't want to just slam the door, right? If a Jehovah's Witness comes by, we don't shoo them away. Who's going to witness to those so-called witnesses? It's sad because they think they're on the right path, but they're headed straight to Hell. We have the truth and it is our privilege as well as our duty to share what we know with those who are headed the wrong way. Why wouldn't we also share what we know with Catholics? Are they headed in the right direction? No, unfortunately they are not! And again, we're just getting started.

The Rosary indulgence is a subcategory, which means it's supposedly not partial but is plenary, or full remission of all your punishment for any particular sin. Again, the Rosary is number four of the plenary options but remember that it's only available to you once a day.

The Rosary consists of a number of specific prayers. First you have the introductory prayers, then one Apostle's Creed, one Our Father, three Hail Mary's and lastly, one Glory Be. It's apparently important how you pray all these parts because it can't be done randomly. You don't just say them. You have a right section and area to be in each step of the way while you're performing it. There is a precise correct order. This information on the Rosary is from their own website. In fact, if you go to the right places, they will even show you a step by step diagram on how to flip through the beads in the right order to get to your goal, which they say is to be rid of your punishment for one sin. This is from their own website:

"The purpose of the Rosary is to help keep in memory, certain mysteries. There are twenty mysteries reflected upon in the Rosary and these are divided into five categories."
The five sections of regular beads represent those five before you get to a big transition bead.

There are: *"the Joyful Mysteries, the Luminous Mysteries, the Sorrowful Mysteries, and the Glorious Mysteries. You may also wish to pray the Rosary online with others or by yourself."*

That of course contradicts what we read earlier. I thought you said you're supposed to do this in some certain place. I guess they must have more revising to do on that one or maybe they'll recreate it completely. Also as suggested by Pope Saint John Paul the Great:

"The Joyful Mysteries are to be said on..."

Listen! Don't miss these specifics or you might end up wasting your time [Though it's all a waste of time]:

"...on Monday and Saturday, the Luminous on Thursday, the Sorrowful on Tuesday and Friday, and the Glorious on Wednesday and Sunday, with the exception of Sundays of Christmas season."

During Christmas you use the Joyful but with the Sundays of Lent, use the Sorrowful. Does that all make sense? Not really? Neither you nor I want to take more time analyzing that mess! But in the case of this indulgence, here's what is expected of Catholics to atone for their sins: If you somehow get all that right, then make the sign of the cross and say the Apostles Creed, with step two, you say the Our Father, then three Hail Mary's, and then the Glory Be to the Father. Next announce the first mystery and then say another Our Father, followed by saying ten Hail Mary's while meditating on that mystery. Next you say the Glory Be to the Father, announce the second mystery, say the Our Father again, and then repeat number six and seven, which is ten Hail Mary's and a Glory Be to the Father with the third, fourth and fifth mysteries in the same manner. Excuse me?! That entire process is punishment! With all due respect: What?! Are you kidding me?

Oh, and then when you're done, you're still not really done because you have to do this Hail Holy Queen prayer thing, which I'm not going to repeat. Also, after each of the giant sections, you must say the following prayer requested by the "Blessed Virgin Mary of Fatima." Who or what is that, you ask? It's one of the demonic apparitions floating around on the planet. Some of these apparitions, which the Bible calls a familiar, foul, or evil spirit, claims to be Mary. So, the Catholic Church is telling its followers to repeat one of those prayers that came from a demonic apparition, which the Bible calls a demon or a familiar spirit. That is all built into the Rosary.

There you go. According to the Roman Catholic Church, those are four ways you can get a full indulgence and four ways to get a partial indulgence. There is more good news for sinners, according to the Catholic leadership, because they decided at one point that plenary indulgence may also be gained on some special occasions, which are not everyday occurrences. These include but are not limited to [remember these are their words, not mine]: receiving a plenary indulgence even by radio or television from a blessing given by a Pope. Wouldn't that be your lucky day? You get a free pass from sitting there flipping through those beads. You can just watch TV! That's what they teach! I'm not making this up! Other alternatives are a bishop being authorized to give out a plenary indulgence three times per year. You can also take part devoutly, which means you have to really get into it, in the celebration of a day devoted on a world level to a particular religious purpose [meaning Catholic purpose] such as their World Day of Prayer or World Youth Day. Have you heard of those? The latter is the Catholics way of sucking in the youth to help promote a one-world religion. They say if you attend those events seriously and devoutly, it will count toward getting rid of your punishment for a sin.

Now, you think: *"Are you serious? It works if someone is just watching the TV broadcast of this Pope guy? It's bad enough that you're saying man can forgive sins but now you're going to sit there and dish out the idea that if I do something you prescribe, you're going to decree that I now deserve, and will receive, less punishment for my sins against God?"*

Yes, that's what they're saying. On top of the earlier CNN article, here's one from CBS News so again, I'm not making this stuff up.

CBS News: *"Vatican: 'Get time off in purgatory by following the Pope on Twitter.'"*

I know much of this sound like I'm kidding, but sadly, I'm not coming up with this stuff! It's their beliefs. But first of all, Purgatory is not real and it's not Biblical! They also claim there are works you can perform to get out of punishment.

CBS News: *"The Vatican is taking a modern approach to one of its oldest traditions by offering indulgences to Twitter followers on the Pope's social media account..."*

Remember, the Catholic Church is advocating indulgences as your way out of this whole sin mess.

CBS: "Aware that some Catholics may not be able to travel to Brazil where World Youth Day is held..."

Remember, if you don't want to go through the beads and all that other stuff, World Youth Day is another church authorized solution to one of your sins. If you want to get a full pardon, you'll need to make it to where ever in the world the conference is. But maybe you're thinking, "Hey, I don't have the money to go to Brazil!" Well that won't be a problem anymore. You only need to sign up for the Pope's Twitter account and one sin's punishment is averted. Seriously, this sounds like rules from a grammar school tree house club but it's not exaggeration. This information comes from their words.

CBS continues: *"...Pope Francis is making a first time offer to the faithful, who follow the events in Rio de Janeiro online. Under Catholic belief, after confessing and being absolved from sin* [from the Catholic Church], *the indulgences granted reduce the amount of time one spends in purgatory... Under the Pope's new offer, those who follow the week's events on the Twitter feed can get* [Listen! These are CBS's words, not mine] *can get a speedier transit through Purgatory, hopefully on your way to Heaven* [see, you don't know if you'll make it to Heaven, even after working for indulgences]. *The notion of indulgence is that you've already been forgiven for your sin, because you've gone to confession..."*

That means confession through the Catholic Church where a priest gets to supposedly grant that forgiveness. They're not talking about Jesus granting it. But oh, by the way, is that what the Bible teaches? Does it say we go to our fellow man to confess our sins in order for those sins to be forgiven? What does 1 Timothy 2:15 say? It tells us there is only one mediator between God and man and that is Jesus Christ. We can only go through Jesus.

There's another strike. And again, this is all dealing with confession of sin and including the forgiveness of sin. But if you're not teaching that you have to go through Jesus for forgiveness, what are you teaching people with Catholicism? You're prescribing a way to end up in Hell! It is of utmost importance! You cannot get the way we deal with sin wrong! It has eternal consequences.

CBS continues: *"...what it does is reduce the amount of time that you spend in purgatory after you die to work off that sin..."*

So even CBS admits Catholicism has a works-based salvation. That quote is from Patrick Hornbeck, who is the chair of the Department of Theology at the University of Fordham in New York, which is a Catholic university. I decided to look up that university and here's what I found: They've got all kinds of information on aspects of Catholicism like how to become a Jesuit. We'll get to the Jesuits next. But also, they have something for the kids that they can get involved in. Your kids can just click on a link to explore their interfaith ministry. What is interfaith about? Interfaith is the buzz word about bringing together all religions. And who wants to control the global religion in the last days? The Vatican does. Also, on Fordham University's site, if you click on interfaith, they say:

"Rooted in our Catholic and Jesuit identity, we are a community where people of all faith traditions are welcome. Whether you're a Catholic, Jewish, Hindu, Orthodox Christian, Muslim, or exploring, we invite you to one of many campus ministry events that we offer through the year and to explore one of the many clubs and organizations that call campus ministry home."

Apparently, these kinds of appeals are working, and Catholics must be getting tired of flipping through beads because the number of Pope Francis Twitter followers has climbed to 27 million. So many of those signing up to follow the Pope think they're going to get something just for signing up. But remember, besides signing up for the pope's tweets, you have other Catholic opportunities to work off sin. Another way is to either be watching television or listening to a radio broadcast when the Pope gives a blessing. Or if you're really devout about it, you can just go to a special event like World Day of Prayer or World Youth Day. And here's another one, which is option three on the list:

"Taking part, for at least three full days in a spiritual retreat."

So, if you make it only two and a half days because you became ill after ordering the chicken, even though you knew better, then it doesn't count. You'll need to start the retreat over.

Option four: *"Taking part in some functions during the week of prayer for Christian unity and special indulgences are also granted on occasions of particular spiritual significance such as the Jubilee Year or centenary* [100 years] *or similar anniversary; such an event as the apparition of Our Lady of Lourdes."*

What is the Our Lady of Lourdes apparition? It's another of their demonic apparitions from around the planet that claimed to be Mary. The Catholic Church gives credence to many of them. For example, the church built a shrine around Our Lady of Lourdes and now it's a place where people can travel to for a pilgrimage. If you go on that pilgrimage, it's going to count as an indulgence against your sins.

"Our Lady of Lourdes is a Roman Catholic title of the Blessed Virgin Mary in honor of the Marian apparition that reportedly occurred in 1858."

This happened before the apparition mentioned earlier called Fatima. The story of Our Lady of Lourdes is that supposedly a 14-year-old peasant girl told her mother a lady had spoken to the girl in a cave. Hey, they should have learned the lesson from Mohammed, right? What happened to him? How did the whole Islam thing begin? It started when Mohammed went into a cave. What happened there was the start of Islam. Mohammed went in there and saw a spirit that he originally felt was malevolent. He sensed it was an evil spirit, so he got out of there. But then his family talked him into going back and checking it out more because they said surely the spirit must have been Allah and Allah wouldn't lie to you. So, Mohammed changed his mind and went back in there a second time. He then came out saying it wasn't an evil spirit. He decided it was the Angel

Gabriel. Over the next 23 years while he couldn't read or write, this supposed Angel Gabriel, which it was not because it was a demon, told Mohammed all this stuff he had to memorize. It ended up in the Quran. That name means recitations. Mohammed couldn't read or write but this familiar spirit, as the Bible calls them (a demon), told him stuff, which he recited until much later when the information was written down. You hope he got it right over a 23-year period but that's where the Quran came from and it's now Islam's basis of authority? Again, stay out of caves!

Similarly, the whole thing with Our Lady of Lourdes is that a young girl goes into a cave and sees this lady. Well it's a demon, or what the Bible calls a familiar spirit. But the cave demon called itself the Virgin Mary, so it had to be, right? Wrong! Demons lie. But the Catholic Church must have agreed that it was the Virgin Mary because:

"In 1862, Pope Pius IX authorized...the veneration of the Blessed Virgin Mary in Lourdes. The image of Our Lady of Lourdes has been widely copied and reproduced."

That brings up the question of why Catholic leadership tore out and threw away God's second commandment, which says you shall not worship idols. They took it out of their version of the Ten Commandments in their catechisms and other literature. Well of course they did that because what is an extremely widespread and popular practice in Catholicism? It is idols. But wait a second, that would only leave them with nine commandments. So how do they still show ten to avoid suspicion? Well, I'll tell you: I actually caught it one day when I was living in Northern California. I saw it with my own eyes. They took the tenth commandment about how 'you shall not covet your neighbor's wife, field, manservant, maidservant, ox, [donkey], or anything', and they split that commandment into two so that [Presto chango!], they got back to having the correct number of Ten Commandments. So Catholic leaders took the second commandment, the idols commandment out of God's Word and split number ten into two commandments to make the number ten again so that people would not notice that they deleted one. That is of course, very deceitful, but unfortunately, it's just the tip of the iceberg, as we'll learn.

Oh, and by the way, I want to mention once again that we as Christians do not pray and listen to so-called dead people because the Bible is clear on that point. When you die you go straight to Heaven or Hell and you aren't coming back.

The Catholic Church celebrates a mass in honor of this Lourdes Lady demon. It's February 11th of each year. This is one of those special indulgence-gaining events that you can do a pilgrimage to, supposedly for getting rid of some of your punishment for sins. They apparently also have a spring of water there that this apparition advises people to drink from and wash in. Tons of people will literally go there every year and supposedly get healings and things of that nature. Lourdes has now become one of those pilgrimage sites. But again, they aren't instructed to go there because you may have nothing else to do at the time, what is most important is to go there while being devout about it so you can get rid of your sins.

I like this statement: *"The Lourdes authorities provide* [the spring of water] *free of charge to any who ask..."*

What I find interesting there is that they make you pay to get out of Hell, but you can have this demon water for free.

This Lourdes place is visited by millions of Catholics every year and again, many or most are going there thinking they're going to get sins forgiven and maybe some kind of secret healing.

This is significant: *"...the plenary [full] indulgence attached to the Apostolic Blessing that a priest is to impart when giving the sacraments to a person in danger of death and which, if no priest is available, the church grants to any rightly disposed* [Catholic] *at the moment of death on condition that that person was accustomed to say some prayers during his life."*

Did you get that one? That's an answer to the worst-case scenario for a Catholic who may experience tragedy while not having his works and indulgences completed up to the second of death. So, let's say you're about to die because someone, who wants to do you in is chasing you. Your back is against the wall but it's okay if you can't find a priest as long as hopefully sometime in your life you did participate in some sort of a prayer. In that case they say, "Okay, we'll let you go." What?!

When we began discussing indulgences earlier, you may have been wondering where you had heard of them before. In our Christian history, this was the straw that broke the camels' back for some in the Catholic Church. The story here gets into our heritage when these sorts of practices are what Martin Luther and many others before him rejected because they were leading Catholics to Hell. This is why we call ourselves Protestants. We protested this stuff and said only the Bible is our authority; not man and not the Pope. Only Jesus Christ is our authority and He said Grace alone, or faith alone, is what saves us. It is NOT our works! And Protestants were murdered horribly for it. Yet we have Christians today backing up into the arms of these false teachings from Catholicism. Rome has never changed and never will. They're waiting for what they call the Protestant experiment to end when Protestants will be duped again and return in mass numbers to the Roman Catholic Church. We're headed back to the spiritual Dark Ages. Listen to how bad it got back in Martin Luther's day and what led up to the Protestant Reformation:

"Indulgences became popular in the Middle Ages as a reward for displaying piety and doing good deeds. The faithful, the Catholics, asked that indulgences be given for saying their favorite prayers, doing acts of devotion, attending places of worship, going on a pilgrimage, and for putting on performances and processions, including giving donations of money for a good cause."

Building projects were funded through all these indulgences bringing in money and other assets including property. But is that what we as Christians are to do? We do things like good deeds, help people, serve in the church, work at this and help that, work together, sing, and pray. Is it all because we want something in return? Is it for a reward or to get our punishment removed? Is that what we teach? No! So, there's another strike! We do it all because Christ's love compels us.

In the Catholic system, along with many other things, but especially indulgences, it became too much and these protesters [Protestants] began to cry out. What had happened much earlier is that Catholic leadership figured out:

"Hey, wait a second. We could not just have these guys flipping through beads, we can get them flipping through their wallets because we can make up whatever will work for us and they'll do it since they think their eternal life is on the line, and even the lives of their dead relatives."

So back in the Middle Ages, the Catholic Church created a vocation called "Professional Pardoners." These guys roamed around to generate and collect money for particular church projects. If the Catholic Church wanted to build a new church facility or maybe something at the Vatican or possibly just store up money in the coffers, these Pardoners were the door-to-door type workers. Because there was no TV back then, they went from town to town letting everyone know the good news about a wonderful list they'd made showing good local Catholic followers what they could do to have their sins forgiven. They had the list of sins all categorized, including appropriate amounts required for forgiveness of certain sins. Did you sleep with a harlot? Well then that will cost you two gold pieces or three silver in order to have that forgiven. Did you get caught stealing something? That'll be one gold piece. That's right, this is your best chance to deal with those pesky sins. The sin store is only available now while we're in town. Hey, these are special indulgences so take advantage.

You think I'm kidding but I'm not. They took all that money and stored it up. We'll get to that later. So, they'd go around to these towns and give promises of rewards. This practice took things even beyond supposedly removing your punishment and shaving time off from your supposed Purgatory experience. It degraded into requests for money to grant promises of rewards like get out of jail free benefits and even salvation. It became all about the money.

In fact: *"The Butter Tower earned its nickname because the money to build it was raised by the sale of indulgences, allowing the use of butter during Lent."*

How about that? There's some good news for all of you popcorn lovers or corn on the cob fans, because I know that when you try to eat corn without butter, it's just not good. But hey, if you give the Catholic Church a dollar fifty, your butter free lent days are over. You can use it all you want. Man, they made a lot of money off that idea! They built a whole Butter Tower. Okay, I am joking about the popcorn and the corn on the cob but I'm not kidding about the premise. Can you believe that?

"The scandalous conduct of the 'pardoners' was an immediate occasion of the Protestant Reformation. In 1517, Pope Leo X offered indulgences for those who gave alms [money] *to rebuild St. Peter's Basilica in Rome. The aggressive marketing practices of Johann Tetzel in promoting this cause provoked Martin*

Luther to write his Ninety-Five Theses, condemning what he saw; the purchase and sale of salvation."

Because that's exactly what it was! And here's an example of what Catholic Pardoners were going around the towns saying:

"In Thesis 28 [of those ninety-five] *Luther objected to a saying that was attributed to Tetzel: 'As soon as a coin in the coffer rings, a soul from purgatory springs.'"*

So, they have indulgences not only for you, but also for your loved ones who are already gone. Do you want to get your deceased mother out of Purgatory faster? Well come on then, help them out. Let's get out your wallet and put some money in the church's hands.

It goes on: *"The Ninety-Five Theses not only denounced such transactions as worldly but denied the Pope's right to grant pardons on God's behalf in the first place: the only thing that indulgences guaranteed, Luther said, was an increase in profit and greed because the pardon of the church was in God's power alone."*

"The sale of indulgences spread to include the forgiveness of sins. Again, not only for the individual but for those people who were already dead."

Listen to part of this sermon from this Tetzel guy, who was selling the idea that coins in the coffer spring your dead relative's souls from purgatory. This is a brutal laying-on of the salvation guilt for money in this works-based false pseudo-Christian cult.

Catholic Pardoner, Johann Tetzel: *"Don't you hear the voices of your dead parents and other relatives crying out?* [Wow! Can you imagine what kind of person would say this?] *Have mercy on us* [they say], *for we suffer great punishment and pain. From this you could release us with just a few alms* [bucks]. *We have created you, fed you, cared for you, and left you our temporal goods. Why do you treat us so cruelly and leave us to suffer in the flames when it takes only a little to save us?"*

Can you see those poor churchgoers who didn't know better? They didn't even have a Bible (that collects dust in our homes), like we have today. They didn't have the Bible that the reformers brought to us at the expense of being strangled, beaten, drowned, and otherwise murdered. Those Catholic followers in the Middle Ages didn't know any better so they would run up and empty their pockets to save dead relatives. It works like a charm. Martin Luther, John Calvin, Ulrich Zwingli, and others had had enough! They stood up against the establishment of the day.

The Catholic Church also raised cash in many other ways besides indulgences. One other way was to sell relics. They sold things like pieces of straw, hay, white feathers from a dove, and supposed pieces of the cross. They would sell these things as items that had supposedly been the nearest to Jesus on Earth. The money went straight to the Vatican and the church's other projects. These holy relics were sought after. People saw their purchases from the Catholic Church as a way of pleasing God. Parishioners thought it showed that they had honored God by spending their money on relics that were associated with the Son.

Remember too that they also made money off of pilgrimages. You couldn't just show up to the pilgrimage destination and grab your indulgence for your remission of sin and punishment (for you or your loved one). You also had to be able to prove you had been there by purchasing a badge. The badges cost money, so these poor pilgrimage people had to buy the badges and of course you'd want to grab some holy water while you're there. Another item you need is a certificate to also prove you had been there and that you had completed your journey. They won't just take a sinner's word for it, right? It's all about the money!

Now was it really that bad? What is the old axiom? Those who don't learn their history are what? They are doomed to repeat it. I've said for years we in the Christian Church are guilty of that very thing. We don't know our own history. What does it mean to be a Protestant Christian? Let me give you a couple of examples.

This is the movement that was rising just before we get to Martin Luther in 1517. It all started with John Wycliffe in the mid 1300's. Wycliffe is known as the morning star of the Reformation. Remember, a lot of these guys who are the reformers were former Catholic monks or priests. They discovered the truth by just starting to read the Bible. What a concept, right? Once they read God's word for themselves, they came to realize what they'd been taught in the Catholic Church is wrong. Man does not have authority to forgive sin. Only God and Jesus can forgive sins. It's not of a man's own works or the whim of any human leader of men:

"Not of works, so that no man can boast", (which is a quote from Ephesians 2:9).

It is only by Grace through faith in Jesus Christ. It is a gift from God!

John Wycliffe began to preach the message of Grace and in fact, he not only preached to His congregants, but also sent out a group of folks called the Lollards. The Lollards were a group of simple Christian preachers who hit the streets and began to evangelize. They just told people the good news. They let folks know God's followers didn't have to go through all this baloney. Wycliffe died a natural death but the Catholic Church got so mad at him afterwards because his deed was already done, forty-four years after his death, Catholics actually dug up his bones, burned them, and threw them into a nearby river.

Oftentimes the Catholic Church didn't wait to do their cruel deeds until a person was dead. John Huss in Bohemia started out in the Catholic Church, but it was the same eye-opening experience for him when he began to read the Bible for himself. He figured out that he was not preaching the correct way to get to Heaven so because he was a faithful preacher, he began preaching the truth. Catholic leadership told him to stop but he wouldn't. So, what did the Catholic Church do? They condemned Huss to be burned at the stake. They stripped him of his clothes before degrading and mocking him with a paper dunce cap put on his head that was painted with devils and an inscription that said: "Ringleader of Heretics."

They then pronounced: *"Now we commit your soul to the devil."*

Wycliffe however, looked to Heaven saying: *"I commend my spirit into your hands, oh Lord Jesus Christ, which you have redeemed."*

The Catholics took him to the stake and lit the wood on fire. In no time at all, Huss was engulfed in flames that leaped high into the air. But as they did, Huss sang a simple hymn with such a loud and a cheerful voice that he was heard above the crackling of the flames and the noise of the crowd. They burned him alive, and he was singing hymns of praise to God! He showed he was not going to budge from his faith in Jesus.

Thomas Hawkes was also burned at the stake. Why? It was the same issue where he wasn't going to submit to a false teaching.

"Just before his death though, several of his friends asked him if he would do them a favor. They were afraid for their own lives. They wondered how long true Christian faith could stand in the midst of the flames."

That is of course because Hawkes was being burned alive for being a Christian.

"So [Hawkes] agreed that if his pain was tolerable and his mind was still at peace, even in the midst of the flames and by the help of God to show them that the most terrible horrible torments could in fact be endured for the cause of Christ and the Gospel, then he would lift his hands above his head."

And in this way, he would give his friends that positive signal.

"When the man had been in the fire for so long that he could no longer speak, his skin had shrunk, his fingers had been burned off, and everyone thought he was dead, suddenly he raised his hands high above his head and in an ecstasy of joy, clapped them together three times."

And from that brave act, the rest of the Christians there took courage and Thomas Hawkes got to be with Jesus because he was a Christian and he wasn't going to budge about Jesus being the only way to Heaven. But it was the Catholic Church that burned him alive.

And if you think they've ever changed, you're in for a rude awakening. We need to witness to Catholics just as much as we witness to anyone else who has a false way to Heaven.

Thomas Harding was just a simple Christian farmer. The church caught him reading the Bible. What did they do to him for reading the Bible? The Catholic Church burned him at the stake. In fact, listen to this:

"The Catholic priest actually told the people that whoever brought the wood to burn this man alive, just for reading the Bible, that the church would give them an indulgence [Listen to this one!] to commit sins for forty days without fear of penalty."

So now you're telling Catholic followers that they can sin up a storm as long as they just bring the wood to burn this Christian man alive! That was just for reading the Bible.

This all leads us to the Bloody Mary Regime. You've probably heard of that English Queen from the middle 1500's. Did you know that during Bloody Mary's reign, many of our fellow brothers and sisters in Christ were burned alive, drowned, strangled to death, and otherwise murdered? There's a nursery rhyme that has to do with that timeframe and you probably have even said it yourself. It goes like this:

*"Mary, Mary, quite contrary,
How does your garden grow?
With silver bells, and cockle shells,
And pretty maids all in a row."*

The silver bells were the Sanctus Bells that the Catholics carried with them, the cockle shells where the badges that the Catholic pilgrims wore to the shrines. The maids all in a row were the nuns, and the garden was what she, Bloody Mary, was trying to grow. The garden part refers to Bloody Mary's forced growth of Catholicism. She and Catholic leadership were shoving it down people's throats. How many times did people sing that rhyme as a reformation song to warn others about Catholicism coming in and doing their dirty deeds?

William Tyndale is another one. He translated the Bible into English for you and I to read. Tyndale was the one who launched the Gutenberg Press. Because of him, people were able to get countless copies of the Bible in English. How did the Catholic Church reward him? They strangled him to death! Then even after Tyndale was dead, it wasn't good enough for the Catholic leadership, so they burned his dead body at the stake.

John Hooper began to read the Bible and had his eyes quickly opened so he too rejected the Catholic Church's false teachings. Listen to what happened to him as a consequence:

"After Hooper forgave the man who made the fire, it was lit, but the fire builder had used green wood and when it had finally caught, the wind blew the flames away from Hooper. A second fire was lit but it only burned low, not flaring up as it should have. Then a third fire was lit but even that didn't do much good

because of the wind. [Listen!] Even when this man's mouth was black, his tongue was swollen, and his lips continued to move until they shrank to the gums, he knocked on his breast with his hands until one of his arms fell off. In fact, he was in the fire for over 45 minutes suffering patiently even when the lower part of his body was burned off and his intestines spilled out."

However, John Hooper's suffering turned out to have great purpose:

"It was this man's writing that had a profound influence upon another group of Christians. In fact, so much so that eventually they decided enough is enough. They decided to find a place to form their own country where they could have freedom in Jesus Christ. Those Christians were called the Puritans."

Now today, knowing all that, still the Pope comes over here to our country that was begun by those Puritans and keeps trying to seduce us into coming back to the Catholic Church. Those reformers, who sacrificed their earthly lives for us must be rolling over in their graves.

Here's some alarming information about the state of the Catholic Church today. If you don't know, Pope Francis is from the Jesuit faction of Catholicism. He's the first and only Jesuit ever picked by the Catholic Church to be their ultimate leader. That is big news! It's ugly enough when we look back at the history of what Rome does to people when they disagree with that church. You may think they've changed but they have not.

Being Pope, Francis is also, of course, at the top of all Jesuits. Here's where it gets very serious: Jesuits have to take something called the Jesuit "Extreme Oath of Induction." With it they pledge themselves to be a soldier of the Pope. But Francis is the first to take this pledge and then become Pope. Listen to just a portion of their present-day oath and what these men pledge to do when they become a Jesuit Catholic Priest:

"I promise therefore to the utmost of my power that I shall and will defend this doctrine of his holiness the Catholic Church and against all usurpers of the heretical or Protestant authority, whatever. I furthermore promise and declare that I will, when opportunity presents, make and wage relentless war, secretly or openly against all heretics, Protestants and liberals, as I'm directed to do, to exterminate them from the face of the whole earth; and that I will spare neither age, sex, or condition; and that I will hang, waste, boil, flay, strangle, and bury

alive these infamous heretics, rip up their stomachs and wombs of their women and crush their infants heads against the walls, in order to annihilate forever their execrable race. Then when the same cannot be done openly, I will [Listen!] secretly [behind the scenes] use the poison cup, the strangulated cord, the steel of the poniard [a spear], or a leaden bullet, regardless of the honor, rank, dignity, or authority of the person or persons, whatever may be their condition in life, either public or private, as I at any time may be directed to do so as an agent of the Pope or Superior or the Brotherhood of the Holy Faith, of the Society of Jesuits."

And how is the first Jesuit soldier Pope, Pope Francis treated when he comes here to America? The media treats him like a pop star! And Rome has never changed. Neither will their beliefs. The Christian Church better wake up!

I'll close the chapter with this: Doctor Mal Couch is now with the Lord. I sat under his instruction at seminary. Doctor Couch said that as Protestant Christians, we'd all better start speaking up and speaking out. He didn't say we need to be nasty, but we do need to speak out about all this we've just looked at because Catholicism has never changed. Doctor Couch warned us years ago that if the Christian Church doesn't call this out, Catholicism would eventually revert to what happened with the widespread murdering of Christians at the time of the Reformation.

Don't kid yourself. We are in the end days and if you fast forward to the Seven Year Tribulation, which could begin any day now, people at that time will be slaughtered like bugs on a truck windshield. Doctor Couch warned that if we don't deal with this issue, we'd be headed back to the spiritual dark ages. We need to call a spade, a spade. Again, I did not say we should get nasty. I'm not saying we should have an antagonistic attitude and get into clashes. We need to treat this as the exact same issue as us wanting to reach out to a woman or man on the street, a Jehovah's Witness, a pagan, Muslim, Hindu, Buddhist, or a New Ager.

We need to start witnessing to Catholics because these are not secondary issues. These are salvific issues so if you get any one of them wrong, like we're seeing here with the wrong Jesus and wrong salvation, it means those who are getting it wrong are not on the path to Heaven, they're going to Hell. How can we sit here, say nothing, and do nothing? How do we, possibly out of fear, keep our mouths shut? I'd rather have someone hate my guts but go to Heaven, than love me and go to Hell. As Christians we need to love others as Christ loves. Did everyone love Jesus? Did everyone like his message even though it was true? We must get prepared and then take the same action Christ did!

Chapter Two

Catholicism is a Cult

In the last chapter we answered the question of whether Roman Catholicism is the same thing as Biblical Christianity. It is NOT the same thing as Christianity. In fact, we saw that Catholicism is a major pseudo-Christian religion with "pseudo" meaning fake or false. In fact, the theme of this chapter, which comes from an intense research of the facts, is part of an accurate description of Catholicism. That word is "Cult." Roman Catholicism is not only a fake and false version of Christianity; it also fits both the secular and Christian definitions of a cult.

I love the way one guy puts it:

"The Protestant Reformation was basically a movement in reaction to and away from the cults. The main focus of that statement is Roman Catholicism. That may sound harsh, but it is only because we've been brainwashed by the media."

Again, nine times out of ten, who does the media drag out for us after saying something like, "And now for the Christian perspective..."It's normally a Catholic priest, right? So, because as secular media perpetuates it, people think Roman Catholicism is the same as Christianity. But it's not and it isn't just a false religion. In this chapter, we're going to see that Roman Catholicism is a cult by the two major standards. Let's take a look at that:

"A cult is sometimes difficult to define as there are many definitions to choose from. The non-Christian definition of a cult usually is focused on sociological, psychological, or behavioral factors. According to these factors, a cult is a religious group that seeks to 'control' its members..."

Does Roman Catholicism seek to control its followers? It absolutely does! It's all about fear and control so it fits the secular definition of a cult.

"...and it does so either by a single individual or the organization."

What organization of Roman Catholicism controls and manipulates people? It's the Vatican, right? So, Catholicism practices both aspects of the secular definition of a cult.

"The cult is manipulative and demands total commitment and loyalty of the followers."

Is that what Roman Catholicism does? It absolutely does!

"Even truly Christian groups can be cult-like in their use of manipulation and demands of loyalty."

In Protestantism, we'd say a group like that would be one that practices legalism or things of that nature, right? A cult-like Protestant group might make pronouncements like:

"You can't go bowling because those holes in the ball are really the eyes of the devil."

Or they may say you can't drink certain beverages and you must wear certain clothes. That's getting into legalisms.

Now let's look at the Christian definition: Here's the standard evangelical definition of a Christian cult:

"Any group that deviates from Biblical Christianity in the fundamental doctrines of the faith."

Does Roman Catholicism do that? Yes! How many strikes did we see in the last chapter? And we were just getting started. There is a long list of false teachings coming from this one religious entity, so it fits the secular definition of how they control their followers from a single individual and it also fits by how that control comes from the organization.

Catholicism also classifies as a cult by the evangelical definition because, over and over again, they deviate from Biblical truth. Some of those very crucial ways they do so are their source of authority, the nature of God, including the Trinity, the person or work of Christ, the nature of man, and the means of salvation. Again, if you get any one of those wrong when you're classifying a group under the evangelical Christian definition, it's a cult. Roman Catholicism is a cult. When a group or individual has a problem with the Trinity, that's a cult. When they get the wrong source of authority, it's a cult. Catholicism doesn't want to use the Bible by itself, they want to lean on and promote the Bible along with this and that. That's what cults do and it's also with Roman Catholicism does.

When you get the wrong version of salvation, that's a cult, right? When you get the wrong version of who God is and the work of Jesus Christ, it's a cult. And that's usually what they get wrong. They alter or completely change the deity of Christ or the humanity of Christ. Instead of following the Bible about things like Jesus being fully God and fully man at the same time, they usually get one or the other wrong. So that's a cult.

As we've now seen, Roman Catholicism fits both the secular definition of a cult and the evangelical definition of a cult. I know it may sound harsh, but they are not just a fake, false, pseudo-Christian religion, they are also defined, on two different levels, as a cult. Yes, it sounds harsh but those are the facts. I think that will be clear by the end of this chapter.

Continuing with a description of cults: *"In many cases these groups may use the same words as true Christians, but they radically redefine them."*

Those last three words are important: they "radically redefine them." And isn't that the truth? Whether it's a Mormon or Jehovah's Witness knocking on your door or a Roman Catholic you're talking with, when you tell them you believe in Jesus, what do all three of those groups normally say? They claim that they do too. But their version of Jesus and their version of salvation are both completely different. They redefine Jesus and salvation. You have to go behind their general proclamation and dig into their true meanings on these issues and the way they redefine these Biblical beliefs classifies them as a cult.

Let me give you some examples and first I'm going to focus on the evangelical definition, which says any group that deviates from Biblical Christianity and the fundamental foundations of our faith, is a cult. So, let me quickly rip through some things that Roman Catholicism teaches and you tell me if it deviates, thereby putting them in the category of a cult.

Catholic teaching: *"The bishops with the Pope as their head, rule the universal church."*

Is that the structure of authority according to the Bible? No! Who's the head of the Christian Church? It's Jesus Christ and Him alone, so they got that one wrong.

Catholic teaching: *"Catholicism believes that God has entrusted revelation to the bishops. Only they [It's called the Magisterium and we'll get to that in a minute] have the right to interpret the scriptures."*

Is that what the Bible says? No! Reading God's word is for our benefit. That's why the reformers were strangled, drowned, buried, and burned alive. It was just for the right to get the Bible into the common person's hands to read for ourselves, so there's another deviation.

Catholic teaching: *"The Pope is infallible in his teaching."*

Seriously? Is a mere man perfect in all he says and does? No! So that's another deviation. Again, these are deviations and what is the definition of a cult? It is any group that deviates from Biblical truth. I've mentioned three already and we've got a long way to go. Again, according to secular definitions and the evangelical definition, Roman Catholicism is a cult.

Catholic teaching: *"Scripture, they believe, and tradition [which includes the Catholic church councils and the early Catholic church fathers] are the word of God."*

Is that what we believe and what the Bible teaches? What is the only word of God? It is only that which is in the Bible, so they got that wrong.

Catholic teaching: *"Mary, they believe is co-redeemer because she participated with Christ in the painful act of redemption."*

What?! That's their teaching. Is it a deviation? Yes of course, and it's a sign of a cult.

Catholic teaching: *"Mary, they also believe, is the co-mediator to whom we can entrust all our cares and petitions."*

Is that what the Bible teaches? No! The Bible says there is only one mediator and who's that? It's Jesus! So, is that a deviation? It absolutely is!

Catholic teaching: *"Initial justification is by means of baptism."*

Their version of baptism is infant baptism. First of all, whether it's a baby or a person of enough age to decide for themselves, are we justified by being baptized? No! It is symbolic. Also, how do babies even know what they're doing in that situation let alone be able to freely choose? So, this one is a double no!

Catholic teaching: *"Adults must prepare for justification through faith and good works."*

Do our works and good deeds justify us? No!

Catholic teaching: *"Grace, they believe is merited by good works."*

Is that how we're to receive God's grace? No! It is by faith that we receive God's grace.

Catholic teaching: *"Salvation, they believe is attained by cooperating with grace through faith, good works, and participation in the sacraments."*

Is that how salvation happens? No!

Catholic teaching: *"With Roman Catholicism, no one can know if he will attain to eternal life."*

What?! What did John say in the Bible? He said, "I write these things to you, children so you may KNOW that you have eternal life (emphasis added)." Is that another Catholic deviation? It absolutely is!

Catholic teaching: *"The Roman Catholic Church is necessary for salvation."*

Does the Bible tell us that we have to be Catholic to attain salvation? No, or course not! They got that one wrong too and we're still going.

Catholic teaching: *"Christ's body and blood exists wholly and entirely in every fragment of consecrated bread and wine in every Roman Catholic Church around the world."*

So, they're saying Jesus' real body is divided up daily into each wafer and wine sacrament when any Catholic priest says it is. Is that in the Bible? No! That's a deviation.

Catholic teaching: *"The sacrifice of the cross is perpetuated in the sacrifice of the mass."*

No, the sacrifice was one event for one time. It was once for all, according to the Bible's book of Hebrews.

Catholic teaching: *"Each sacrifice of the mass appeases God's wrath against sin."*

Excuse me?! The mass appeases God's wrath against sin? No, it does not! But what does appease God's wrath for sin? It was the one time sacrifice of His son, Jesus on the cross, who appeased sin. Is the Catholic idea of this a deviation? Yes!

And again, these aren't secondary issues like robe-wars where you're into black robes and I like blue robes. These teachings by Roman Catholicism, every single one we've just listed are salvation (salvific) issues. These are all major deviations from the Biblical truth. Again, labeling Catholicism as a cult is not my definition, it is the secular definition and the evangelical definition. Roman Catholicism by its own belief system, just like Mormonism and Jehovah's Witnesses, fits the category of a cult. According to the Catholic teachings themselves, it fits exactly in that camp.

I want to mention something that really bugs me. "Righteous indignation" is what we think we're doing with an excited word yelled at the other driver when we're cut off in traffic. We think that strong feeling coming out of our mouth is righteous indignation. But no, that's probably not what's going on there. It's called having issues with our flesh. Here's what bothers me though: While we can get worked up in everyday traffic with what we think is righteous indignation, typically when we see God's truth defamed and people being led (deviated) down the wrong path toward Hell, that doesn't seem to fire us up as much!

Another practice that really fires me up, is when I see people in the media bearing false witness by more often than not, dragging out a Catholic priest to comment on the latest news story. They say something like, "And now for the Christian perspective..." But it's a Catholic priest. I have nothing against that guy, per se, as a person, but that's not Christianity! They should at least be honest and say, "Now for the Catholic perspective..." But even with that, if the media allows him a widely heard voice and if in fact Catholicism's teachings are diverting people from the only way to Heaven, which it is, doesn't that rile you up?!

So Roman Catholicism exactly fits the classic definition of a cult. It's not just in their belief system, but also in their verbiage. Their verbiage shows more ways they are deviating from the truth, which again makes them a cult.

Catholic term: *"Absolution"*

According to Catholicism it is, *"the act of releasing someone from their sin by God through the means of a priest."*

Is that how we're forgiven, and our sins are removed? No! Who do we go to for forgiveness of sins? We take it to Jesus! Do we go through a man or a priest? We absolutely do not!

Catholic term: *"Assumption"*

According to Catholicism it means *"the taking of the body and soul of Mary by God into glory. Catholic doctrine does not state whether or not Mary died but tradition holds that she died and was immediately afterward assumed into Heaven, both body and soul."*

What?! You've got it all wrong! Is that what we Christians believe and what the Bible teaches? No! That's another deviation.

Another one involved baptism. We believe in baptism but what is the Catholic version of *"Baptism"*?

Catholic Baptism is *"one of the seven sacraments that takes away original sin and actual sin."*

Does baptism remove any kind of sin? No! That's a deviation.

The Catholic version of *"Beautification"* means *"an official declaration of the Roman Catholic Church concerning a particular man or woman who, due to a holy life, may be venerated by a particular group of people."*

Is that what the Bible says? When we do good deeds, is it all about being venerated by people long after we're dead? No!

And Catholic doctrine gets even worse with the veneration stuff. They take it to stage two with what's called *"Canonization"*, which is *"an infallible declaration by the Pope..."*

Wait right there! Is the Pope infallible? Is any person on the planet infallible? No, of course not! The Bible says the heart of man is deceitfully wicked. Who is the only one who can know and does know that He's infallible? It is God alone. None of us are perfect, including the popes.

Back to Canonization: *"...which is an infallible declaration by the Pope that a particular Catholic, who was previously beautified [the first step—beautification] is worthy now of veneration by the entire Roman Catholic Church."*

There is another deviation, which again, is from their own verbiage.

What about the Catholic version of *"Confession"*? Is confessing of sin a positive thing? When we confess, the Biblical Greek word translates to tell us we're "saying the same thing." What does that mean? It means God already knows our sin and He's just waiting for us to confess. It's like when your parents catch you doing something wrong. They already know and many times you know they know just by the way they are looking at you. So, in that case, what is it that your parents are waiting for? They already know you did it, but you need to "say the same thing", which is to confess. You need to own up to it. That's the Biblical definition. By confessing, we're saying the same thing that God already knows about it. You say, *"It was wrong and I'm sorry. Would you please forgive me?"*

Catholicism's version of *"Confession"* is *"telling sins to a priest and the Lord forgives the person through the priest."*

Is that the same thing? No, it's not!

How about the Catholic *"Confessional?"* Is it Biblical? Their confessional is the little compartment you slide in to confess sins. You can only confess your sins in this small booth, and it must be to a priest. So, they prescribe confession to be only in a certain religious atmosphere, inside a religious building, in a religious box, while talking to a religious guy wearing religious garb. Is that how we get rid of sins? No!

Catholic *"Confirmation"* is *"a ceremony performed by a bishop that is [Listen!] supposed to strengthen a person to enable him to resist sin."*

Excuse me?! How do we resist sin? We do so by the power of the Holy Spirit. When saved, we become indwelt by the Spirit of God. You then walk, live, and keep in step with the Spirit. In that way you shall not fulfill the lusts of the flesh. It's the work of the spirit and not some ritual you go through.

"Catholic Confirmation is usually done at the age of twelve. The bishop dips his right thumb in holy oil and anoints the person on the forehead by making the sign of the cross and says [Listen!]; 'Be sealed with the gift of the Holy Spirit.'"

Is that how we receive the Holy Spirit? Wow!! It absolutely is not! How do you receive the Holy Spirit? Ephesians says that at the moment of salvation, you're sealed with the Holy Spirit. The Bible says it's God's guarantee. It's His pledge. In fact, it's the Greek word "Arrabon", which means engagement ring. You get that at the moment of salvation. It's not when you turn twelve and some guy puts some oil on your head. That's wrong! That's extremely misleading!

"Dulia" is the Catholic word for giving *"honor to saints and angels."*

Do we worship and/or give honor to saints and angels? No!

In fact, Catholicism has another related term called *"Hyperdulia"*, which refers to their *"honor and praise given to Mary."*

Mary, I'm sure was a great godly woman, and we'll cover this in more detail later, but in the first chapter of Luke, speaking at the time of Jesus birth, Mary says: 'Praise God, my Savior.' This is from when she states her full "Magnificat" in Luke 1:46-55. She admits she needs a savior, so she is saying she's just like the rest of us. We all need a savior, including her. Again, I'm sure she was a great and wonderful woman, who had an amazing ministry and it must have been an amazing privilege to be the vessel which the messiah arrived in. I get that, but guess what; she needed a savior just like the rest of us!

Do we worship saints and dead people? No and by the way, "saint" is the Greek word "hagios", which means "holy one." When we look at it in Scripture, that word includes all Christians, so we are all saints. On that note, if you're married try this exciting technique at home: Turn to your spouse and say, *"Hey, you're a saint!"* That would be especially hard to do right after a disagreement that caused another one of those intense moments of fellowship, right? Though telling them they are a saint, is probably good for your relationship so do it anyway.

It's also correct Biblical teaching because the Bible says anyone, who is a born-again Christian, is a saint (hagios or holy one). We have the imputed righteousness that is the holiness of Christ, which is laid upon us. You don't become a saint the way Catholic doctrine claims. They teach that after you've long since died, some religious entity determines that you're now a saint and then tells other people to pray to you and worship you. What?! That is a complete misunderstanding and another deviation.

As we've already seen, Catholicism gets communion wrong in what it is, but they also get the name wrong. They call it *"The Eucharist."* Wait until we get into where their practice of the Eucharist came from. It's a real eye-opener. But *"Eucharistic Adoration"* is their idea that the *"Blessed Sacrament"*, or Eucharist, supposedly becomes the literal body and blood of Jesus Christ right then and there every single time, repeatedly all over the world whenever a priest wills it so.

The Eucharist *"is displayed and adored by Catholics."*

Do we literally adore the elements as if they are the actual body of Christ? No! Jesus said to *"Do this in remembrance of me."* It is an awesome special time, but we do it in remembrance. It is not his literal body. It's only symbolic.

Well known of course is the traditional Catholic prayer: *"Hail Mary"*

Again, do we pray to deceased people even if it is supposedly praying to the Virgin Mary? From Biblical teachings, we are told not to!

"Holy Orders" is *"one of the seven sacraments, by which men, bishops, deacons, and priests are given the power and authority by another man, a bishop to offer sacrifice and forgive sins."*

What?! That is what Holy Orders means. Is that Biblical? No, it is not and that's another deviation.

Again, what's the theme we are seeing? I'm not the one saying this stuff. I'm just going with the bare-bones secular and evangelical definitions. If you're involved with something that deviates from Biblical truth, what is it you have then? You have a cult!

"Holy See" is *"the final seat of authority for the entire Roman Catholic Church located in Rome and positioned under the headship of the Pope."*

So again, is that where we get our final authority? Do we look to some headquarters to tell us what to do? No, we don't!

How about the *"The Immaculate Conception"?* Catholicism's Immaculate 'Conception' does not involve the birth of Jesus Christ through the Virgin Mary. A lot of people confuse Catholicism's Immaculate Conception with the virgin birth. That's not what it is. The Immaculate Conception is supposedly this:

"That Mary was conceived herself without original sin."

Is that true? Is that what we believe? It absolutely is not. But that's what they call the Immaculate Conception where they believe Mary was conceived without sin. It is of course not true!

We talked about *"Indulgence"* in the last chapter. It is their idea that there are certain actions you can take that are works and behaviors, which allow you to supposedly remove the punishment for all or some of your sin. But how is the punishment of sin removed? It is only through Jesus Christ!

"Infallibility" is their teachings that the Catholic church in Rome has basically the same authority carried by the Bible. Is that true and Biblical? It absolutely is not! That's another deviation.

Earlier we mentioned the *"Magisterium."* What is that?

"The divinely appointed authority in the Catholic church, consisting of the pope and the bishops, the Magisterium alone has the right to interpret the word of God."

Again, they're saying they are the only ones who can tell us what the Bible means. Is that what the Bible teaches? No, it absolutely does not!

"In Roman Catholicism, 'Penance' is a means by which all sins committed after baptism are removed. The means are assigned by a priest and usually consist of special prayers or deeds performed by the sinner."

Is that even how we get rid of sins at all, let alone every sin you commit after baptism? No! How do we get rid of sins? It's always the same way whether before or after baptism. It is only through Jesus Christ.

There is also the whole thing with Catholicism calling their popes the *"Vicar of Christ"*, which means popes are supposedly acting in place of Christ. Can a pope replace Jesus? And again, they say each pope becomes head over everything and supposedly whatever he says, rules on, and does, is infallible.

Is that what the Bible teaches? It absolutely is not!

There is also the idea of *"Purgatory."* Is there really a place of temporary punishment where you go and "purg" (purge) your sins in a place of "tory" (sins)? Do you suffer and burn until your relatives can give the Roman Catholic Church enough cash and/or pray them out of there sooner? And the Catholic church still teaches this today.

Is that what we teach? Is that what the Bible tells us? No, it is not! That's a deviation and if you deviate from Biblical truth, by definition, you're in the category of a cult.

I'm telling you, we have to develop a heart that won't claim Roman Catholicism is the same thing as Christianity and then we need to take this next step: You probably already have a heart to witness to the Mormons, the Jehovah's Witnesses, and the other cults, but we need to have the same heart for the Catholics who truly believe these false teachings. Why is this so important? It's because they're not going to Heaven. I didn't say that. They did. By the definition of their so-called faith, it's not the same thing as Christianity, which is the only way. Where does the penalty of getting it wrong put you for all eternity? You end up in Hell. This is a serious issue because Roman Catholicism is a pseudo-Christian group that is a cult.

Here's another one: The Catholic *"Requiem"* is a mass offered for the dead.

But once a person is dead, is there anything you can do for them? Do we pray to them? We certainly don't! Can we do anything for them or for ourselves through them? No.

Now I'm not saying you should be mean and tell people things like, *"Hey, your loved one is burning in Hell!"* Sometimes as a pastor, we're asked if we would say a prayer for someone's deceased relative or friend. You may have been asked to do this. Well we're not going to say, *"Too bad! I'm sure they're engulfed in flames!"* But it is an opportunity you can use. I'll normally say something like this:

"Listen, what's done is done, but the Bible is very clear: When you're in Heaven, you're in Heaven and when you're in Hell, you're in Hell. I don't know the person's heart but that's what the Bible says. What we can do is we can pray all right, but we need to pray for the folks who remain and pray that they get saved so that they can know for sure that they can have eternal life. We can pray that they will know that, and they can then know they're headed to Heaven."

So, you can flip that around to help in your witnessing. But praying for the dead and speaking to the dead are practices taught to Catholics. In fact, there are *"sacramental special prayers, special deeds, and special objects used to gain spiritual benefits from God."* Is that how we get benefits from God? Do we go through those kinds of rituals? No, it is not!

Here's a tragic story which should challenge all Christians to witness to Catholics: I worked with a guy while going to Bible college whose mother in law was a Catholic and had passed away. He and his wife were all tore up about it. But he came to me with this confidence that she was in a better place. Of course, I didn't rub his nose in it. I'm not joking, his idea of what happened to her literally broke my heart. Here was a guy, who had this conviction and confidence that his mother in law was in a better place. He offered me this piece of information that he was sure to be the truth: With a total straight face, he told me why he felt so sure she was now in Heaven. He said it was because she went to Mass on a pretty regular basis, (the following was supposed to be the shoo-in), she had a lot of figurines in her house, and she even had a priest come over and bless them. I looked at him and was speechless. It just busted my heart.

The *"sign of the cross"* is sacramental in Roman Catholicism. You probably know this as the movement of your index finger in the sign of a cross while pointing back at your own face. But will that give you some sort of blessing? Hey, if that's a blessing, we need to come up with all kinds of crazy hand movements and gyrations. I'd be doing those all day because I need as many blessings as I can get. What? Rituals and behaviors don't help. That's not how you get a blessing. It's only through Jesus Christ.

Now we're covering all the cult aspects of Catholicism so let's next do a comparison of Roman Catholicism with those groups I would assume most everyone has no problem categorizing as a cult. For example: Are Mormonism and Jehovah's Witnesses cults? Yes, and so is Catholicism. In case you think what we've already seen is not enough, let's take a look at some interesting similarities.

How about mentioning the specific church leaders around the planet? Catholicism has the Pope, Mormonism has the Prophet, and Jehovah's Witnesses has the Watchtower Organization. How about Christianity? It has no one except of course, the headship of Christ, which is a whole different thing.

How about the source of theology, or where they get their truth? Catholicism says theirs is from the Bible, but it is also from tradition, the Pope, the rulings of the church councils, and other things of that nature. Mormonism says their authority is the Bible, but it's also the Book of Mormon and other writings. Jehovah's Witnesses also say the Bible is their authority, but their Bible is a twisted perverted Bible. They literally changed the Christian Bible. They also stand on the authority of the writings of their Watchtower Organization. Again, as Christians what do we rely on as our sole source of truth? Clearly and simply, it is only the Bible.

Here are some other quick samples of the similar nonbiblical teachings. Catholicism has purgatory, penance, indulgences, praying to Mary, and Mary's supposed assumption. Mormonism has many gods, god from another world, goddess mother, and the idea that you can become a god. Jehovah's Witnesses say that Jesus is Michael the Archangel, they don't allow blood transfusions, they say there is no Hell, and they teach that 144,000 will go to Heaven. We in Christianity teach none of that because if it isn't in the Bible, we don't believe it, right?

How about their methods of salvation? Catholicism, Mormonism, and Jehovah's Witnesses are all works-based salvation. With Christianity our salvation is through faith in the work of Jesus Christ on the cross.

What about the concept of the true church? Catholicism, Mormonism, and Jehovah's Witnesses believe their respective church is the one and only true church. Christianity believes all who are saved by grace through faith in Jesus Christ are a part of the true Church in Christ. That is totally different.

What about their claim of authority? Catholicism has what's called *"Apostolate Succession"*, which is a line of bishops, who supposedly stretch all the way back to the Apostles. Is that where we should get authority? Mormonism is the same thing where they have an apostolic succession. Jehovah's Witnesses succession is by being a faithful servant. So, with Jehovah's Witnesses, I guess you earn that authority. What about Christianity? Our authority is in Jesus Christ alone! That is a major difference.

What about church assets? Catholicism has great wealth and power, Mormonism has great wealth and power, and Jehovah's Witnesses have great wealth but not much power. How about you and I as Christians? What are our assets? We have treasure in Heaven! Amen?

What about having a goddess-like figure? Listen to these similarities: In Catholicism, Mary has god-like abilities. She supposedly has the ability to hear and answer all prayers of all people of all time anywhere on the planet and she intercedes with God. That's what Catholicism teaches. Believe it or not, Mormonism has that too. Their "Goddess Mother" has supposedly populated this world with spirits who inhabit human bodies. This point is one where Jehovah's Witnesses and Biblical Christianity agree. They don't buy into the goddess stuff and neither do Christians.

How about images of God, Jesus, Mary, etc.? Catholicism uses a lot of those images in their so-called churches and services. Mormonism has all kinds of images they use in their temples and headquarters. In one of the last books we'll put out in this overall study of World Religions, Cults & The Occult, we'll look at another group that uses all kinds of symbolism. That is Freemasonry. Jehovah's Witnesses and Biblical Christianity do not use a lot of imagery. To summarize some of this comparison information, listen to what this guy says:

"I find it disturbing to see the similarities between Roman Catholicism and the cults. The Protestant Reformation happened for a reason; to get back to Biblical theology and to be rid of extra-biblical teaching. The Protestant Reformation was the [Listen!] ***counter-cult movement****."*

That's pretty interesting, isn't it? It was a counter reaction to what? It was against a major cult called Catholicism.

So far, I've shared just a little information on the Protestant Reformation and how reformers tried to get away from false teachings of this cult. In fact, we Christian Protestants still maintain some of our traditions begun by our Protestant reaction while getting out of that cult. I'll just share a couple of them. Again, these are certain traditions we have that were created as a result of leaving Catholicism:

In Protestant Churches, why do we always have the pastor's pulpit right smack dab in the middle, and typically the Bible as the centerpiece? Well that was part of what happened because a lot of the reformers were former Catholic monks or Catholic priests. Where do you suppose they started their teachings after leaving Catholicism? They went right back into their Catholic cathedrals and began to teach the Bible. They started teaching straight from the Word of God.

Prior to the Reformation, the lecterns (pulpits), where the Catholic priests and others stood, were typically high above the people. They would be high or higher than the balcony area. The priest was normally up there projecting his booming voice down at the little people below. Along that line, if you go into a Catholic service today, it's all symbolic. It's all about emotion because you have to feel religious, right? They foster that atmosphere with the acoustics, accompaniment, burning incense, candles, the vestibule, statues, and all the regal clothes. It's all meant to give you that deep reverential experience. It's all setup for the sake of an emotional religious appeal.

So, the first thing Protestant reformers did was rip down the lecterns and plop them right smack dab in the middle of the stage in front of the people. Then they put the Bible in front of them right on top of the lectern/pulpit. That symbolized the Bible alone being our source of authority.

The other thing the reformers did right away had to do with mass. In the Catholic experience, when they had mass there typically was a wooden partition separating the people from the priest behind who was doing the Eucharist thing. Because the reformers became aware that we are all one in Christ, they ripped the partitions out. As they discovered from the Bible, Christians have direct access to God. We don't have to go through a man. We go through Jesus Christ. The reformers also got rid of the candles, statues and all that other ceremonial and religious stuff.

In fact, at the beginning of the reformation, they even got rid of all the pews and any other kinds of seating. Imagine if you went to a Protestant Church back then and the entire church was completely gutted. When you walked in all you would see is a podium with a Bible on it. The guy preached from it and you stood there for a long time. Apparently over time the Church learned the old axiom that the mind can only absorb what the seat can endure, but in this case, it was the feet. So eventually the benches came back and that's why we have them today.

But much of what we do in the modern-day Protestant Church is part of that reactionary movement long, long, ago, which was a counter-cult movement against and away from the Roman Catholic church.

At this point, a very important question to look at is: Where did all of this deviation from the Bible originate? How in the world did the Catholic Church get into this stuff, because Catholicism makes claims that they're the true church going all the way back to the Apostle Peter. They say they've always been this way as the one true mother church. Is that true? No. We're going to look at their history and easily connect how it is being repeated today.

Catholicism is a counter movement against Christianity that started after the rule of a guy named Constantine. Roman Catholicism is not and has never been, the true church. They are a spinoff from Constantine's reign. Let me lay that out for you:

The Catholic Church proclaims itself to be the Church that Jesus Christ died for, the original church, the true origin, etc., but is that true? Even a cursory reading in the New Testament will reveal that the Catholic Church did not have its origins in the teachings of Jesus, his Apostles, the New Testament, the Bible, or the early Church beliefs because there is no mention in the Bible from Jesus or the Apostles or the early Church of what Catholicism teaches. There's no mention of the papacy, the worship and adoration of Mary, the immaculate conception of Mary, the perpetual virginity of Mary, the assumption of Mary, Mary as the co-redemptrix and mediatrix, the petitioning of saints in Heaven for their prayers, the apostolic succession, the ordinances of the church functioning as sacraments, infant baptism, confession of sin to a priest, purgatory, indulgences, or the equal authority of the church tradition with Scripture. So, if the origin of the Catholic church is not in the teachings of the early Church, Jesus, the Apostles, or in the New Testament, then how can you say it's the original church?

It's not. Then how did it develop? Constantine laid the groundwork for Roman Catholicism. Here's how:

For the first 280 years of Christian history, Christianity was banned by the Roman Empire and Christians were terribly persecuted. It all changed after Constantine appeared on the scene. He reigned as Roman Emperor from 306 to 337 A.D. There is a debate with some saying he became a Christian, but others don't think so. I'm one of those who lean toward the idea that he probably wasn't saved but whatever; we'll let God be the ultimate judge on that. Now remember, the Christian Church was birthed into heavy duty persecution during its first two to three hundred years and that persecution came from the Roman Empire.

The first official persecution of Christians came in AD 64 when Emperor Nero attempted to blame Christians for the great fire in Rome and according to Church tradition, it was during the reign of Nero that Peter and Paul were martyred in Rome. Christian Church history would say Peter was crucified upside down per his request and Paul was beheaded because he was a Roman citizen and back then you couldn't crucify a Roman citizen.

Christians suffered persecutions for two and a half centuries, almost 300 years for the refusal to participate in the imperial cult. With the imperial cult, as citizens moved around through an average day, they would basically take a pinch of incense and burn it to Caesar. It was to give and pledge their worship to Caesar. Is that something we as Christians could participate in either then or now? No! So, Christians, because of their beliefs did not get along well with Roman laws concerning Caesar worship. It wasn't a whole lot different than what went on with the Catholic Church's attitude of reverence for the Pope. The popes are all-important since Catholicism teaches that he is infallible, so you need to worship him, kiss his ring, kiss his feet, and do whatever he says. It was the same with pre-Catholic Rome under the Caesars. Christians rightly refused certain practices, resulting in the following consequences:

Christians refused to do that, Rome considered it an act of treason, and thus was punished by execution. The most widespread official persecution of Christians was carried out by a guy named Diocletian and that was during 303 to 311 A.D. The emperor ordered Christian buildings and the homes of Christians to be torn down. Their books were collected and burned. Christians were arrested, tortured, mutilated, burned, starved, and condemned to the gladiatorial contests to amuse the spectators. They were thrown to the lions, right?

Constantine came on the scene shortly after that in 311 A.D. People say Constantine's mother Helena influenced him toward Christianity. Sources record that Constantine had a dramatic event happen to him in 312. This is the year right after Diocletian subjected Christians to their worst persecution ever. It had been going on for a long time, but Diocletian's time was the major one. Here's the event and why people say he became a Christian:

"The event, in 312 was the battle of the Milvian Bridge, after which Constantine claimed the Emperorship of the West."

Listen to what Constantine attributed his victory to: *"According to these sources, Constantine looked up to the sun before the battle and saw a cross of light above it."*

How many of you made the unfortunate mistake when you were a kid, and I would assume you haven't done it since you've been an adult, of looking straight into the sun? If you've done that, you know it causes you to see crosses, dots, spots, dogs, and all kinds of things. But anyway, Constantine looked into the sun and supposedly saw a cross with Greek words above it that mean:

"In this sign you will conquer."

So, before the battle took place, Constantine commanded his troops to adorn their shields with the Christian symbol; chi (X) and rho (P). Chi and rho are the first two letters of the Greek word, "Christos", which is where we get "Christ." Christ means, "Anointed One." It's the same thing as the Hebrew word, "Moshiach", which means "Messiah." So, if you overlay the "X" on the lower half of the "P", you'll have the symbol he had put on the shields and it's a symbol we see today.

Constantine won a decisive battle and the story goes that he thought the Christian thing worked for him. Does that sound like a conversion? I don't know. Not to me, but whatever. After the battle he came out with what was called the "Edict of Milan." That was an order Constantine put out that basically stopped the Christian persecution, which was wonderful. Unfortunately, though, that was not all it did. The edict also created what was called, "universal belief." There's a similar word we use today because of what he established then, is still happening now. It's called "tolerance" of all religions and at that time it included Christianity which was being persecuted. So now with this Edict of Milan, people could practice whatever beliefs they wanted.

Constantine said it was proper that the Christians and all others should have liberty to follow that mode of religion, which to each of them appeared best; granting tolerance to all religions including Christianity so he opened up the door to tolerance.

Then just before his death in 337, Constantine was 'baptized' into Christianity. He believed that if he waited to get baptized on his deathbed, he was in less danger of polluting his soul with sin and not getting into Heaven.

Does that sound like he really understood the gospel? It doesn't look that way, so I have a problem with that. But what Constantine did bring in with the Edict of Milan in 313 was this attitude of tolerance. At the same time, Constantine attempted to unify Christianity:

"He envisioned that Christianity could be a convenient religion that could unite the Roman Empire."

The Roman Empire at that time was beginning to fragment and divide so Constantine thought maybe this religion could help them pull together as a country. We know that Rome went down the tubes by 476, which was about 150 years later.

"While this may have seemed to be a positive development for the Christian Church, the results were anything but positive."

Basically, what he did was stop the persecution of the Church and that was admirable, but he also established a tolerance for all religions so what developed was that anyone could believe whatever they want and because of that the different views could then merge. Does that sound familiar? Are churches today trying to merge with other religions? Yes, in fact let me give you some modern-day examples of that:

This happened recently in Sacramento: *"Representatives of the Jewish, Catholic, Protestant, B'hai, Mormon, Sikh, Vedic Druid, and Muslim beliefs are all reading their scriptures and religious texts together."*

That was in combined inclusive services where they were all together and included reading from verses in the Koran. They are promoting all faiths living together in harmony. This is going on in the Church but is that what the Bible teaches? Here's another account:

"Hundreds of Christians, Muslims, Jews, Hindus, Buddhists, and Atheists have convened at the Northwoods Church in Texas, which is a Baptist church, in an effort to try to understand one another."

It's just what Constantine did. He brought in this tolerance that says let's all just come together, merge, and unify. And as you can see, that idea gave birth to the Catholic Church.

"A bishop right now is urging Christians to call God, 'Allah'. The Catholic leader believes it would help ease tension between the religions [Let's all just merge together, right?]. Christians are now being invited in the United States to celebrate 'religious diversity' on Pentecost Sunday. It's called 'Progressive Christianity.' They say, 'We don't claim that our religion [These are supposed to be Christians!] is superior to all others.'"

Yeah, but Jesus does. John 14:6 says Jesus is the way, the truth, and the life. Nobody comes to the father except through Him. I didn't say that. Jesus did. Here's another:

"We can grow closer to God in deeper compassion. We understand our own traditions better through greater awareness."

Another example has been happening since 2007. It's always on the first Sunday in May and they call it "Pluralism Sunday." It's an annual event to bring all the religions together. Again, this is just what Constantine did. He did not Christianize Rome but instead brought in this tolerance of all religions to pull all beliefs together under Rome's unified power. Here's more alarming developments:

"Right now, in the Church, one in four professing born again Christians believe that all people are eventually saved or accepted by God."

That's 25% of the Christian Church today who are infected with this tolerance. Also, 26% say a person's religion doesn't matter because all faiths teach the same lesson. And you wonder why we're going through this study? That's over a quarter of professing born-again Christians in the Church, who now believe it doesn't matter what faith you follow. But if that's really what you believe and you think you can get there somehow other than through Jesus, are you even saved? That's scary ground, man. And listen to this:

"An even higher proportion, 40% of born-again Christians say they believe that Muslims and Christians worship the same God."

Is that what the Bible teaches and what we believe? Again, these are the same teachings Constantine brought in. Yes, it stopped the persecution of the Church and that was wonderful, however, he brought in this attitude of universalism, tolerance, and the need for a Roman figure to control it all. In that way he sought to unify the empire, not just the government, but now it could also include the religions. Is that starting to sound familiar?

During his time, Constantine began to paganize the Church. In his unification process, he would basically look for ways to merge Christianity with Paganism. He worked at ways to take these pagan beliefs and turn them into Christian practices so Rome could invite the pagans to join Christians in this universal worship. As mentioned, it did stop the persecution, but overnight, paganism came in and the Christian Church became polluted. There is an old axiom about growth in the Church:

"The blood of the martyrs is the seed of the Church."

Why did the Christian Church grow so fast? Back then it was because your life was on the line for being a Christian. Why is the Church growing so fast right now over in China and Iran? There your life is on the line for being a Christian. So typically, where there's heavy persecution, when they gather for church services in those kinds of places, do you think you'd find a lot of phony Christians? No! So, imagine an atmosphere where every single person is seriously on fire, dedicated to Jesus Christ because his or her life is on the line. You either mean it or you don't. So, when they get together, can you imagine the Spirit of God moving and what happens in those services? Can you imagine the power?! It's because there is no mixture. It's God's pure word. Let me give you an analogy:

"A 2,000-member Baptist Church was filled to overflowing one Sunday morning, and on this day, the preacher was about ready to start the sermon when two men dressed in long black coats and black hats entered through the back of the church sanctuary. One of the two men walked in the middle of the church while the other one stayed at the back. All of a sudden both of them reached into their coats and pulled out machine guns. Then the one in the middle shouted to the whole 2,000-member congregation: 'Everyone willing to take a bullet for Jesus, stay in your seats.' Well naturally, the pews emptied fast, followed by the choir. Then all the Deacons ran out followed by the choir director and the assistant pastor. In just a few moments there were only about 20 people left in the church along with the pastor, who was holding steady in the pulpit [Of course he was! Hey, it's my story.]. Then all of a sudden, the men put their weapons away and said gently to the preacher: "Okay pastor, all the hypocrites are gone. You can start the service now."

Right? In reverse order, that's what Constantine did to the Church. Yes, he stopped the persecution but then added the idea that now anything goes in the Church. Does that sound like today, or what? Because of those actions and whether he realized it or not, Constantine laid the foundation for the birth of the Roman Catholic Church. Let me finish this chapter with that:

Constantine found that with the Roman Empire being so vast, expansive, and diverse, not everyone would agree to forsake his or her religious beliefs to embrace Christianity, so Constantine allowed and even promoted the Christianization of Pagan beliefs. Completely Pagan and utterly unbiblical beliefs were given Christian identities to merge them into a universal religion. And the idea was for Rome to eventually control this universal religion in order to help control the Roman government that was starting to fracture but also to keep all the religions together. It was basically done to unify the Roman Empire. That was what Constantine did.

Now I said all that to get to this: Where did Roman Catholicism start? The Catholic church says, *"Oh, it started with Peter through a long line of succession."* No, it didn't! Or they say, *"Hey, we're the one true church. We are the remnants of the early Church."* No, you're not!

We see the birth of the first pope was about AD 540. His name was Gregory the Pope, or Great or whatever. He's the first and Rome falls about 35 years after he is born. So, the first pope basically gets his start out of this universal religion movement and then when Rome falls, guess who continues on? It's the Catholic Church.

Let me give you some examples of what he did, and this will explain where they get many of their false teachings and false practices. These are some of the religions that Constantine merged together by Christianizing pagan practices so all could worship together. The first one is the cult of Isis. Listen to this:

The cult of Isis was an Egyptian mother goddess religion and it was absorbed into Catholicism by replacing Isis with Mary. Many of the titles that were used for Isis such as 'Queen of Heaven', 'Mother of God', 'Theotokos' [meaning] God-bearer, were now attached to Mary. Mary was given an exalted role in the Catholic Church way beyond what the Bible describes. In order to attract Isis worshipers to a faith they would not otherwise embrace, this is what they did. In fact, many temples to Isis were converted at this time into temples dedicated to Mary.

So, there you have the birth of "Mary Worship" and "Mariology" in the Catholic Church. It was because Constantine stopped the persecution, which was good, but he brought in this tolerance, which sought to merge all religions together, so he started to Christianize paganism and these are the leftover remnants of that time which have found a home in the Catholic church. Let me give you a second one:

Mithraism was another religion at that time of the Roman Empire, which was very popular for the first through the fifth centuries among the Romans, especially the soldiers. Mithraism was another pagan religion they merged together with Christianity. One of the key features of Mithraism was a sacrificial meal, which involved the eating of the flesh and the drinking of the blood of a bull. Mythras, the god of Mithraism was present in the flesh and blood of the bull and when consumed, granted salvation to those who partook of the sacrificial meal.

What does that sound like?! That is the Eucharist, which Catholicism today teaches is the actual blood and the actual body, not of Mythras, but of Jesus Christ. Also, just like Mithraism, Catholicism says their Eucharist is how you can gain salvation. Its just pagan Mithraism carried forward to further paganize Catholicism. It was also known as, "the eating of one's God." So, the Eucharist and the worship of Mary were both from pagan practices.

On top of that: *"Mithraism had seven sacraments"*, just like the Catholic church does today. That's interesting. A second practice Catholicism adopted from Mithraism appears to be "The Seven Sacraments." As one guy put it:

"...the similarities between Mithraism and Roman Catholicism are too many to ignore."

So here again, Catholicism took the Christian act of communion and merged it with pagan Mithraism. Here's another one:

"Roman emperors and citizens were what was called Henotheists."

A Henotheist means you have only one god though you believe in a plurality of gods. They basically pick one as their favorite god. They would say the one they picked is the most powerful god. Let me give you some examples from back in that time period:

The Roman god, Jupiter was considered supreme over the Roman pantheon of gods. Roman sailors were often worshipers of Neptune, the god of the oceans. When the Catholic church absorbed Roman paganism, it simply replaced the Roman practice of the pantheon of gods with 'saints.'

Catholicism doesn't call them the Roman pantheon of gods anymore. They call them the saints. And just as the Roman pantheon of gods had a god of love, god of peace, god of war, god of strength, god of wisdom, and on down the line, guess what the Catholic church has? They have saints in charge over what? It's all those same categories as the Roman pantheon of gods. They have Saint Michael for soldiers and mariners and Catholicism teaches that you can pray to the long list of saints for help with luck, money, stopping the rain, or whatever.

So, at their origins, that's what Catholicism did with adding the saints. It's just a rip off of the Roman pantheon of gods. Again, these practices don't come from the Bible, they come from a merging of groups and acceptance of each other's beliefs after promotion of this tolerant attitude that is being repeated in the Church today.

Another interesting example from today, is a church that used to be called Christ Community Church but has now changed their name to "C3 Exchange." They have removed their cross and here are some of their beliefs:

They are now preferring to be identified as 'neither Christian nor church'; rather, they seek to be an 'inclusive spiritual community', promising to 'honor all spiritual paths' and accept you 'for who and where you are.' They say the cross is just one symbol of the many faiths. What?! This is being repeated today and was what gave birth to the Roman Catholic Church.

Here are some other examples of paganism at the origins and foundation of Roman Catholicism: Where did the papacy, which is about having a pope, come from? Why do you need a guy in charge like the pope who is supposed to be that all-supreme ruler? Well, that was from the tradition of Roman emperors. Keep in mind that the name is "Roman" Catholicism. It is not just Catholicism.

Where is Roman Catholicism headquartered? Today and always, it has been Rome. Listen to this:

With the city of Rome being the center of government for the Roman Empire and with the Roman emperors living in Rome, the City of Rome rose to prominence in all facets of life. Constantine and his successors gave their support to the Bishop of Rome as the Supreme Ruler of the church. At the time, other Christian bishops and Christians resisted this idea [because it's not Biblical] of the Roman bishop being supreme, but the Roman bishop eventually rose to this supremacy and due to the power and influence of the Roman emperors, he basically took charge of the religion and this is how Roman Catholicism birthed the popes. Now listen this:

"In fact, there was a title the Romans called the Roman emperors. They were called, 'Pontifex Maximus.'"

That's the exact title for Roman Catholic popes. So, you had the Roman Catholic Church headed by a guy with the same title as the Roman Caesars. Why? It was because that's what Constantine wanted to do. He wanted to merge and unify the power bases of the governments and the religions.

Roman Catholicism is not Biblical Christianity. It didn't come from the early Church, the teachings of the Bible, the New Testament, Jesus, or the Apostles. It came as a spinoff of a tolerance movement trying to get all religions to come together. They blended in the pagan terminology and even pagan practices so that then and today their roots are in Paganism. Yet our media is obsessed with trotting out the Catholic priests and bishops before the cameras while saying, *"And now, for the Christian perspective..."*

The origin of the Catholic Church is the tragic compromise of Christianity with pagan religions and instead of proclaiming the Gospel and converting pagans, the Catholic Church Christianized pagan religions and paganized Christianity.

To summarize, basically Roman Catholicism is not sharing the Gospel, it's a pseudo-Christian group, they've deviated from Biblical truth, and they've merged with pagan religions to create a universal "church." By the way, are you familiar with the definition of the word, "Catholic?" It means "universal." So, the

Roman Catholic church means the "Roman Universal Church." If you do your homework, this is all available to discover.

We've looked at a lot of what gave birth to the Holy Roman Empire. The Holy Roman Empire is basically what Western civilization calls The Dark Ages. Rome fell in 476, and the first pope, in practice, was in 440. So, when Rome fell, these guys just continued on and shortly after that the Dark Ages began in Western civilization. Why did it go dark? It was because the Holy Roman Empire took over with the ecclesiastical structure of the Roman Catholic universal church, which then not only controlled the religions, but also the governments. This is where the Dark Ages came from. It was not from Christian Scripture.

That continued on and then there was eventually a split in 1054. The Eastern Orthodox split with the Roman Catholic church over some of these issues and the western church, Catholicism, continued on even up to this day. Then what happened was the popes began to go beyond their religion and began to choose those who would be the rulers of countries and their governments. At that point they were controlling both. Why? It's because that is just what Rome had done. Catholicism is built in their structure. By the way, what does the Roman Catholic Church want to do right now? It's the exact same thing. Why is it that, even in the United States of America, for a long time now, every president elected eventually goes to visit the Pope? Have you ever thought about that? With all due respect, what does the Pope have to do with American policy? What is this about the U.S. checking in with the popes? Rome has never given up its ultimate desire.

Again, Roman Catholicism looks at you and I as what's called the Protestant Experiment. To them, we're just a weird aberration. Their ultimate goal is to bring it all back together. Not just all the religions on the planet, though that's what they're doing right now, but they also want control over the governments. Fast forward to the Book of Revelation in the Bible where it talks about the woman that rides the beast. The Beast is the Antichrist with his One World Government system. Who's riding on top of the Beast initially and controlling the Beast? That is the One World Religion, which is Babylon the Harlot. So, if in fact that's who we're dealing with in this study, the religion that becomes the entity in Revelation, then it's true that they will have finally gotten back what they lost at the Protestant Reformation. The Bible also says it's the worst time in the history of mankind and you don't want to be there. It's the Seven Year Tribulation.

Right now, you're seeing the groundwork for history to be repeated. Today we have this attitude of tolerance making inroads all over the world and even in the Church where we're merging with other religions. In doing so, the Church is backing up into the Roman arms again to facilitate Roman Catholicism taking control of the whole system.

The Dark Ages continued on with Roman Catholicism dominating but what was it that finally busted out of it for a period? It was the Protestant Reformation, which was a "counter-cult" movement. I love that accurate description! Martin Luther normally gets the credit for the Protestant Reformation and of course he rightly deserves the accolades, though it actually started before him. That said:

In the 1500's Martin Luther launched the Protestant Reformation. John Calvin became a Reformation leader based in Geneva, Switzerland, and others, including Huldrych Zwingli and a large Anabaptist movement helped reform religion in the Western world. The Holy Roman Empire continued to hold power, but the seeds of its demise had been sown after the Reformation. The church's imperial influence waned and the authority of the pope was curtailed. Europe for a time emerged from the Middle Ages.

The Middle Ages are also called the Dark Ages. Later we'll get into certain things from that period like the Inquisitions, which amounted to doom for those who dared disagree with Roman Catholicism. It was also during the time of the Holy Roman Empire when they controlled the governments, that they launched military campaigns, which were called, "The Crusades." I've said this before but here it is in context: Christian, you do not have to justify, you shouldn't try, and there is no justification for the Crusades. Don't justify, give an answer, or give an excuse because it was the Roman Catholic Church, who did that. It was not Biblical Christianity so don't fall for the trap where those who haven't studied the issue say things like, *"Oh, you Christians are just as bad as the Muslims. You've committed horrible atrocities."* Wait, I didn't do that! And the Bible doesn't condone it. And true Christianity didn't do that. Roman Catholicism did it and I agree with you that it was horrible, egregious, and wrong! But the Crusades were not carried out by Christianity so don't fall for that.

For a time, we broke out of the Dark Ages, but now what's happening? We are heading back toward the spiritual Dark Ages with the Roman Catholic

Church making inroads at taking back control. The present-day Pope comes to North America and is treated like a pop star. Yet Catholicism has never wavered from their false teachings and they are still the same cult they've always been. They're coming over to North America in an attempt to suck in all religions. Their ultimate desire and goal is for what they had back in the day and what they were birthed from. They want to control all religions and all governments around the world.

Chapter Three

Catholicism is Demonic

So far, we've seen that Roman Catholicism is a pseudo-Christian religion. Pseudo means fake or false, so Catholicism is not Christianity. In the past couple chapters, we took a look at the facts to learn that they are defined, both secularly and Biblically, as a cult. They flunked the possibility of being Christian on both tests. In this chapter we'll see, believe it or not, that they're not only fake and pseudo-Christian, they're not only a cult all the way around, but frankly and unfortunately, they are demonic! In fact, an even more accurate description is "devilish", in their behavior. I didn't say that, Jesus did, so let's take a look at those facts.

Remember that all false philosophies (religions, psychological, etc.) are Satan's creation. Notice I said ALL false philosophies. How many does this apply to? It includes ALL false philosophies, whether religious, psychological, or whatever. If it's a lie, who does it ultimately come from? It's from Satan. So that's the premise we need to look at here. Is Roman Catholicism something that is actually satanic? Is that a fair statement? Or is this just someone's terminology that we're buying into? No, it's not something we've been sold on! This is from Jesus!

In John, Chapter 8, Jesus is the one who lays this out for us. So again, these are not my words, Jesus says that anything false comes from Satan and if it comes from Satan, that makes it satanic, demonic, devilish, etc. We will not only see where lies come from, but we're also going to look at another aspect of Satan, which is his murderous behavior. Jesus talks about Satan's murderous behavior in this Chapter of John and teaches that those who hold onto a falsehood and refuse to listen to the truth are acting like their father, the Devil. Here it is beginning in John 8, verse 31:

"To the Jews who had believed him, Jesus said, 'If you hold to my teaching, you are really my disciples. Then you will know the truth and the truth will set you free.'"

Then some skeptical Jews say something like: Hey listen, we're Abraham's descendants and we've never been slaves to anyone. How can you say we shall be set free?

Jesus replied: *"I tell you the truth; everyone who sins is a slave to sin. Now a slave has no permanent place in the family, but a son belongs to it forever. So, if the Son sets you free, you will be free indeed. I know you are Abraham's descendants. Yet you are ready to kill me..."*

Jesus is not just telling the truth, He is the embodiment of truth. He is the way, the truth, and the life. He, the truth, is right there in front of them. They did not want to receive the Truth so what did they want to do instead? They wanted to kill him. They weren't looking for just an argument that might end later with agreeing to disagree, they would like Him dead. So, Jesus calls them on the carpet in public for not receiving His word no matter what He says:

"Yet you are ready to kill me because you have no room for my word. I am telling you what I have been in the Father's presence, and you are doing what you have heard from your father."

Uh, oh! What do you think Jesus is saying there about who their father is? Let's read on from Jesus after the Jews say Abraham is their father. Jesus answered them:

"If you were Abraham's children, then you would do the things Abraham did. As it is, you were determined to kill me, a man who's told you the truth that I heard from God. Abraham didn't do such things. You are doing the works of your father."

So, a second time Jesus says they don't belong to God the Father because of their murderous behavior. He says to them: You're holding on to a lie, you refuse to receive the truth, and you want to kill me even though I'm just trying to share the truth with you. You're acting like your real father. So, they come back at Him saying they're not illegitimate children and the only father they have is God himself. Now let's look at how Jesus responds:

"If God were your Father, you would love me..."

Yes, you would love Jesus, including his truth, right? And Jesus is the truth.

"...for I came from God and now I'm here. I have not come on my own; But He sent me. Why is my language not clear to you? Because you are unable to hear what I say. You belong to [Listen!] your father, the Devil."

At that point, would you say those guys probably got upset? Yes, but that's okay because Jesus spoke the truth. Where does their desire to kill Jesus come from? Why do they want to get rid of the truth-messenger? The answer can be found by looking at who their father is. It's Satan and they want to carry out their father's desire. That's where this murderous attitude is coming from. It's coming from the Devil. Jesus continues:

"The Devil was a murderer from the beginning, not holding to the truth for there is no truth in him. When he lies, he speaks his native language, for he is a liar and the father of lies."

What's the first point we started with in this chapter? We said ALL false philosophies, all false religions, and everything that is a lie, comes from whom? It is from Satan and we're hearing that straight from Jesus' words in the Bible. This is not just some anti-Catholic thing. It includes anything false, whether it's Catholicism, Mormonism, Hinduism, Buddhism, Islam, or whatever. If it's a lie, it's ultimately coming from Satan. He's the father of all lies! Jesus continues in verse 45:

"Yet because I tell you the truth, you do not believe me! Can any of you prove me guilty of sin? If I'm telling the truth, why don't you believe me? He who belongs to God hears what God says. The reason why you do not hear is because you do not belong to God."

Whoa!! The Jews answered Him: *"Aren't we right in saying that you are a Samaritan and demon-possessed?"*

Again, it's not just that they disagree. They literally and vehemently want to annihilate the messenger here. They are following a lie and first of all, that in itself is satanic. Satan is where all lies come from. Secondly, they want to get rid of the truth. They want to kill it and that is also satanic. That's also what Satan does. Number three: They name-call and the sad irony is that they are so duped, they believe a demonic lie. They are telling Jesus, who is giving them the truth out of love, that Jesus is the one who is demonically deceived, so there are three different satanic aspects involved.

You're going to see every single one of those aspects with Roman Catholicism. They're not just a fake pseudo-Christian cult, they are also demonic, which means devilish. This is the way they act with those who disagree. Catholicism is not okay to leave it at just a verbal conflict. They are out to kill the messenger. We're going to see that's true all throughout history and, believe it or not, it's still in effect today. What we're going to take a look at are the devilish things they did.

Remember too, that you and I as Christians don't have to give an answer for any of this which the Catholic Church did, because Christianity was not responsible for any of it. We saw that with the Crusades and you also don't have to give a response for the Inquisitions, which were an absolutely demonic, devilish attempt to literally kill, murder, and get rid of the truth of Biblical Christianity. That's what we're going to see with the Inquisitions, so let's take a look:

The Inquisitions, or Tribunals were established by the Roman Catholic Church in order to try to seek out and sentence people that the Roman Catholic Church believed to be guilty of heresy. The purpose of the Inquisitions was to secure and maintain religious and doctrinal unity according to the Roman Catholic Church and throughout the Holy Roman Empire through the conversion or persecution of alleged heretics.

Basically, they would torture you until you recant the truth. If you did not recant, you would die! Is that how we Christians today handle someone that disagrees with us? I hope everyone is thinking "No!", and if so, then praise God because that is being Biblical. But that's not what Catholicism did and I'm telling you, their same practice has not gone away today. We'll get to that in a little bit.

With the marriage of church and state that arose in the fourth century, people who the Roman Catholic Church considered to be heretics also came to be considered as enemies of the state. And that merging of church and state is going to return again in the Seven Year Tribulation with the Harlot Woman that rides the Beast, who is colluding with the Antichrist's governmental system. In Revelation, we see that Harlot church is going after every believer in God. If you read about the first half of the Seven Year Tribulation during the Fifth Seal, there is mass martyrdom. Those people are being slaughtered like flies. Christians will become an enemy of the state. What the Holy Roman Empire lost at the Reformation is all going to come back to them and believe it or not, I don't think we're that far off from the return of Catholicism's control over religions and governments. And at that time, it won't be that you're just labeled a heretic, you will literally become an enemy of the state, which means the government comes and hunts you down, and they don't just hunt you to throw you in jail, they capture you and then because you're a supposed heretic, who doesn't believe what Catholicism says you need to believe, you will die! Christians will be tortured until they recant or die. Do you think that could happen? Well folks, we're seeing it right now.

What are the two things that even evangelical Christianity is being severely persecuted for around the world? Even here in the United States we see the telltale signs. First is the moral issue of homosexuality. If you disagree with that, what are you called? You're basically a heretic to them. You're labeled a bigot, homophobe, and hater. Now you can even be prosecuted for a hate crime. They want to have you put away. The second thing we're persecuted for is our belief that Jesus is the only way. We didn't make that up. It's John 14:6, right? They are calling that exclusivism. They say, *"What gives you the right to think your religion is the only way?"* But I didn't say it, Jesus did. Take it up with Him. Since I'm a follower of Jesus, and now we're referring back to John 8, I love Jesus. And a sign that I love Him is I believe what He says because He is THE truth. I can't recant that!

But those are the two things I believe are going to be part of the last nails in the coffin as things ramp up with secularists and other religions claiming, *"We need to do something about these 'so-called' Christians. They are right-wing fundamentalists and terrorists."*

With the Inquisitions, you might be wondering if they were really that bad. Yes, they were horrid! I want to share just some of what was happening.

Keep in mind that what I'm about to give you, as gross as it is, will only demonstrate the mild stuff. Now what is the point of listing these horrible atrocities? It is to show that Roman Catholicism is devilish and demonic. It isn't that you are even allowed to disagree with them and walk away. No, no, no, they will torture you until you recant, or you'll be tortured until you die. This really happened in history a multitude of times. Once they took control and implemented these despicable enforcements of their false doctrines, the world was plunged into what came to be known as the Dark Ages. But listen to some of these:

"Strappado", also known as "Corda", was a torture technique they used during the Inquisitions. It was a method of torture involving binding the victim's hands behind their back and then suspending them by the wrists. Sometimes a series of drops would be added. It would force your arms out of your sockets. As you can imagine, at some point your arms are going to pop right out. Also, weights could be added to the victim's body, making it even more excruciating.

As Jesus said, you [torturers] want to do what your father the devil does. You want to kill Me just because I'm telling you the truth. Roman Catholicism is not just pseudo-Christian and not only a cult, but they're devilish in their behavior with those who disagree.

The "Rack" was one of the most well-known methods of torture. The victim had their hands and feet bound to rollers at the opposite ends of a big frame. The torturer would turn the rollers so that the chains attached to the victim's arms and legs would dislocate the joints of the victim. They'd finally just pop them. If the torturer continued because you didn't recant, they'd turn the rollers until the victim's arms and legs would literally be torn off. They would not stop until you either recanted your disagreement with Catholic doctrine, or you would die. The mindset was: We're going to kill you because you don't believe what we believe. You, Christian, are the one who is demonic and we Roman Catholics have to get rid of you. As we just read in John, Chapter 8, these attitudes where the same that ancient Jews had for Jesus.

"Toca", or "Waterboarding" is still used today and involves securing the victim to an inclined board and binding them so they cannot move. Then the victim is gagged and has a cloth placed over his or her face. Water is then poured over it, which gives the victim a feeling of drowning even if no water enters the nose and the mouth. The CIA actually uses this today as part of their training. On average, a person can only last fourteen seconds before they are begging to be released. And the Holy Roman Empire would do that so someone whose only offense was saying they don't think they believe what Catholics do.

"Mancuerda" is another one, you can look up pictures online but I don't recommend it. It's a process where the torturer ties a tight chord around the victim and then grasps both ends of the cord. The torturer then throws his weight backwards and this causes the chord to cut through the flesh, the muscle, and into the bone. It begins to shred the person. This would be repeated many times in several areas of the victim's body.

The "Head-Crusher" was exactly that! I saw a picture and just thought, *"You've got to be kidding me. Who would do such a horrible thing?"* As the name suggests, it crushes the victim's head. The victim's chin is placed on a metal bar and a cap is placed on top of the head. Then the torturer turns a screw, which causes the head to press down against the bar. This causes the teeth to shatter, jaw bones to break, the eyes to pop out, and eventually leads to a slow excruciating death.

And let me mention again that I'm sharing just the milder torture methods. As if what you've already heard wasn't sick enough, there are some that literally made me ill.

"Water Cure" involved forcing the victim to imbibe up to 30 pints of water, resulting in intense pain and often death. They would just keep the water going into you until it kills you. Again, you either recant or you're going to die.

The "Maiden of Nuremberg" was also known as the "Iron Maiden." This was a sarcophagus looking thing which had blades inside. The victim was locked inside the coffin for hours while blades pierced the body in non-lethal areas, causing extreme pain.

This one was gross: The Spanish Tickler was a metal claw, sometimes attached to a pole. I saw some pictures of a couple different forms of it. One of them was basically a big old metal pole that had these three large long curved prongs. The prongs came to a sharp point like a giant metal bird claw. Some had more than three prongs, but it was in the shape of a claw. On a naked and bound victim, what the torturer would do was put the sharp claw (the tickler) on the person and literally rake their body and shred them. It would also break their bones. Usually it started with the arms and then they would move to the chest. Then they would flip the victim over and rake their back. They would then get their neck and finally flip them over again to get their face, which almost always resulted in death. They would literally rake and shred them with these razor-sharp tools.

That's horrific enough just to think that this happened, but could these monstrous practices ever return to use? Yes, they will, and it'll all be coming back during the Seven Year Tribulation. I wonder what religious organization is going to be a part of it? Let's move on:

"When an Inquisition was set up to investigate heresy in a particular area, the Holy Roman Empire..."

Isn't that an oxymoron; "Holy" Roman Empire?

"...the Pope would appoint two 'inquisitors', each of which had equal authority. These inquisitors had the power to investigate and excommunicate even princes. They wielded enormous power and influence."

Did you catch that? These inquisitors had the power to even confront princes, who were rulers of countries. Rulers of governments could be threatened with torture. This is why I said Rome not only got ecclesiastical control over spiritual things, but they also got control over the governments of the countries. They held sway over both. And again, that's what is ironic. When you see the Harlot Woman (a religious entity) that rides the Beast in Revelation 17, that's what she is doing. The Antichrist with his One World Government system is being led at first by the harlot religious system until God destroys her. At the beginning, she's the one in control over the Beast system. So, all at the same time, she's back in control of the religions and the governments.

That's what the Catholic Church had and it's what they will be getting back. Again, these inquisitors had the authority to approach powerful people and figuratively, as well as literally hold their feet to the fire. When the Reformation really began to take place with Martin Luther, John Calvin, and others, secular princes would rescue them and hide them out in their castles. It was not because the princes were necessarily convinced of Biblical truth, it was because they saw a way out of the stranglehold of the Catholic Church which was controlling their secular governments. Through reformers gaining ground, maybe people would realize the popes did not deserve the authority and certainly not to round people up at random including princes who disagreed with them. Actually, it wasn't just telling the truth, which Catholicism called heresy that landed you on the bad side of the Holy Roman Empire, it was whatever the Pope felt like commanding you to do. If you declined, disagreed, or disobeyed, he could label you a heretic and have you brought in to learn which torture you'll get.

This was the kind of society the Holy Roman Empire built and the age of it became known as the Dark Ages. So, what did we Christians protest against? It was about fighting for the truth, but it was also against this horrid behavior. Why was America so vehement about freedom at our founding? It was because of what we came out of. It was this treatment where if you disagreed, you were tortured to death. You were not allowed to just disagree and walk away. There was no seeing them the next morning in the office around the water cooler for round two. You were tortured to death. This is what we protested against and what we founded our country on. Now after looking at that history, it's crazy that we've get the Pope coming over here and being treated like a rock star. The Holy Roman Empire has never changed. Let's continue:

"The inquisitors were known to subject people to cruel and unusual punishment including torture. They could imprison subjects that they thought were just lying."

So, you only needed to lie, or be thought to have lied, and they had reason enough to torture you. Here are some torture techniques with explanations. We'll quickly look at how they used a few of these torture devices and then we'll move on. Remember, all you'd have to say is something like, *"I'm not sure I really believe what you believe."* That's all it would take for you to be facing one of these consequences:

The Heretic's Fork was an insidious device designed to induce long periods of sleep deprivation and often used as a punishment or as a means of gaining a confession. It was very simple; consisting of a double-ended fork, which was placed between the chin and the breastbone. A leather binding was then used to secure it around the neck. Often the victim would be hung from the ceiling or positioned in such a way as to prevent the wearer from speaking or indeed, sleeping. Inevitably tiredness and fatigue would take over and the victim's head would eventually fall forward, forcing the four prongs into his throat and chest resulting in excruciating levels of pain. Combining both fatigue and severe pain, the heretic's fork became an invaluable tool during the war on witchcraft and became a favorite amongst witch hunters and interrogators alike.

The Knee Splitter was yet another hideous device used during the Inquisition. As the name suggests, its sole purpose was to split the knee although it was often used on other joints such as elbows, wrists, and ankles. They ranged in size but usually consisted of two wooden blocks, each supporting a number of wooden or metal spikes and finally joined by two threaded bolts. It would be placed either side of the joint and slowly tightened like a clamp. This forced the spikes into the knee, shredding both bone and flesh. As a result, the joint was completely destroyed leaving the victim in excruciating pain. This rendered the leg completely useless and if you were lucky enough to survive the interrogation, developing an infection was almost a guarantee, thus the victim would often succumb to gangrene and if the limb was not amputated, which in itself was a life-threatening procedure, then death was almost a certainty.

The Witches Chair, or Chair of Torture was yet another diabolical device conjured up in order to gain a confession. They could vary in design but were normally a simple hard wooden chair similar in construction to the dunking stool, although were covered in metal spikes which the victim would be forced onto, bound, and left to suffer. Although the spikes punctured the flesh, they were carefully positioned to miss vital organs and because the victim was skewered and unable to move, they also served to plug wounds stemming the flow of blood. In some variations, hot coals could be placed beneath the seat in order to burn the victim. However, regardless of the design, a timely death was never a condition of this hideous device. Thus, its unfortunate occupant could survive for anything from a few hours to several days. There was yet another side to the Witches Chair. Interrogator's quickly realized the psychological power they could wield by simply threatening a subject or in more extreme cases, by forcing an individual to watch the torture of another, often a neighbor, a friend, or even a member of one's own family. Therefore, a confession was often gained simply by threatening the victim with its use.

The Spanish Donkey. Here we have yet another insidious device that's sole purpose was to inflict tremendous amounts of pain and dreadful injuries, predominantly on women. Similar to the Judas Cradle, the Spanish Donkey was basically a triangular piece of wood or metal with a point facing upwards. In many instances, an increasing amount of weight was placed on the victim's legs and feet, thus increasing the amount of pressure placed on the genitals by the point. As a result, many victims had hip joints ripped apart and some even ruptured under the pressure. Regardless, an encounter with a Spanish Donkey had only one guaranteed outcome: An insidiously painful death.

How did Jesus put it? Like this: *'Why do you want to kill me? I'm just trying to tell you the truth. You want to kill me because you're doing what your father desires and your father is not God the Father, it's the Devil and you're acting just like him.'*

So, it's not just a pseudo-Christian cult. It's also demonic. We all make a big deal, and rightly so, about the jihadists in Islam, but how long has the Roman Catholic Church been doing the same? It was long before the Islamic jihadists even showed up on the scene. While Catholicism does the same thing, they are never called on the carpet for it because a lot of people have been duped into thinking that Roman Catholicism is the same thing as Biblical Christianity, but it's not! And the Christian Church is even chumming up to Catholicism again. I don't know about you, but I don't want to cozy up to those folks. That said, I'll witness to them for sure and at the same time hope they don't return to some of these horrible persecutions again in our lifetime, but I'm not going to budge on the truth and I'll just hope they don't go there again soon. I know this torture stuff is hard to think about, but this is what they do. Let's continue on about the inquisitors, who practiced these obscene cruel punishments on behalf of the Catholic Church, and you'll notice another oxymoron in the first few words:

"In 1252, Pope ***'Innocent'*** *IV officially sanctioned torture as a way of extracting truth from subjects. During the Spanish Inquisition alone, as many as 2,000 people were burned at the stake. The Spanish Inquisition of course was set up by King Ferdinand and Queen Isabella of Spain in 1478..."*

Does that time period sound familiar? Columbus sailed a bit later in 1492.

"...and also, with the approval of Pope Sixtus IV, it focused mainly on the Jews..."

So, at this point they not only want to get rid of Christians, but also the Jewish people.

"...who were suspected of having continued to practice Judaism. Later on, with the spread of Protestantism into Spain, the Inquisition also began to persecute

Protestants who broke away from the Catholic Church. The Inquisition essentially became more like a secret police. [a Nazi-style Gestapo] That secret police is still in effect today."

Can you guess what the name of the secret police is for the Catholics? They are called; the Jesuits and they're the Pope's army. We'll get to more on that in a minute. Oh, and by the way, as we mentioned, Pope Francis is a Jesuit and the first Jesuit pope ever. So that's double trouble. Anyway, let's continue on:

"The secret police would investigate and retaliate against internal threats. One historian estimated that over the course of the Spanish Inquisition alone, they tried a total of 341,021 people, of whom at least ten percent, 31,912 were executed."

So, one question I have is how in the world did the Gospel survive during all this and then continue all the way up to the birth of the Catholic Church? Catholicism's persecution of Christians went all the way up to the Reformation in the 1500's. When the Christian reformers started to break away, shortly after that, the Puritans and then the Pilgrims came to the United States, which gave us what we have today. But in the span of all history, Christian's reprieve from persecution has been kind of a short blip. That's why Catholicism calls Christians the "Protestant Experiment." They want their world power back and unfortunately, they are making inroads with the Church. They're gathering us back as we're being duped. Roman Catholicism has never changed.

But how in the world did Christianity survive with this kind of devilish behavior happening? They'd say if you disagree, we, the state, are going to hunt you down and kill you. You've then become an enemy of the state, which is the Holy Roman Empire. Well let's trace the trail explaining how Christianity was preserved on up into the time of the Protestants in England, who eventually came here to the United States to establish what we have today. I think sometimes we take this God-orchestrated preservation of Christianity for granted. Here is how we survived and by now you understand why the Middle Ages were called the Dark Ages:

Throughout the centuries, God has preserved his Word. He's raised up men and women, even during the Middle Ages, often called the Dark Ages. The truth of the Gospel was still available. The Roman Catholic Church, the Holy

Roman Empire was at the height of their power and the common language of the Bible was suppressed. The language of that day began to change into English, but the Catholic Church deliberately kept the Bible in Latin so even if you could come across a copy of it, you couldn't read it because people no longer spoke or read Latin so these translations got the reformers killed. They took the Latin version of the Bible, the Vulgate, and translated it into English. For that they were subjected to the Inquisitions. They were tortured, murdered, and all kinds of horrible stuff.

God's word was still active. God's hand is never shortened that it cannot save [Isaiah 59 - His truth was marching on, right?]. The Church had already survived much persecution of the Roman emperors.

In the last chapter we saw the Christian persecution by the Emperor Diocletian, which was the worst of it, but for the first couple hundred years from the Church's inception, there was also heavy persecution. Though that persecution had a way of keeping the Church pure because your life is on the line. There was no phony Christian stuff, easy believeism, and easy Christianity. If you mentioned you're a Christian, you could die. But what persecution did was keep the Church pure. Powerful amazing things took place from a pure Church without all the falsehood, baloney, and fake believers. With a purer Church, the Spirit of God moves, right? So, Christians were used to persecution since the Church's inception. Acts, Chapter 2 talks about how persecution broke out early with the Church and it's been that way ever since.

As we talked about in the last chapter, Rome, under Constantine, began to consolidate its power. Again, what he did was start merging paganism with the Christian Church and shortly after that was the birth of the first pope. Then the Roman Catholic Church, the Holy Roman Empire held power all the way up through the Dark Ages and on up to the Protestant Reformation.

Now during the time when Catholicism was starting to take off from Constantine and as you look throughout Christian Church history, there were Christians who spoke up like Bishop Alexander and Bishop Athanasius. Even back then, they begin to translate the Bible and spread it throughout Europe. Even during the Middle Ages, which again were the Dark Ages, small groups of Christians tried to do the Lord's work, but it mostly had to be in these smaller groups because the Catholic Church literally hunted them down like animals and slaughtered them by the tens of thousands just because they believed in the Gospel.

As in John, Chapter 8, the same type of persecution was happening during the Holy Roman Empire's Dark Ages, which were called that because it was dominated by the Catholic Church. At that time there was not only the Inquisitions with the devilish behavior of torturing people for disagreeing with the Roman Catholic Church, but there was also something called The Crusades. Now with the Crusades, just as with the Inquisitions, if someone comes up to you as a Christian and states an old false narrative like:

"Oh, you Christians, I tell you what, you guys are just as bad as those Islamic terrorists. I can't believe you're even mentioning the jihadists when you guys killed so many people in the Crusades."

No, we did not! The Roman Catholic Church did. And I'll be the first one to agree with you that it was horrific, non-Christian, ungodly, and certainly nothing that Jesus would do. You and I as Christians should never have to or even try to defend something that we're not responsible for like the <u>Catholic</u> Crusades.

Again, the other thing Christians are falsely accused of is the Inquisitions. They'll say we Christians tortured people and that Islamic terrorists are bad, but Christians did the same thing with the Inquisitions. Again, no, we did not! The Roman Catholic Church did that, so I don't have to defend something our people didn't do. Besides, who was it that the Catholic Church oftentimes killed, not only during the Inquisitions but also with the Crusades? It was both Christians and Jews so don't fall for that trap. It was all the behavior of the so-called "Holy" Roman Empire. Here is some of that:

In the 11th and 12th centuries, you had a group called the Petrobrussians and they rejected infant baptism. They became known as the Anabaptists. They re-baptized believers who had been baptized as infants, maintaining that baptism is only valid if it was a conscious act of faith by the adult believer. The Anabaptists survived intense persecution and from the Anabaptists we had the English Baptists, which became prominent in the mid 1600's here in the United States.

That's our heritage, which includes escaping from being murdered by Catholicism. Again, I think the Church is guilty of an old axiom: *"Those who do not learn their history are doomed to repeat it."*

This is our history and we didn't just protest against falsehood, we protested against this torturous murderous behavior brought on just because we disagreed with Roman Catholicism. And yet, everyone wants to chum-up with Catholicism so that all of us can just get along. Christians are actually saying it's all the same and that Catholics believe the same things we believe. But no, they do not!

The Waldensians was a group founded by Peter Waldo in Lyon, France in the 1100's. Waldo valued the necessity for all Christians to preach the Gospel, which of course is Matthew 28 that talks about the Christian's great commission to witness to non-believers. Well, in 1184 a Papal Bowl was issued against all Waldensians to hunt them down and kill them. Of course, it was just because they said, "We need to share the Gospel!" Again, how did Christianity survive with all this murderous behavior where Catholicism would literally hunt you down, torture you, and kill you for being Christian? Well these are the ways Jesus kept His Church alive.

Other reform groups that existed before the Protestant Reformation were the Novatians, the Albigenses, the Petrobrussians, the Paulicians, the Cathari, the Paterines, the Lollards, and more. Long before Martin Luther posted his 95 Theses on the door in Wittenberg, Germany in 1517, there were men [and women] who stood up for true [Christian] reform and the true Gospel. That's what we saw before with the account of John Wycliffe and John Hus. The 16th century is when you begin to see the Reformation but notice all the Christians furthering the Gospel long before that. It all led to the Reformation and what was it that Christians were rejecting? It was not only standing for biblical truth, but it was speaking out against this murderous behavior.

"During the 16th century, other godly men stood in opposition to the Church of Rome--Jakob Hutter (founder of the Hutterites), John Knox of Scotland, William Tyndale..."

Tyndale was murdered by the Catholic church simply for translating the New Testament into English so that anyone knowing English could read the Bible.

"...John Calvin of France, Ulrich Zwingli of Switzerland, and the English reformers; Cranmer, Latimer, and Ridley, all burned at the stake."

They were burned just because they disagreed with Roman Catholicism. A ruler named "Bloody Mary" burned them to death. Before Bloody Mary showed up on the scene and took power, it was a Protestant England in that area. When she took over, she ruled that the citizens would go back to being Catholic. If you disagreed with her decision, she did what Catholics do because it's built into their doctrine. It's how Catholicism deals with truth tellers they label heretics. They kill them. So of course, that's what she began to institute and it's where the name, Bloody Mary came from. She murdered tons and tons of our brothers and sisters in Christ. These men who were burned at the stake were reformer leaders who translated the Bible so that anyone could read it and not just the elite.

God has remained faithful in every age. Those faithful Christians were used by God to contend earnestly for the faith that was once and for all delivered to the saints.

Let me give you a little more information from this narrator on a television program about that period of time, and specifically what the Catholic Church was up to:

"For centuries, to disobey the pope was heresy punishable by death. JH Ignaz Von Dollinger, a leading 19th century Catholic professor of church history, confessed; 'Since 1183, the view of the Catholic church had been...that every departure from the teaching of the Catholic church...must be punished with death and the most cruel of deaths, by fire..."

For 1000 years before the Reformation, there were Christians who refused to give allegiance to Rome and who were slaughtered by the millions. Everyone knows of the Crusades to retake the holy land, but few know that even larger and more numerous crusades were fought in an attempt to exterminate Christians all over Europe, who out of conscience to God and obedience to the Bible would not submit to the authority of the popes or embrace wrongs and heresies. Of these martyrs, historian Will Durant wrote: *'The Roman church, the martyrs were sure, was the Whore of Babylon.'*

The popes promised instantaneous entrance into Heaven for those who gave their lives slaughtering the heretics. It took about a century to exterminate the Albigensian Christians, who at one time were the majority of the population of southern France. Among the cities wiped out by Pope Innocent III, was Beziers, France. 60,000 were massacred there, including women and children. In the infamous St Bartholomew's Massacre in August 1572, 70,000 Huguenots were killed. Another 200,000 were slaughtered over a period of months, causing 500,000 to flee to Protestant countries for refuge. The Waldenses were all but exterminated, as were the Hussites.

Here is an excerpt from Pope Martin IV's letter to the King of Poland in 1429, one hundred years before the Reformation: *"Know that the interest of the Holy See, and those of your crown, make it a duty to exterminate the Hussites. Remember that these impious persons dare proclaim principles of equality...that all Christians are brethren...that Christ came on Earth to abolish slavery; they call the people to liberty. While there is still time, then turn your forces against Bohemia: burn, massacre, make deserts everywhere for nothing could be more agreeable to God, are more useful to the cause of kings, than the extermination of the Hussites."*

To mention the horror of the tortures and murders of the Inquisitions that terrorized Europe for centuries would take volumes. There is no city on earth that has shed more blood, both of Christians and Jews, than Rome. Pagan Rome threw Christians to the lions and killed them in periodic persecutions during the first three centuries. That was nothing however compared to the slaughter of both Christians and Jews by Catholic Rome. Historian Will Durant wrote candidly: *"Compared with the persecution of alleged heresy in Europe by the Roman Catholic Church...the persecution of Christians in the first three centuries after Christ, by Pagan Rome, was a mild and humane procedure."*

Yes, this woman is indeed drunk with the blood of the Saints and the martyrs of Jesus and no other city comes even close to Rome in this regard.

Notice he said the pope guaranteed entrance into Heaven, if you do what? It was if you went after the so-called heretics and killed them. Does that ring a bell? What does that sound just like? It's exactly what Islam teaches, right? But this had been going on from Catholicism a lot longer and well before Muhammad appeared on the scene, so in essence, although it may not be politically correct, is it fair to ask: Who is the original, and still today, the ongoing jihadists? It's Roman Catholicism. That's just going with the facts.

Now let's break down the Inquisitions. History traditionally says there are four periods of inquisitions, but I believe what we're going to see is five. And the fifth one is still in place today, which is the bombshell we'll see at the end of this information:

The first of the inquisitions is known as the Medieval or Episcopal Inquisition and refers to the various tribunals that started around 1184. The second major inquisition was the Spanish Inquisition set up by King Ferdinand and Queen Isabella of Spain in 1478. Third, was the Portuguese Inquisition, which was established in Portugal in 1536 and operated much like the famous Spanish Inquisition. Later, in 1560, in India and other parts of the Portuguese Empire of Asia, these inquisitions dealt with converts from Hinduism who were suspected of continuing to practice some of their Hindu beliefs.

The last period, which they call period four, is what they call the Roman Inquisition. Listen to this:

It was established in 1542 when Pope Paul III established the Holy Office. That is their term and it is still used today, as the final court of appeals in all trials of heresy. This group was made up of cardinals and other officials whose task was to maintain and defend the doctrines of the Catholic Church. This group played an important role in the counter reformation and it was also this body that condemned Galileo for grave suspicion of heresy and banned all his works in 1633 for teaching that the sun was the center of the Universe and that the Earth revolved around the sun.

There's another lie Christians are often accused of. They'll say the Christians taught that the Earth was flat or that Christians were trying to hold back true science and even eliminated Galileo. But Christians had no part in all that! Again, Roman Catholicism was at the center of it.

So that was all part of what they would consider the last inquisition called the Roman Inquisition. During that time the basic headquarters for the inquisition was named The Holy Office so as we continue, remember that it was set up in the mid 1500's.

The next phase happened during the time of Vatican II in 1965. A lot of people want to excuse the Catholic Church by saying they used to be that way but today they've radically changed and they're now more like us Christians. That's extremely naive at best and a lie at worst! All they did was change the terminology and repackage themselves. It's still the same belief system. I'm telling you, Rome will never change and has no intention of changing and they're not going to change their behavior either! I'll get to that in a minute. First listen to this:

"In 1965 [during Vatican II] Pope Paul VI reorganized the Holy Office and changed it to the "Congregation for the Doctrine of the Faith", and it remains in effect today."

So, this doctrine and power of inquisition is still in effect. It was called the Holy Office until they changed the name to the Congregation for the Doctrine of the Faith, which is still in effect today. Those are not my words. Again, it's from their literature. So technically this power structure to implement inquisition-type torturous murderous behavior against heretics who disagree with the Catholic Church, is still in effect today.

Now let me further explain the workings of this Congregation for the Doctrine of the Faith, which until 1965 had always been known by Catholics as the Holy Office. When you hear them say Holy Office, maybe because the new name is just too long, that's what they're talking about. In their own terminology, they say this Holy Office is part of the Universal Inquisition, so they admit it has not ended. The Inquisition against Protestants continues up to this day. Here is more on that:

"Its headquarters is at the Palace of the Holy Office just outside Vatican City. It serves as the final court of appeals in trials of heresy and serves as an important part of the counter Reformation."

So, because of the Reformation, the Catholic Church lost their controlling grip on the states and countries, they tried their best to crack down and murder all the dissenters, but many escaped to other countries and spread too fast. The reformers got out of control (in Catholicism's mind), and then came over to America where reform could really gain a foothold. I'm sure Roman Catholic leadership was wondering what to do with that. Sadly though, Catholicism is back making inroads into North America and all over the world.

They are pulling in Europe, which has gone dark again for a multitude of reasons, the greatest of which is getting away from Biblical Christianity. So, Catholicism's influence is coming back. It's all part of their Counter Reformation. And they still have this inquisition against you and I in full force to this day. Let's continue.

In 1981, guess who headed up this Holy Office, which again, is now also called the Congregation for the Doctrine of Faith? Who led this office for the ongoing inquisitions against the Protestants, which has as its tenets, that it will kill heretics? In 1981 Joseph Ratzinger took control of it. Who is he? You probably remember him as the previous pope to the current Pope Francis. That is Pope Benedict, who was Pope from 2005 to 2013. He was in charge of this inquisition office.

"In 1988, Pope John Paul II reaffirmed the Holy Office's authority. On November 11th, 2014 Pope Francis set up within them, a 'special body to expedite the consideration of appeals.' In 2015, Francis established an Ecclesiastical Judicial Commission, which has its own staff."

It appears that they are getting geared up for something. And the term that's been popularized lately is "last days extreme vetting." Are they conditioning our minds to be prepared for a world where anyone who disagrees with this universal religious belief system needs to be eliminated? Could that happen? It looks like the machinery is being put into place.

So, in their own words, this ongoing inquisition is still in effect to this day, blessed by the Vatican, expanding in the Vatican, and waiting for the right time. Listen to what they say they consider a crime:

"This includes investigations into 'grave derelicts', i.e., acts which the Catholic Church considers to be the most serious crimes."

Let's look at a few of those "most serious crimes" they are going to come get you for: If you say anything against the Eucharist, they're coming for you. Again, the Eucharist is their version of Communion and we saw earlier that it is blasphemy. So, from this secular information and not from me, the Holy Office is on the books saying they are going to get you. Does that sound like any other religion you're familiar with? If you say anything against Mohammed, what's going to happen to you? You die! If you say anything against the Koran, what's going to happen? You die! If you convert someone away from Islam, what happens? You die! And this goes on and on. So, who are the original jihadists? Roman Catholicism is. Islamic Jihadists are being called to the carpet for their behavior but how come no one is talking about Catholicism?

Remember, Roman Catholicism wants their state control back. They want to control the governments again. Again, after a presidential election, why is it that every American president goes over to see the Pope? With all due respect, who cares about the Pope? What does that have to do with us? Why are you going over there? What's going on with that? Who's in charge and pulling the strings here? Who's submitting to whom? If you disagree, according to what these guys have on their books and what they've been adding to those books, they're planning to come get you. If you speak against the Eucharist, according to Catholicism, you're a 'grave derelict' who is guilty of the most serious crimes.

They also say you are guilty of the most serious crimes and a grave derelict if you say anything against the sanctity of the Sacrament of Penance. Do you remember what we looked at with their idea of Penance? It's basically their works-based system to work off your own punishment for sin. You need to do all these things, including category "2" of subset "F" on a certain day of the week while kneeling and thumbing through beads at a Catholic altar, and blah, blah, blah. If you, anyone, or I say anything against that, you're a grave derelict and they're coming after you!

Now I'd like to point out the obvious to Roman Catholicism: You, Catholicism, will sit there and take people to task, putting them under this ongoing [your terms, not mine] Universal Inquisition against Protestant Christianity just because they disagree with your false teachings. You promote non-biblical blasphemous things like something you call the Eucharist, that people need to work their way into Heaven, and that they need to work off their punishment for sins, but you apparently don't care to do much of anything about the pedophile priests in your own organization. Does anyone find that ironic? How in the world is that allowed to continue? Who's pulling the strings behind the scenes? How come that one hasn't been put to rest? If any Joe Schmo public was guilty of that, they'd be going to jail lickety split. How do these guys continue and continue and continue to get away with it? Who's pulling the strings? Right?

After the Protestant Reformation and besides the Holy Office, facts came out about another alarming faction of the Catholic Church, which is also continuing to this today. The Reformation led to these guys forming in 1540. Their name is the Jesuits and they're also known as the Papal Elite Troops. This is the Roman Catholic army. It's the army of these Catholic guys who are responsible to handle those who disagree with the Catholic Church.

Earlier, I introduced you to the last couple paragraphs from the present-day Jesuit Extreme Oath of Induction. That oath is what they have to pledge to do as a Jesuit in the Catholic Church. What I want to do now is take a bit more time as we finish this chapter, to give you the first part of the oath starting with what the Superior says and then much of the rest of the oath including the part you saw before. Again, these guys are the army of the Vatican that is still supporting their Catholicism's inquisition against Protestants and whomever else disagrees with them. This is all in place as Catholic doctrine today and is still enforced today. Here's what the Superior says in this ceremony:

"Heretofore, you have been taught to act the dissembler and to be a spy. Among the reformers, to be a reformer; among the Protestants, generally to be a Protestant, obtaining their confidence, to seek even to preach from their pulpits..."

They always want to say, "Oh, but aren't we all the same?" No, we are not! What are these Jesuit guys pledging to do? As a weasel amongst you, they are promising to lie to your face and also get their tacit approval for Catholicism from being in your midst. They hope to even be able to get behind your pulpit to lead your sheep. Why do they want to obtain our confidence? That's where it continues:

"...that you might be enabled to gather together all information for the benefit of your Order as a faithful soldier of the Pope."

Now here's how the oath taker responds to the Superior and again, this is the Jesuits Extreme Oath:

"I (name), declare and swear, that his holiness the Pope is Christ's Vice-regent and is the true and only head of the Catholic or Universal Church throughout the earth; that he has the power to dispose heretical kings, princes, states, commonwealths and government,..."

Oh, I see. You're going back to what we escaped from with our Reformation. This oath is talking about a global program. So, is this why people keep meeting with the Pope? Are you threatening people, or something? Are you putting things back to the way it used to be? What's going on here? The oath continues:

"...commonwealths and governments, all being illegal without his sacred confirmation and that they may safely be destroyed."

So, anyone that doesn't agree with them and they consider illegal, they believe they have the authority to act against them, and these Jesuits are the army to do it secretly like assassins. They are saying, "We will come and take you out." This is what they believe the Pope has the authority to do on the entire planet.

"Therefore, to the utmost of my power I shall and will defend this doctrine of his Holiness' right against all usurpers of the heretical or Protestant authority whatever..."

"I furthermore promised and declare that I will, when opportunity presents, make and wage relentless war, secretly or openly, against all heretics, Protestants, and liberals as I am directed to do, to [Listen!] exterminate them from the face of the whole earth; and that I will spare neither age, sex, or condition; and that I will hang, waste, boil, flay, strangle..."

Wait, they wouldn't do that, would they? Well, what did we just see earlier? They have certainly done it all and worse. And they are doing it and will do it as long as it takes to exterminate all who disagree. We are fooling ourselves if we think they would never go back to this!

"...I will hang, waste, boil, flay, strangle, and bury alive these infamous heretics, rip up the stomachs and wombs of their women and crush their infant's heads against the walls, in order to annihilate forever their execrable [repulsive or disgusting] race. That when the same cannot be done openly, I will secretly use the poisoned cup, the strangulating cord, the steel of the poniard [dagger], or the leaden bullet, regardless of the honor, rank, dignity, or authority of the person or persons, whatever may be their condition in life, either public or private, as I at any time may be directed to do so by any agent of the Pope or Superior of the Brotherhood of the Holy Faith, of the Society of Jesuits."

And we now have a double whopper seated at the top of the Vatican. We not only have Pope Francis, who is the Pope, but for the first time in their history, Francis is also one of the Catholic Jesuit army who has taken that oath. So now when Mr. Rock Star Pope comes here to talk to us, what should we be reading between the lines? We should understand he comes from the following point of view:

'I have the authority to, openly or secretly as the Pope and a Jesuit, do what I want to do to any heretic anywhere on the planet. We will do so to whatever government or person we deem to be illegal, according to our belief system.'

Is that wild? And the not so crazy coincidence is that the Bible talks about how this is going to come to fruition. It will be in the Seven Year Tribulation and it all revolves around the issue in Revelation 17 with this picture of the Woman, Mystery Babylon the Harlot who rides the Beast Antichrist for a time, takes ecclesiastical control, and grabs governmental control on the whole planet as a part of that Seven Year Tribulation. Could it be that Roman Catholicism is a part of that? I kind of think so but we'll get to that in the next chapter. Then we'll look at their whole belief system and why it's messed up. Folks, as always with false teachings, these are serious issues. This debauchery has never gone away. I'll finish with a quote about the Holy Office, which, as mentioned, is their ongoing version of the Universal Inquisition:

"It is the Court of Appeals for heresy and was reorganized in 1965, renamed, and it remains in effect today."

So, the irony is; it isn't just that the Catholic Church did this in the past, it's still in effect today. After these first three chapters, you may be getting a better feel for why I harp on the righteous indignation that hopefully is what's happening to me when I see this kind of thing said so much on the news:

"And now for the Christian perspective..."

And then who do they put up on the screen? It's a Roman Catholic. So, people are falling for their scam, right and left. And you still hear people, even in the church saying,

"Hey, listen, Catholics believe the same things we do."

You know what the reformers would be doing if they heard all these statements like that from Protestant believers today? They'd be rolling over in their graves. They be telling us:

"You guys are digging your own graves. After all we did and all our sacrifice, what in the world are you doing? And when did you get so chicken livered that you can't call a spade, a spade? Why can't you stand for the truth?"

This is the boldness that we Christians need to get in these last days. We don't need to be antagonistic and we certainly don't want to go to, an eye for an eye. But we need to be prepared because this is the level of deception spreading across our planet.

Chapter Four

The Harlot

We've already seen how Catholicism is a pseudo-Christian cult. In Chapter One we learned they are not the same thing as Christianity. In Chapter Two we found that they are also a cult. They are a cult as described by the secular definition as well as the Biblical definition. Again, I didn't say that, the facts tell us so.

In the last chapter we also saw that the Roman Catholic Church is also demonic, which means devilish. Why? We see in John Chapter 8 that Jesus, who is the truth, the way, and the life, was sharing the truth but what was the reaction of those who believed in falsehoods? They wanted to murder Him! Believe it or not, that same demonic attitude toward the truth continues with the Catholic Church. Their doctrine does not allow you to just walk away from an argument with them. Just like what we see in the Gospels from Jews who wanted to kill Christ, they want to murder Christians who proclaim Christ's truth. This we saw in the last chapter about the Inquisitions, which are still in effect today. Inquisition is basically the Catholic version of murder and slaughter of those who disagree and begs the question of whether the first jihadists were Muslim or Roman Catholic. Catholicism has actually been on a jihad for their faith a lot longer than Islam has.

We talked about the different inquisitions throughout history. There was the Medieval, Spanish, Portuguese, and Roman Inquisitions. Remember, the Roman Inquisition was primarily directed towards Protestant Christians during the Reformation. You'll hear that the Roman Inquisition is technically the last one and distant history, but that's not true however, as we uncovered by looking at the facts, the Roman Inquisition is still in effect today. They only changed the terminology. It's now called the Universal or Ongoing Inquisition and is administered out of their Holy Office. With the change in names, today, the ongoing inquisition against Protestant Christians is called the Congregation for the Doctrine of the Faith, and again, it is still in effect today. They ultimately still have this demonic devilish doctrine commanding them to murder people who do not go along with their version of the truth, so Roman Catholicism is not just a pseudo-Christian group or just another cult, it is also full of lies, demonic, and murderous.

In the next couple of chapters, I want to explain where all this is leading. From doing the research, I'm convinced, believe it or not, that all this is leading to the emergence of future events outlined in Revelation 17 where Earth's population is dealing with the Woman, or the Harlot, who rides the Beast. Who in the world is this Woman the Bible describes?

If we look at Revelation 17, the Woman rides the Beast and the Beast is the Antichrist. Well then, who and what is this Woman? I don't think anyone really disagrees that the Woman clearly represents the One World Religious System that is going to come on the planet in the last days. And that religious system (the Woman) is going to work with the Antichrist. So, it is said that she, at least initially, rides the Antichrist Beast. Then at some point the Beast destroys her during the bowl judgments of Revelation, which takes place towards the end of the Seven Year Tribulation. But who is this Woman, what are her characteristics, and do we see any entity today lining up with the description in Revelation 17? Let's take a look:

"One of the seven angels who had the seven bowls came and said to me, 'Come and I will show you the punishment of the great prostitute, who sits on many waters. With her the kings of the Earth committed adultery, and the inhabitants of the Earth were intoxicated with the wine of her adulteries.'"

So, people got caught up in her corrupt and morally decadent ways. It becomes a worldwide feeling that everyone's getting involved with the corruption and loving it.

"Then the angel carried me away in the spirit into a desert. There I saw a woman riding a scarlet beast that was covered with blasphemous names and had seven heads and ten horns. The woman was dressed in [What?] purple and scarlet, and was glittering with [What?] gold, precious stones, and pearls. She held a [What?] golden cup in her hand, filled with the abominable things and the filth of her adulteries. The title was written on her forehead: 'Mystery, Babylon the Great, the Mother of Prostitutes and of the Abominations of the Earth'. I saw that the Woman was drunk with the blood of the Saints, the blood of those who bore testimony to Jesus. When I saw her, I was greatly astonished. Then the angel said to me: 'Why are you astonished? I will explain to you the mystery of the Woman and of the Beast she rides, which has seven heads and ten horns. The Beast [Antichrist], which you saw, once was, now is not, and will come up out of the abyss and go to his destruction. The inhabitants of the earth whose names have not been written in the book of life from the creation of the world will be astonished when they see the beast, because he once was, now is not, and yet will come. This calls for the mind of wisdom. The seven heads are seven hills on which the woman sits. There are also seven kings. Five have fallen, one is, the other has not yet come; but when he does come, he must remain for a little while. The beast who once was, and now is not, is an eighth king. He belongs to the seven and is going to his destruction. The ten horns you saw are the ten kings who have not yet received a kingdom, but for one hour will receive authority as kings along with the beast. They have one purpose and will give their power and authority to the beast. They will make war against the Lamb, but the Lamb will overcome them because...'"

Why? Here's a Crone translation: It's because He is Jesus. He is the Lord of lords and the King of kings.

"...and with him will be His called, chosen, and faithful followers."

That is Revelation 19 where Christians are coming back with Jesus at the end the Seven Year Tribulation.

"Then the angel said to me, 'The waters you saw, were the prostitute sits, are peoples, multitudes, nations, and languages [it's over the whole world]. The Beast and the ten horns you saw will hate the prostitute. They will bring her to ruin and leave her naked; they will eat her flesh and burn her with fire. [Why?] For God has put it into their hearts to accomplish his purpose by agreeing to

give the beast their power to rule until God's words are fulfilled. The woman you saw is the great [What?] city that rules over the kings of the earth.'"

So, from Revelation 17 we see that in the last days, during the Seven Year Tribulation, it's going to culminate in a One World Religion System that is going to obviously be considered an abomination to God. Why? It's because it is spiritual adultery. It is fornication and that term in Scripture means to go astray, follow idols and pursue false religious belief systems. This One World Religious System is going to seduce people around the world to be a part of it and the planet's population is going to be intoxicated with it. This One World Religious System, this Harlot system, is going to be working with the Antichrist System, which is the Beast, or the One World Government System. The latter will ultimately be split up into ten areas, who will give their power over to the Beast so at some point he'll have full control over the entire system.

It is also saying that these two systems, government and religion, are something you cannot opt out of. Apparently, it's going to get so bad that if you don't like either the One World Religion or the One World Government, you will die. We see this in Revelation 13 where if you don't take the Mark of the Beast from the Antichrist and False Prophet, you will die. Four times in Revelation 13, it says you'll need to worship the Antichrist, but also, with the One World Religion, if you don't go along with it, the Bible says she is drunk with the blood of the saints so they will come and kill you. Would you say that's something you don't want to be part of? That's a timeframe you definitely want to avoid! The good news is that you can through Jesus Christ.

But this is what's coming to our planet and it was written down nearly 2,000 years ago. I see five things that need to happen for Revelation 13 to be fulfilled. I'll take you through the first two in this chapter and the final three in the next.

Here is number one: First you need a religious figure, who is drawing together all the world's religions. That person will be playing the role of this Harlot. Who is that and what religious system also has a specific person as the false prophet? Secondly, I believe you need some sort of a pluralistic movement that is seducing people to go along with and embrace this One World Religion because the Bible says humans across the world are intoxicated with this Harlot system. So where is it? You need to see people beginning to warm up to that Harlot religion. Third, you need some sort of a woman or female figure. You need a feminine representative in some form or fashion involved with this One World Religion system. Fourth, you have to have an Antichrist figure to work with the Harlot, and fifth, you need a global authority system to punish those who don't do what you want them to.

Let's start with the first one, which is the religious figure. Now I wonder what religious person is at the head of a large world-wide religion, that happens be a city and works with the governments around the planet while viewing themselves, even to this day, as being in control of those governments. Who could that be?? Yeah, I think we all know. I like what one guy said:

"Hey, if the Pope is not the False Prophet, he's working very hard to get the job."

Right? But do we see any signs of all this? Let's put it to the test. Now we hear people discount the idea by saying something like, "Oh, everyone's always saying it's the Pope, the Catholic Church, and blah, blah, blah." Well, let's check into it and do our homework. Do we see any signs of this guy being a part of an abomination, harlotry, and drawing together of the world's religions all into one? Folks, the Catholic Church has been doing this for a long time. They want to control all the religions on the planet, and they want to dominate the governments as well. They want what they lost at the time of the reformation. Let's take a look at the different popes exhibiting this behavior. Here's the first evidence in this report:

"John Paul II has gathered leaders of the world's major religions a number of times and embraced them all as worshipers of the true God, including Hindus, Buddhists, Muslims, Animists, Shintoists, Shamans, Witches, and others. He told Hindu audiences in India that he had not come to teach them anything, but to learn from their rich spiritual heritage to which the entire world ought to give heed. Everyone is embraced by Rome except Evangelical Christians, whom the Pope calls sects, and warns Catholics against their errors as he did in Mexico City in May 1990 and elsewhere since that time. One need only read the 'ecumenical' documents coming out of the Vatican from the Pope and cardinals, such as Cardinal Cassity, president of the Pontifical Council for Promoting Christian Unity and Cardinal Arinze, president of the Pontifical Council for Interreligious Dialogue, to realize that by ecumenism, Rome means all religions uniting under the Pope. This was clear in the general report of Cardinal Arinze to the Extraordinary Consistory of Cardinals at the Vatican in April 1991. As it

is in Arinza's new book, "Religions For Peace", the deception is such that the Lutheran World Federation signed, with the Vatican, a declaration saying that Lutherans and Catholics were now in agreement and basically renouncing the Reformation. Yet nothing in Catholicism's false gospel of works and rituals has changed. The prophesied world religion is in the process of being formed before our eyes. And the Vatican is the headquarters of the movement. Is this not spiritual fornication?"

So, the Harlot Woman commits spiritual fornication in the last days, apparently drawing all the world's religions together into one and those religions are intoxicated with it. Well, what's that? Is that a fit? Now you might think: *"Well, that's probably just the old pope. That's Pope John Paul II, which is two popes removed. This new guy is not doing that kind of thing."* Well, here's some information on the present pope:

"Right now, Pope Francis and the Vatican are vying for control over Jerusalem and the Temple Mount."

He's not the first pope to do so. They've been trying to pull this together for decades. Why? It's because a lot of people are talking about building a Universal Temple in Jerusalem where the whole world can worship. Pope Francis is also taking a lot of trips to Israel. He's actually working and praying with Jews, Muslims, and Eastern Orthodox while putting out the message that we're all one and all brothers and sisters in Christ. He's also making it very easy for anyone to be a part of the developing One World Religion Harlot System. Francis is even making statements about how a person can be an atheist, homosexual, or non-repentant and don't need to repent at all as long as they become a Catholic. That way it's easy to add them into the system, right? Is what the pope advocates the same as what the Bible says? It absolutely is not! Let's quickly take a look at 1 Corinthians 6:9-11:

"Do you not know that the unrighteous will not inherit the kingdom of God? Do not be deceived: Neither fornicators, nor idolaters, nor adulterers, nor homosexuals, nor sodomites, nor thieves, nor the covetous, nor drunkards, nor revilers, nor extortionists, will inherit the kingdom of God. And such were some of you..."

Now does that mean a person is doomed even if they were an atheist but then accepts Christ as their Savior? Is it true that repentance doesn't matter and you're damned forever once you become an atheist? Are you cut off at that point? No, you can always repent and get right with God. Does it mean a person who's involved with homosexuality has committed the unpardonable sin so they can never be saved? No, they can repent of that. Notice he didn't cite just homosexuality, he mentioned many others like liars and thieves so denying salvation is not the point. It even says, 'such WERE some of you.'

But that's not what the Pope is saying. He's telling them they can skip God's decree that they must repent. The Pope's "infallibility" apparently puts him above God. The Pope is saying they don't need to change, or even acknowledge an issue at all. You can even be an atheist, who acknowledges nothing. As long as you're part of a Catholic Church, you can join this One World Religion Let's continue in Corinthians:

"But such were some of you; you were washed; you were sanctified; you were justified in the name the Lord Jesus Christ and the Spirit of our God."

Now remember, this is no longer Pope John Paul II. We are talking about the current pope, Pope Francis, who goes on to say the following:

"It's dangerous for you and I and anybody on the planet to think that you can go to Heaven apart from the Catholic Church." Speaking to a crowd of 33,000 people he said, "There is no such thing as do-it-yourself Christians or free agents. It is a dangerous temptation to believe that one can have a personal direct immediate relationship with Jesus Christ without communion and mediation with the Catholic Church."

Is that true? Folks, that is not the Gospel! How do you get around that one? And he keeps saying it on many different occasions around the world so on the one hand, Catholicism is saying everyone can and should become a Catholic whether you're atheist, non-repentant, homosexual, or whatever, and you don't need to repent of any kind of sins. You only need to become a Catholic. However, on the other hand you're not welcome to go straight to Jesus Christ.

This is the seduction going on everywhere and they've been building on it with successive popes for decades. Now lest you think Pope Francis is not really working toward corralling all the world's religions, I have to point out that he is not only working toward that very goal, this guy is in turbo mode. He's making what Pope John Paul II did look like child's play. I'm going to include two reports, back to back. The first is from when he came to America in the last few years and was treated like a pop star. It was the time he went to ground zero and the 9/11 memorial. At that time, instead of just showing up to affirm that it was a horrible event and maybe say his Catholic prayers, which I'm not necessarily promoting either, he used it as a springboard to promote all religions coming together as one. He basically said we need to unite the religions because of these atrocities.

The second transcript is a commercial they pumped out around the same time and it's directly from their own Catholic television program. So again, it's not my words. You tell me if they're not a main part of this One World Harlot Religion System and are making sure that they will come out at the top to govern the whole thing. So, let's examine that evidence from this interfaith commemoration ceremony for 9/11 that was held at Ground Zero in New York City:

Pope Francis: *"We gather today on this hallowed ground, the scene of unspeakable violence and pain."*

Hindu Woman: *"May God protect us. May God nourish us. May we work together."*

Japanese Woman: *"Victory begets enmity. Defeated dwell in pain."*

Muslim Woman: *"That truth is above everything and the highest deed is truthful living."*

A Pastor: *"For theirs is the kingdom of heaven. Blessed are those who mourn."*

Muslim woman: *"Grant us to live with the salutation of peace and lead us to your abode of peace."*

Choir sings: "Let there be peace on Earth and let it begin with me..."

Now here is the Catholic commercial:

Pope Francis: *"Most of the planet's inhabitants declare themselves believers. This should lead to dialogue among religions. We should not stop praying for it and collaborating with those who think differently."*

Lama Rinchen Dandro: *"I have confidence in the Buddha."*

Rabbi Daniel Goldman: *"I believe in God."*

Catholic Priest Guillermo Marco: *"I believe in Jesus Christ."*

Islamic Leader Omar Abboud: *"I believe in God, Allah."*

Pope Francis: *"Many think differently, feel differently, seeking God or meeting God in different ways. In this crowd, in this range of religions, there is only one certainty we have for all: we are all children of God."*

Lama Rinchen Dandro: *"I believe in love."*

Rabbi Daniel Goldman: *"I believe in love."*

Islamic Leader Omar Abboud: *"I believe in love."*

Catholic Priest Guillermo Marco: *"I believe in love."*

Pope Francis: *"I hope you will spread my prayer request this month: 'That sincere dialogue among men and women of different faiths may produce the fruits of peace and justice.'"*

Wow! I'll say it again: If the Pope is not the False Prophet, he's working really hard to get the job! It's right out there for anyone to see. Two thousand years ago, we were told some entity is coming to the planet and it's specifically an entity in a city. We'll get into more details on that last point in a minute. This entity will corral the world and the world will become intoxicated with it even though it's spiritual fornication and is the Harlot One World Religious System.

Now let's take a look at some further proof. First, remember again that the Harlot commits spiritual fornication. In the Old Testament when God talks about harlotry, adultery, and spiritual fornication; he's speaking about lusting after false religions that are not of Him. It's also specifically linked with idolatry.

Do you know of any religion linked with idolatry? Catholicism is full of idols and so much so that they ripped out the second of God's Ten Commandments. Of course, they did because that one focuses on idols. It simply says you shall have no idols. After removing one of the Lord's commandments, Catholicism covered their tracks and patched up God's commandments by splitting number ten into two separate commandments. Now they were back to Ten so what they had done wasn't so obvious. It certainly fits the worship of idols. They're practicing the same kind of spiritual fornication.

A second proof involves what Revelation says is a city on seven hills. Guess what city has historically been called The City on Seven Hills? It's Rome. And where is the Vatican located? It is of course in Rome. Let me give you the historical names for those seven hills: Aventine, Caelian, Capitoline, Esquiline, Palatine, Quirinal, and Viminal. In fact, if you don't want to believe that from the historical names and the number of hills, listen to this direct quote from the Catholic Encyclopedia:

"It is within the city of Rome called the City of Seven Hills that the entire area of Vatican State proper is now confined."

So, this Harlot is in a city. She's in a city on seven hills. And she's controlling the kings of the earth. Does that start to sound familiar?

How about Mystery, Babylon the Great? If you look back in ancient history from the Old Testament, we see people of Earth gathering together at Babylon and its Tower of Babel. After a worldwide flood, you think you'd have people's attention and you would have convinced them to worship God and do what he says. But no, it's the same story throughout history. These Babylon people went into idolatry and those Babylonian ideas have historically and Biblically been the source of the harlotry, abomination, and spiritual fornication for many later religions. And it's exactly what we see with the Catholic Church where they have latched themselves onto that same mindset.

An interesting discussion has gone on for a long time with some saying Revelation must be talking about a literally rebuilt Babylon in the same area where the Tower of Babel was. I don't necessarily buy into that. I think that the Bible is talking about a spiritual Babylon. For just one proof text, we'll look at 1 Peter 5:13 where Peter says this:

"She who is in Babylon chosen together with you sends her greetings, and so does my son Mark."

Here's the question: Where was 1 Peter written? Peter wrote it in Rome. So, Peter here, in the New Testament is again equating Rome with Spiritual Babylon. It also says she's in bed with the world's rulers and reigns over the kings of the earth. We clearly see that in the text. Is that what the different popes and the Catholic Church are up to? Yes, it is! Let me share some of that with you:

Not only do the popes call themselves the Vicar of Christ, but the Vatican is obsessed with earthly enterprise, as history proves. The popes have built an unrivaled worldwide empire of property, wealth, and influence and nor is that abandoned today. Vatican II clearly stated that the Roman Catholic Church today still ceaselessly seeks to bring under its control, all mankind and their goods.

Hey, that's from Vatican II, which wrapped up in 1965. That's very recent relative to Catholic Church history. They believe all mankind and their goods belong to Catholicism. What's interesting, as we get into Revelation 18, is the destruction of the Harlot's wealth, goods, and all her possessions. Chapter 17 is the spiritual destruction and 18 is the material destruction. This mirrors Catholic leadership's thinking and actions. They're not only involved spiritually in this harlotry, but they believe they own all the wealth of the people on earth.

Popes have long claimed dominion over the world and its peoples. Pope Gregory XI's papal bull of 1372 claimed papal dominion over the entire world, secular and religious, and excommunicated all who failed to obey the popes and to pay them taxes. It was confirmed by subsequent popes and in 1568 Pope Pius V swore that this was to remain an eternal law.

So, their eternal law decrees that the Roman Catholic Church will forever be in charge of the planet, including all kings, rulers, and all their wealth. They still believe this today. It is an eternal law for them.

Popes crowned and disposed kings and emperors, exacting obedience by threatening them with excommunication. Again, as we saw in the last couple chapters, this is a lot of the reason why some of the Protestant Reformers like Martin Luther and others, were whisked away to safe keeping by royalty. It was not necessarily because the kings were so convinced of the Gospel, it was more often because they saw these reformers as a way out of this stranglehold from the Catholic Church.

At the time of the First Vatican Council in 1869, they warned that Catholicism would make it infallible dogma that they could force kings and magistrates, by excommunication and its consequences, to carry out their sentences of confiscation, imprisonment, and death. So here again we see that they believe they have the authority to eliminate people. If anyone anywhere on the whole planet doesn't do what they say, they believe they have the authority to take them out. This is their writings and rulings.

One eighteenth century historian counted ninety-five popes who claimed to have divine power to depose kings and emperors. Now why am I pointing this out? It's because this Woman from Revelation, in our future, is in bed with the world's rulers and she's in charge. This Woman on Seven Hills of this city [Vatican City] in Rome is in charge of the kings of the earth. This all fits with what the Catholic Church believes.

Historian Walter James wrote, *'Pope Innocent III held all Europe in his net. Gregory IX thundered that the pope was lord and master over everyone and everything."* Wow!

Another historian said during the whole medieval period there was in Rome a single spiritual and temporal authority [the papacy] exercising powers which in the end exceeded those that had ever lain within the grasp of a Roman emperor.

Notice again their name is not just the Catholic Church. It's the Roman Catholic Church. Catholicism came out of Constantine, the Roman Emperor, when faiths were encouraged to blend together, which begins to ruin the Christian Church and also birthed the Roman Catholic Church. And this new Roman Catholic Church kept that same mindset of the Roman Caesars, who felt entitled to rule the whole planet. Carrying that attitude forward and adding in the spiritual aspects of man, the Roman Catholic Church feels they are in charge over the whole world.

Vatican City is the only city which also exchanges ambassadors with nations, and she does so with every major country on the planet. Ambassadors come to Vatican City from every major country, including the United States, not out of courtesy but because 'the Pope is the most powerful ruler on Earth today.'

Here's just one example of a United States president: When Bill Clinton greeted the Pope, Clinton addressed him as "Holy Father" and "Your Holiness." Excuse me? That's crazy stuff.

Unlike any other city on the earth, the Vatican is acknowledged as a sovereign state in its own right, separate and distinct from the nation of Italy surrounding it. So, the Vatican is its own entity, smack dab in Rome.

There's no other city in history that it has been true of, and such is the case today: Only the Vatican is said to be 'a city' reigning over the kings of the earth. There is no city upon Earth past or present, which meets all the criteria, except Catholic Rome and Vatican City. And that city was written about two thousand years ago in Revelation 17.

Now let's talk quickly about the clothing that was mentioned in Revelation, as well as the decadent wealth and the golden cup, which is filled with abomination, or filth. The incredible wealth of this woman John saw:

She was dressed in purple and scarlet, she was decked with gold and precious stones and pearls and she had a golden cup in her hand, full of abominations and filthiness of her fornication.

What about the colors of purple and scarlet? Those were the same colors used by the Roman Caesars and which the soldiers in the Gospels mockingly robed Jesus Christ with as King of the Jews. Of course, we know that happened just prior to the crucifixion and was described in Matthew 27 and John 19. So those colors were not only used by Roman Emperors, but guess who adopted them when taking over from Constantine? It was the Roman Catholic Church. The woman's colors, scarlet and purple are the same colors even to this day of the Catholic clergy.

Here's a quote from the Catholic Encyclopedia:

"The Cappa Magna is a cloak with a long train and a hooded shoulder cape...it was purple wool for the bishops; for cardinals, it was scarlet watered silk."

Another one is called the Cassock, or the Soutand:

"This is a close fitting, ankle-length robe worn by the Catholic clergy as their official garb. ...The color for bishops and other prelates is purple, and for Cardinals it's scarlet."

And they still wear them to this day. What about the golden cup? The 'golden cup in her hand' again identifies with something that goes on in the Catholic Church. And by the way, during their Eucharist, what is in the cup when Catholic priests hold up their golden cups, or chalices? Is that an abomination to God because they claim it is the actual blood of Jesus Christ in there? They are saying the liquid inside is literally Jesus being sacrificed again and again and again, every time they do their Eucharist ceremony with that golden chalice and wafer in every one of their churches. That's an abomination! So then, what is the cup filled with? It's full of abomination. But listen to what the Catholic Encyclopedia says about the golden cup (golden chalice):

"It is the most important of the sacred vessels. It may be of gold or silver but if it's silver, it has to be surfaced with gold."

So Roman Catholicism is specifically big on golden cups, which Revelation 17 specifically mentions.

"The Roman Catholic Church possesses many thousands of golden chalices around the world."

Now let's talk about the wealth:

"Rome [the Catholic Church] has practiced evil to gather her wealth. Much of the wealth of the Roman Catholic Church was acquired during the Inquisitions."

Here's another aspect of what Catholicism did, and can you even imagine some organization actually designing and carrying out these deplorable acts? Then again, it doesn't get much worse than what they were already willing to do with torture, but when you went to those Catholic torture dungeons, they also took everything you had. And if a person had much wealth, they were always in fear. All someone would have to do is accuse you of something against the Pope or that you disagreed with Catholicism. Just with that suspicion, you would be done, and they would come and confiscate everything you had. And you may be wondering if that affected the victim's family. It sure did. Listen to this:

Even the dead were exhumed to face trial and property was taken from their heirs by the Roman Catholic Church. One historian writes: *"The punishments of the Inquisition did not cease when the victim was burned to ashes or imprisoned for life in the dungeons. His relatives were reduced to beggary by the Roman Catholic law when all his possessions were forfeited. The system offered unlimited opportunities to loot and steal from anyone."*

That includes kings and other rulers. It's no wonder those leaders wanted a way out of the Roman Catholic stranglehold. This source of gain largely accounts for the revolting practice of what was called Corpse Trials. The practice of confiscating the property of condemned heretics produced all kinds of acts of extortion. No man was safe whose wealth might arouse suspicion or whose independence might provoke revenge. People were always wondering if Roman Catholicism was going to come and accuse them next. And as if relocating you to a dungeon for torture and murdering wasn't bad enough, they also wanted to steal everything you and your loved ones owned. This is the major way they amassed the wealth that they had, so the Inquisitions were the first way they amassed obscene amounts of wealth.

The second way they've racked up the riches is with Indulgences. Again, Indulgences are the way Catholics can supposedly pay their way to Heaven and it's still going on today. Untold billions of dollars have been paid to the Roman Catholic Church at Vatican City from those who are told they're purchasing Heaven on an installment plan for themselves and their loved ones, or to get their deceased friends and family out of this fake place called Purgatory. Listen to this:

A cardinal in the 16th century complained about the sale of indulgences. The church hierarchy was indignant and accused him by saying: "Are you wanting to turn Rome into an uninhabited desert, to reduce the papacy to impotence, to deprive the pope of the resources indispensable for the discharge of his office?"

Let me translate that from the Latin: *"Are you trying to cut off our money supply?!"*

Wow! So, she has great wealth and she's ripped it off from people throughout the years with the Inquisitions and she's still raking in the dough because people are deceived into thinking:

"Man, I've got it made. I can just work hard and pay my way into Heaven, as well as purchase my loved ones out of torture."

You might describe that as Catholicism's fake spiritual inquisition for your loved ones who've died and supposedly all ended up in a Catholic conceived phony place called Purgatory. The account of Catholicism's finances continues with this:

In addition to such perversions of the Gospel, which has led millions and millions of people to Hell, there are further abominations of the Catholic Church: [And this is all on record] Corrupt banking practices, laundering of drug money, trading in counterfeit securities, and dealings with the mafia. This is all documented in police records. In fact, a guy named Nino Lo Bello, who is a former BusinessWeek correspondent in Rome and Rome bureau chief for The New York Journal of Commerce, writes that the Vatican is so closely allied with the Mafia in Italy that many people believe Sicily is nothing more than a Vatican holding. Wow! So, you have the Jesuits and the Mafia to do your... Wow! That's more craziness.

The wealthiest institution on the planet is what the Roman Catholic Church is. They have innumerable sculptures such as the masters of Michelangelo, paintings from the world's greatest artists, countless other art treasures, and ancient documents. And it's not just in the Vatican. It's literally on church property, including cathedrals all over the planet. There's no way to estimate their wealth because it's so vast. At a world synod of bishops in Rome, a cardinal proposed that the Roman Catholic Church sell some of their vast treasures and give the proceeds to the poor. *"His suggestion was not well received."* By the way, have you seen the throne this guy sits on? Melt some of that gold, baby. How much food could that supply for the planet's poor? The Catholic Church has so much wealth; I don't know if they even know how much it is. Their loads of treasures, gold, silver and cash are tucked away all over the planet.

There is no church, no city, which is a spiritual entity, no religious institution past or present that even comes close to possessing the wealth of the Roman Catholic Church.

Now let me give you this from a newspaper article in Lourdes France:

For years it had been rumored that the Catholic Church there, just in a small area and not the Vatican or all the other cathedrals around the planet, but this one little area, had a priceless collection of gold chalices, diamond studded crucifixes, silver, and precious stones. The Catholic authorities let reporters take a sneak peek and listen to what they found:

"Floor to ceiling were cases and cases opened up revealing massive amounts of solid gold chalices along with rings, crucifixes, statues, and heavy gold broaches; many encrusted with precious stones. Also hidden among the treasures was the crown of Notre Dame studded with diamonds. For just that crown, they said, 'We have no idea. It is of inestimable value.'"

That's just one little crown out of how many massive amounts of boxes of who knows what else is in there. Again, this is not the Vatican or Vatican City. It's just one little area. It's not all the cathedrals around the world or all the other dealings they have with all the other money deposits they're doing, apparently even with the mafia and whatever other kinds of banking procedures. The Roman Catholic Church has wealth beyond imagination! Oh, and:

"Across the road is a building housing hundreds of antique ecclesiastical garments, robes, miters, and sashes."

You think, "So what? Priests need robes." Well, this rare garb is not just made of fine cloth. They are literally sown with heavy gold thread. Can you imagine having so much cash; you sew your clothes together with gold? Oh, and again, this is just one location. It's just a minuscule insignificant part of the entire wealth and the treasure just described is only a part of what's kept in the one location.

How about what John said in Revelation describing the Harlot being drunk with the blood of the saints? Remember, that was another aspect of the One World Religion he mentioned. John knows she's drunk with the blood of the saints. It's not with an alcoholic beverage. She's actually drunk with the blood.

The picture is a horrible one. It's not merely her hands that are red with this blood, she's drunk with it. That means the slaughter of innocents, who for conscience sake would not yield to her totalitarian demands, so refresh and exhilarated her, that she reels in ecstasy. Again, what is it that she's in ecstasy and exhilarated from? It's from the murdering of people, whose offense was to disagree.

"One only has to think of the Inquisitions. In the history of the Inquisitions, it is estimated that in Spain alone, the number of condemned exceeded three million."

That's half the Jewish Holocaust! And again, that was only in Spain and just during that time. What about the other countries? How about what's gone on and is going on that we don't even know about? I would say it far exceeds the Jewish Holocaust. Why isn't anyone talking about this and how come the Pope isn't apologizing for it? We had Obama going around the planet for eight years apologizing, including for us being Christian. Yet Catholicism never apologized for this, which was something worse than the Jewish Holocaust. And it's all on record.

"And in the same [Spanish Inquisition], over 300,000 people burned at the stake."

It was not three or three hundred, or even three thousand. It was three hundred thousand burned. That's just in one area. That's just Spain.

Another historian says this of events leading up to the suppression of the Spanish Inquisition in 1809:

"When Napoleon conquered Spain in 1808, a Polish officer in his army reported that the Dominicans in charge of the Inquisition blockaded themselves in their monastery in Madrid. When Napoleon's troops forced entry, the inquisitors denied the existence of any of the torture chambers."

Now this was in 1808. That's three hundred years after the Reformation. Remember, this inquisition stuff wasn't supposed to be going on anymore. But listen to this:

"The soldiers searched the monastery and discovered them underneath the floors. The chambers were full of prisoners all naked and many insane. The

French soldiers [who are used to blood and cruelty] could not even stomach the sight. They emptied the torture chambers, they laid gunpowder to the monastery, and blew the place up."

Doesn't that kind of remind you of what happened in World War II when the Americans finally made it to Germany and into the Jewish camps? The soldiers forced the local Germans to go out and look at the atrocities committed there, and this same savage mass murder happened at the hands of the Roman Catholic Church. She is drunk with the blood of the saints and it still going on today. How come no one is talking about it?

"To ring out confessions from these poor creatures, the Roman Catholic Church devised ingenious [if you want to use that word] torture techniques so excruciating and barbarous that one is sickened by just even reciting them."

Isn't that how you felt reading the last chapter? And again, I really only shared the mild ones. Even researching it for this book, I finally had to stop reading about it or looking at it.

Another historian said: *"The most ghastly abomination of all was the system of torture. The accounts of its cold-blooded operations make one shudder at the capacity of human beings for cruelty. And it was decreed and regulated by the popes who claimed to represent Christ on Earth."*

That's an abomination! And listen to this depraved practice they instituted:

"Careful notes were taken, not only of all that was confessed by the victim, but of their shrieks, cries, lamentations, broken interjections, and appeals for mercy."

How sick is that to even be able to sit there and record torture sounds?!

"The remnants of some of the chambers of horror remain in Europe and still can be seen today. They stand as memorials to the zealous outworking of the Roman Catholic dogmas, which remains in force today."

Whoa!

"And Catholicism claims their victims to be infallible [deserving of what they got] and to this day say they [Catholicism] have the right to justify this barbarism."

Again, this is just Spain. It's that one small area. Listen to this:

"And to these three million victims, should be added the thousands upon thousands and thousands of Jews deported from their homeland. In just one year alone, the Holy Office..."

Remember, Holy Office is their name for the Inquisition, which is still in effect today.

"...[in Spain] in just one year alone, the Holy Office burned two thousand persons and the bones and effigies of another two thousand and another sixteen thousand were condemned to varying sentences."

Here's an ex-Catholic priest of seven years:

"Peter de Rosa acknowledges that the Catholic Church was responsible for persecuting the Jews, for the Inquisition, for slaughtering heretics by the thousands, and for reintroducing torture into Europe as a part of the judicial process."

Now that's interesting because Revelation also tells us a lot of the people who don't go along with the system, get their heads chopped off. Isn't that's a gruesome murder technique? I mean, surely there was nobody on the planet who would arise to bring that kind of horrible punishment back, let alone start to use it as an official government sanctioned form of punishment where they torture people and slaughter them by chopping their heads off. There's no way that could have become a part of judicial process again, would it? Yes, Catholicism is the one that brought back judicial torture in Europe.

Now if that isn't bad enough, check this out:

"Yet the Roman Catholic Church has never officially admitted that these practices were evil, nor has she apologized to the world or to any victims or their descendants."

Roman Catholicism has not changed her heart no matter what sweet words she speaks when it serves her purpose and she is guilty of spilling more blood than pagan Rome. You know as Protestants and Christians, we talk about how the early Church, even before Catholicism, was being slaughtered, stoned, thrown to the lions, and whatever else. But the Roman Catholic Church has clearly surpassed those terrible persecutions by a long way! Still nobody wants to talk about that. No one mentions it! Why not?! Here's more perspective on that:

Pagan Rome made sport of throwing Christians to the lions, burning them, killing thousands of them, also Jews, yet Catholic Rome has slaughtered many more times the Christians and Jews than Rome ever did. Besides the victims in the Inquisition, there were the slaughters of the Huguenots, the Albigenses, the Waldenses, and other Christians who were massacred, tortured, and burned at the stake by the hundreds of thousands, simply because they refused to align themselves with the Roman Catholic Church and its corruption, heretical dogmas and practices. Out of conscience, these Christians tried to follow the teachings of Jesus Christ and the Apostles, independent of Rome, and for that crime they were maligned, hunted down, imprisoned, tortured, and murdered.

So that's our heritage as Protestants and Christians. But who's guilty of this despicable persecution and murder even more than Pagan Rome? It is the Roman Catholic Church! Why would Rome, the Pope, and Vatican City never once apologize or even admit their culpability in the holocaust they've been carrying out for 1,500 years? Well here's another little piece of history and maybe this is why: The Vatican also had dealings with Hitler. Did you know that? And what was Hitler guilty of? It was a holocaust. Let me show you something very interesting:

"It was thoroughly known, and is still to this day, that Pope Pius XII was completely silent during World War II in the atrocities of Hitler. Had the Pope protested as the representatives of the Jewish organizations and the Allied Powers begged him to do..."

But he couldn't do so because he would have also been condemning the Catholic Church. And listen to this:

In 1936, a Bishop talked with Adolf Hitler for over an hour. Hitler assured the Catholic bishop that there was no fundamental difference between

National Socialism [the Nazis] and the Catholic Church. Hitler told the Catholic bishop: "I'm only doing what the Catholic Church has done for fifteen hundred years, only more effectively." The reason why the Roman Catholic Church has neither apologized nor repented of these crimes, the execution of so-called heretics, including the Jews themselves, was because executions were decreed by 'infallible' popes. The Catholic Church herself claims to be infallible, thus her doctrines could not be wrong.

So, they could not call Hitler out on the carpet for his horrible slaughter, because guess who is guilty of the same? And the Catholic doctrine that says it is impossible for a pope to make a mistake, keeps them from admitting even the tiniest of papal shortcomings or misjudgment. They can't admit a pope could be wrong because the core doctrine is that popes are infallible, so Catholicism kept its mouth shut and let the Nazi atrocities continue.

What's scary is trying to talk about this in the Christian Church today. They look at you like you just grew another eyeball, which for me personally, I think could come in handy in certain situations. But anyway, the Church does look at you strangely when bringing up the subject. You'll hear things like:

"What are you trying to do? Don't you know Catholics and Christians teach the same thing?"

But listen to this:

Protestants are not only failing to call the Roman Catholic Church into account for this behavior [for example, where's the apology and the Catholic ownership of what they've done], but Protestants have now forgotten the hundreds of thousands of fellow Christians who were burned at the stake by the Roman Catholic Church for simply embracing the gospel of Jesus Christ [and refusing to bow to this harlot system]. Amazingly, Protestants are now embracing Catholic Rome. Remember, they look at us Christians as the Protestant Experiment. We're just a small aberration but we'll come back to the Catholic fold soon enough.

"...and she is trying to reconcile us to her on her unchangeable terms."

The only ones changing doctrines here are the Protestants. The Catholic Church is not changing yet:

"Many evangelical leaders are intent upon working with Roman Catholics to evangelize the world."

No, you're not! You may intend to but you're not evangelizing the world because Catholicism does not have the Gospel. What you're doing is working together to build this One World Global Religion that the Harlot is planning to rule over with the help of the Antichrist.

The Protestants don't want to hear any negative reminders of the millions of people tortured and slain by the Roman Catholic Church, which Protestants now pay homage to, or the fact that Catholicism has a sacramental false gospel of works.

Sadly, that's what's going on in the Church today and this leads us to the second sign that we'll look at in the next chapter, which involves why the Protestant church is doing this. The reformers must be rolling over in their graves because of this strong seduction going on. There's an intoxication happening. Remember the words used in Revelation 17 about how the world will be caught up and intoxicated by her adultery? That is what's going on right now, even in the Church. It's called Ecumenical, Pluralism, or whatever you want to call it, but it's basically:

"Can't we all just get along", and "We all believe the same."

What did the Catholic commercial say that played around the time of the 9/11 memorial at ground zero? It was:

'I believe in Buddha. I believe in God. I believe in Jesus Christ. I believe in Allah. But we all believe in love. We all just need to love and come together.'

That's a seduction and a very intoxicating one! And the Church has been falling for it. In the next chapter, we're going to take a look at how the Protestant Church is getting sucked up into that intoxicating lie as they back up straight into the arms of Rome. Then we're going to deal with why the false religion is called a woman and explore whether we see signs of an Antichrist appearing on the scene, as well as a global government entity that can wield the hammer that will come down on people around the whole planet.

Now I have to reiterate something and then give you more interesting timely information. It's a Woman who rides the Beast. It's a Harlot One World Religion System that rides the Beast and that Beast is the Antichrist, who controls the One World Government System. So, it's global religion combining with global government. That's interesting because of who recently became the new United Nations Secretary General. The U.N., which you know is supposed to be controlling the governments around the world, has a new leader as of January 1st, 2017 and his name is Antonio Guterres. He's from Portugal and is a socialist. Wait, what was Hitler? Hitler was also a socialist. In fact, Antonio is so deep into socialism, he has even been serving for many years as international president of the socialists. That is the guy who is now the U.N. leader.

Oh, and have you heard another interesting characteristic of Antonio Guterres? Antonio also happens to be a Catholic. That's the head of the United Nations! So, do you think the governmental system is going to have a problem working with the religious system? Do you think they'll work together? Well again, what does Revelation say? The Woman rides the Beast! So, the Socialist Catholic U.N. head they would need, is now in place! You know it's almost like we're living in the last days and we need to get motivated. Is anyone else coming to that conclusion?

Chapter Five

Christianity Cannot Coexist

First, you need a religious figure if Revelation 17 is going to come to pass. Now secondly, I believe you also need a pluralistic (coexistence) movement. This pluralistic movement must be in place and have people falling for its baloney. The Pope, the Vatican and the Catholic Church are out there saying,

"Hey, can't we all just get along?", "We all need to get along!", "Oh, by the way, just let us be in charge of that.", and "We'll all get together and bring peace to this planet."

And it's one thing to promote those pluralistic views but it doesn't mean anyone is going to buy into it so what's another way we know when we're getting close to Revelation 17 times? We're approaching that time when the pluralistic ecumenical movement message is starting to work, which it is. There's even a very large movement now in the non-Catholic realm of this world. People and religions are getting sucked up into it. Revelation 17 says people will be getting 'intoxicated' with it. The feeling of coming together is all so wonderful. What are the buzzwords we hear today? They tell us we just need to love and tolerate. Isn't that so intoxicating? The world loves those words; love and tolerate. If we want to bring peace and stop the fighting in the world, we just need to love one another, right? It's the spirit of the Beatles all over again. Just love! That's all you had to do. That's what is happening now so this heavy attraction to the pluralistic movement is already in place today.

Obviously, the problem with this idea of melting into the love of this religious pluralistic movement is that the Bible tells us (Crone translation): "Don't you dare! Don't even think about going along with this baloney because there's only one way to Heaven and that's through Jesus Christ!" How many times have we quoted John 14:6, which is so simple but constantly disregarded in our society, even in the Church? Jesus says he is *the* way, *the* truth, and *the* life. Nobody comes to the Father other than by Jesus. You can't go along with this One World Religion. You can't go along with the Pope when he says we're all basically the same so get together and let Catholicism be in charge. We can't go along with these false teachings that blur the lines and ask us to compromise our principles for the sake of working together. That's because every one of those other paths, every single one, leads straight to Hell. Jesus is the only way out of this mess. So how in the world could we work and yoke ourselves together with that pluralistic movement?

Now again, I didn't say that. God said so and that's our first Scripture to look at in 2 Corinthians, Chapter 6. What kind of relationship with unbelievers does the Bible say we should have? Certainly, the most important thing is witnessing to them, right? But that's not what's happening today. Most of the time witnessing does not take place. Christians are only 'yoking together' [teaming up] with non-believers on all these nifty projects because we're told we just need to love and tolerate one another. But that is clearly going over the line for a true born-again Christian. The Biblical truth is that you should never ever do that! God has strong words about not being yoked with unbelievers. Who are the non-believers? Well, just call out any religious group other than Christianity. We're talking about Muslims, Roman Catholicism, Mormons, Sikhs, Buddhists, New Agers, Wiccans, Satanists, and so many others who are all unbelievers. We definitely need to reach them for Christ but notice what we are not to do with the word used by Paul in Corinthians. We are not to "yoke" with them. He doesn't say not to witness. Someone should witness to them. But the key word here is "yoke." Don't get to that point where you're yoking—and I'm not yoking about that. Don't yoke. Yeah, let's just move on. Here's Paul in 2 Corinthians 6:14-17:

"Do not be yoked together with unbelievers [non-Christians]. What do righteousness and weakness have in common? What fellowship can light have with darkness? What harmony is there between Christ and the Devil? What does a believer have in common with an unbeliever? What agreement is there between the temple of God and idols? For we are the temple of the living God. As God

said: 'I will live with them. I will walk among them. I will be their God and they will be my people. Therefore [What must you do?], come out from them and maintain separation, says the Lord. Touch no unclean thing and I will receive you.' "

That's what God says about partnering with unbelievers. Now of course we balance that out with Scripture's challenge of the Great Commission, which unfortunately is treated like the Grand Suggestion, but witnessing to unbelievers is a commission, an order that tells us to get out there and share the Gospel to the whole world. Get out there, teach them, make disciples, and baptize them in the name of the Father, Son, and the Holy Spirit (Matthew 28). We need to witness to people, right? Yes, and we do so because we have the truth. As Paul says in Romans: How beautiful are the feet who bring the good news. He says, how are nonbelievers going to know the truth if there's no one to tell them. It's just common sense that we must witness to people.

But that's not what Paul is warning against in 2 Corinthians 6:14-17 concerning our relationships with unbelievers. Again, he uses the word, "yoked." So of course, we should love them enough to tell them the truth, that what they believe is false and you don't have to be nasty or beat them over the head, but they need to know that they're on the wrong road and that there is only one way, which is through Jesus. So, when we encounter them, we are not to yoke together (team up) with them, but we do want to be there to witness to them and warn them in love that they're on a path which is leading them to Hell. However, the good news is there's one path, but only this certain path, that will get you out of your hopeless situation. So that's what our relationship should be.

However, if you want to add to the great commission, as one example, Jesus also said we should help those whom are hungry. If we run into a Muslim or Buddhist who needs food; hey, I'll get you a cheeseburger, right? If I see a guy with a flat tire on the side of the road and he appears to be a New Ager, in Christ's name I'll help with his trouble. Or maybe you need some clothes. Ok, yes, I'm not against that. But what's the goal besides doing the right thing in helping your fellow man? Do we just help with that flat tire and then leave? No! With the chance to help in an act of kindness I'm given an opportunity for what? When they say, thank you, how do I respond? I say,

"Hey, don't thank me. Thank Jesus because as a Christian, I try to treat others as Jesus would."

So, you should use those incidents as an opportunity to share the Gospel.

However, when interacting with non-believers, God says do not get yoked to them. Yoked is basically when you're developing a relationship that has nothing to do with the Gospel. You're not pointing out that their path is leading them to Hell. You're not telling them the exclusive message (that we didn't make up) about how Jesus said he exclusively is the only way to Heaven. So, if you're not even attempting to get that message across to them but your only desire is to work together with the unbeliever on something other than saving them, that's yoking. And the Scripture is very clear that you do not want to do that.

The word yoke literally means to be bound together with, or to have fellowship with another. Why does God have such strong words in telling us we shouldn't do that? He says, yes, we should witness but don't bind together with them and don't have fellowship with them. The reason is because it's worse than oil and water. It does not mix, and it can't mix. Why? You cannot mix with a lie. Their belief system is a lie because their father, who is the origin of deceit, is Satan and he's also been a murderer from the beginning. That's John, Chapter 8 and comes straight from Jesus. You can't mix God's holy truth with a lie and that certainly includes that Jesus is the only way. Mixing with it and thereby helping to imply that their way is an alternate way, cannot work. He says you can't mix that together and eternity is on the line! You can't get to the stage where you start blending Satan's LIES with God's TRUTH. It can't work and it won't work! Again, it's because eternity is on the line and God takes it seriously. I heard this many years ago when one person said:

"Listen, I'd rather have you hate my guts and go to Heaven than for me to just love and tolerate until you end up in Hell because I never mentioned Jesus."

What kind of a friend doesn't care about that? It's the worst kind. I don't want a friend like that! Is that really being, loving? No, it's not so don't do that! Witness to them! This is the most serious issue any of us face in our lives so share the truth with them. They're following a false path and headed to Hell. Use that flat tire, bring them a sandwich, or do something, anything as an opportunity. One way or another, share the Gospel!

Unfortunately, that's not what's going on today with the pluralistic ecumenical movement trying to gather Christians and non-Christians together under one yoke without any thought to saving non-Christians from Hell. And that's what Paul says. For those who would do something like that, Paul says (Crone translation), 'What are you doing?! Did somebody spray chicken juice on you?' Paul goes into this long teaching where he points out the problem in many different ways. Have you had your parents do that? They tell you about something you did wrong, but that's not good enough. They have to impress upon you about why it was so wrong from a few different angles. You think they're done making the point but then they switch it up to another angle. Finally, you want to say, "Okay! I got it. I'm wrong!" It's the same in this passage. First Paul asks what righteousness and wickedness have in common. That should get your attention right there, but Paul is thinking: 'Let's make sure you get this point because it comes straight from God, our heavenly Father!' Paul says,

"What fellowship can light have with darkness? What harmony is there between Christ and Belial [the Devil]?"

Let me break that down into today's vernacular: What's going on and it's even in the Church today? How can we really get along (be yoked), with those who believe we ourselves are gods or that we will burn in a mythical place called Purgatory where we purge away our sins in order to get to Heaven? The latter is denying the cross! What?! How can we join hands with those who would have you and I believe that sin is an illusion or that Hell is only make-believe and that Heaven for some men will be to endlessly satisfy their lusts with as many virgins as they want, which only happens after you kill a bunch of people for Islam in the Jihad? How do you team up with that? How can you have 'unity' with those claiming to be Christians, yet they claim you have to keep the sacraments in order to be saved, which is another denial of the cross of Christ? How can we come together with those who say Satan doesn't exist or Christ's work on the cross is not enough? How can you have fellowship with those who would have you and I believe that Jesus is not God but merely the Archangel Michael? Or worse yet, as the Mormons teach, he's the spirit brother of Lucifer. How do you yoke yourself up to that by getting along, joining hands, having unity, or being in fellowship with that? What are you doing?! Come out! Get out of that! Be separate! All that stuff pollutes and it's a false path that leads people to Hell. You've got the truth and Christian; YOU are responsible for letting them know that while doing so in love, so don't be yoked with unbelief. Do not do it!

Are you getting the flavor of our clear directive from God for our Christian responsibility when dealing with other people on this planet? Yes, we are to witness to them, but you don't go in there and start blending in. And you don't sit there and work on projects together that have nothing to do with Jesus. Now, here's an example: I won't say what church it was, but this was a family member. They attended a certain church but stopped going when they learned more about the church's community service programs. With all those programs and efforts, which the church organized to do in the community like helping the homeless, feeding low income people, or doing building and cleaning projects for others, not once did they ever share the Gospel. In fact, they had no plans to share the Gospel and when they were confronted about why they don't mention the Gospel, their response was: 'Oh, we just want to show them Christ's love.' Well, it's good that you're trying to demonstrate God's love but what's the premise of even doing these good deeds for others? It's to share with them how Christ's love is why I love you enough to tell you the truth. The truth is that you're going down a false path, which ends in Hell and Jesus is the only way out it!

What that church was doing is called the "Social Gospel" and that's what is happening these days as the practice is rapidly returning throughout the Church. The social gospel is not the Bible's Gospel. The social gospel is just doing good deeds and working with other religions to do good things. That is not what the Bible tells us to do as far as our great commission we've been given to share the Biblical Gospel. That's what is coming back today with this ecumenical movement. But God says to come out from among that baloney and be ye separate.

Now I want to take a look at some of the evidence for whether this movement is really in place. What foundation needs to be laid, to allow Revelation 17 to come to pass? Are we getting close to those Revelation 17 events being able to be fulfilled during the Seven Year Tribulation? Well first, you need the religious figure and I think we definitely see that has already been established. Secondly, you need a pluralistic movement where people are violating the Scripture, including those who profess to be Christians. They would have this sort of attitude:

"Let's all just get along and work together on these projects. We're not talking about Jesus and not sharing the Gospel, but we did go over the line and yoke ourselves to each other as we're getting intoxicated with this (Woman) One World Religion message of love and tolerance which is going to bring peace to the planet. We are putting our hope in that outcome from man instead of looking for Jesus, who is coming back as the Prince of actual Peace!"

Let's take a look at that evidence for a rising pluralistic ecumenical (unity) movement. Again, the question is whether we see our world is being sucked up into this intoxicating feeling that we all just have to get along and specifically, maybe a good idea is for us all to snuggle up under the Vatican.

First of all, we see pluralism all over Europe. As far as pluralism in Berlin, Germany, they have created what's called "The House of One", at a cost of sixty million dollars. What is it for? It is to be used for Christians, Muslims, and Jews to pray under one roof. In Berlin, Pastor Gregor Hohberg explains its purpose:

"From the beginning, we wanted it to be an interreligious project,"

Okay, what's that buzzword? Inter-religious is the same as Interfaith and Inter-religion. It's all about drawing closer together toward a One World Religion. When you see those kinds of terms, you'll know that is what those terms are about. Gregor continues:

"...not a place built by Christians in which Jews and Muslims would be added, but a place for all three religions to have equal prayer space on the same floor with each floor leading to a common room where the different religions would be able to converse."

This is happening now in Europe and they are very excited about it. Here's the transcript from their promo video for that facility:

"'We have inherited a large house, a great world house, said Martin Luther King. We all inhabit this world house, our Earth. We see that the world is growing together and that we have to learn to live with each other. Increasingly religions are colliding, as strangers, as friends, often also as rivals or enemies. For this reason, Jews, Christians, and Muslims have come together in Berlin to dare to attempt something new. We want to build a completely new sacred building, a synagogue, a church, and a mosque under the same roof. And at its center, a meeting place, the House of One. It shall be located in the heart of Berlin, in the place where the city was founded eight hundred years ago. It shall be a unique peaceful place for encounters, meetings, and exchanges between people from different religions and also for those who are removed from religion. Everyone is invited to come; every interest, every question, every support is

welcome. With every peaceful dialogue and every good wish, the cloud of blessing will grow, one earth, one mankind, one home, The House of One."

Really? That's the One World Religion happening right now in Europe. Remember that the Seven Year Tribulation starts with Revelation 6:1 with the opening of the first seal in Heaven as well as Daniel 9:27 about how during that same timeframe on Earth, the Antichrist makes a peace treaty with the people of Israel. I'm not going to say, 'Thus saith the Lord', but some people believe that part of the incentive to get Israel into this treaty is the promise of a new temple because right now that is what the Jewish people are vehemently praying to be able to build.

And now today there is conversation behind the scenes and the behavior of the Pope and the Vatican as it relates to Catholicism vying for control over Jerusalem and the Temple Mount. Again, I'm not saying, 'Thus saith the Lord', but some of the reports out there are that the Vatican wants to build a "Universal Temple" in Jerusalem for the major religions to worship at just like the House of One they've got happening in Berlin.

We can see that groundwork being laid and then fast forward halfway into the Seven Year Tribulation when the Antichrist goes up into the rebuilt temple and declares himself to be God. So maybe the temple in Jerusalem will be more like a one-world type temple, while of course including Jewish people. Or maybe it will be a Jewish temple and more. It's very interesting to see what is unfolding right before our eyes.

How about the youth today? I've said this so many times and I'm telling you again, that the younger generations are falling for this stuff hook, line, and sinker. It's because they've been indoctrinated into this stuff through their schools since first grade. We'll get to the schools aspect more in a minute. But the indoctrination especially includes the millennial and generations after them. The propaganda is all they've ever known. They've been taught to desire globalism, forget American sovereignty and ignore Christianity because we're all one. They've been lied to at a level of being brainwashed. The globalists are co-opting the energy of our youth. Remember the days of youth when you had lots of energy to do all kinds of stuff without getting tired? Then as we get older, we're just kind of dragging more and more, well they're using the energy of the youth to steer and push toward this One World Religion. Let's take a look at that:

"With the help of the World Council of Churches..."

Wow, a world council made up of churches has to be Christian, right? No, it's not! That is one of the biggest sewer pipes of this Ecumenical One World Religion Movement.

"...a group of Christian, Muslim, and Jewish youths have now formed a multifaith community to protect the earth, which they say is a concern for all faiths."

Oh, so you're using this lie of global warming, which by the way can't be called "Global Warming" anymore because you got caught with the scientific data showing Earth is not warming. When your fraud was exposed, what did you do then so it wouldn't blow up in your face? You changed the terminology to "Climate Change." Now I don't know about you and I'm not a scientist, nor the son thereof, but I noticed that the climate changed since yesterday and I have a feeling tomorrow it will have changed again. They reinvented the terms because they got caught. Of course our climate changes. But they picked that innocuous term so you can't catch them on it. That whole climate change issue is the global excuse to gather all the world's religions together to deal with this fictitious planetary crisis that we supposedly need to fix, so the answer is to get all the religions together to make that happen. It's the excuse to blend them. And as long as we're getting them all in one big group, we'll have to have someone to control that huge conglomerate of world religions. I wonder who that might be?

Now let me give you a couple of quotes from these people promoting it, including Tariq Abdul Akbar, who is a 21-year-old Muslim:

"People of all faiths must put aside their religious differences and come together to raise awareness about climate change, which affects all people."

Again, we see climate change as a crisis being used as an excuse to unify religions. It's a lie but it's being used to form a One World Religion, as well as a One World Government. Mark Edwards is a so-called Christian student from Sri Lanka:

"The responsibility to respect creation is common to all faiths. Earth is a gift to us all and we are responsible for its well-being."

So, we all need to work together. Let's yoke ourselves together. That's what they're saying. Liron Alkolombra is a Jewish woman:

"Living in a multifaith [There's that buzzword again.] community is an eye opener. Our visit to a synagogue, a church, and a mosque in Switzerland moved me so much that I realized we all believe in God and we're all part of humanity."

Now I will grant you that we're all part of humanity, but we do not all believe in the same God! There's only one God and that is the Biblical one. What does James, Chapter 2 say? It tells us that even the demons believe in God and they shudder. Are demons saved? No. Make sure you get the right God and follow what He says, which has been recorded in the Bible. But that's what this interfaith movement is pushing; We're all the same. That's pluralism.

What we just looked at is going on in Europe, but how about America? Are we safe from all that? Unfortunately, the answer is no because it's spreading out everywhere around the world. Here's an example from the Bible belt and specifically Nebraska, which is right above Kansas where I used to live:

Even here in America we now have what's called the Tri-Faith Initiative in Omaha that is combining Christians, Jews, and Muslims into an interfaith [There's your buzzword again.] dialogue as well as an interfaith facility. It's a multimillion dollar effort to bring all three religions onto a 35-acre campus. The city's religious leaders say, *"We want to form a relationship between all Jews, all Muslims, and all Christians. It's an opportunity not only to learn to tolerate [There's another buzzword] different faiths but to find ways to celebrate all we have in common and join with those who call God by different names."*

What do you have in common? It rhymes with nothing. And that's because Jesus is the only way! But that's the lie because we all have to get along, so if everyone says, "God", then we're set, right? Well, so what? Which God are we talking about? Is it your god, the environmental god, Allah, or one of the millions of Hindu gods? God is a generic term nowadays. It doesn't mean the one and only God, the Christian God. They take these things like a generic "God" or the fact that we all pray and just lump them together as if waving a magic wand to make them all the same. So, what if we all pray? Does that mean we're praying to the same entity or praying the same kind of prayers? But this is how they seduce people into the ecumenical movement.

Now I want to go back to what's happening in the schools, even in the United States. Here's some actual examples right now happening across America:

Just in case you don't live anywhere near Berlin or Omaha [to be corrupted by this baloney], we now have High School students in Colorado being encouraged to recite a pledge in Arabic, stating, "One Nation under Allah." In New York, kids are now observing Muslim New Year holidays and possibly soon the Hindu Festival Diwali. Diwali is a festival of lights Hinduism celebrates. It's supposed to be about the light and the darkness and all those sorts of beliefs.

But wait a second. Aren't we told as Christians that there is a separation of church and state? They are endlessly saying we can't have religion in schools. Well then what is this stuff involving Islam and Hinduism in U.S. schools? And that's just a couple of examples of hundreds. Also, December used to have what's called "Christmas Break." It's apparently not that anymore. What is it now? They changed the name to "Winter Break." Along with that, we used to have a holiday named, "Easter Break", which they changed to "Spring Break." So, you even went so far as to rip out the Christian terms, but you bring these other religion's practices in and then call them by their actual names. Their version of separation of church and state is to keep Christianity out while everything else goes! That is really what's going on. And here's what is happening in California:

"School kids in California are bowing down to the Sun God as a part of the [Listen to this!] 'liturgical ritual religious practices'..."

That's a clear blatant violation of what you keep telling us about keeping religious practices out of school. What are you doing? The answer is they really mean 'anything but Christianity' is acceptable.

"...liturgical ritual religious practices aimed at having them [This is our children!] 'become one with god through yoga.'"

Now here's what is ironic: Our passage there in 2 Corinthians tells us not to be yoked with unbelievers but the term, "Yoga" means "yoked." You are yoking with the Hindu deities. That is very interesting.

"The founder, Sonia Tudor Jones says she wants to 'spread the gospel of Ashtanga Yoga through the country and even internationally.'"

And where is this that she is being allowed to spread it? It's in our schools. I thought you weren't supposed to do that. But let's continue on.

That's in schools but how about the government? Well it wasn't that long ago, and you might recall it was in the news:

"The Dalai Lama was allowed to open Senate meetings with prayer. Senators bowed their heads in prayers as the Dalai Lama prayed: 'With our thoughts we make our world.'"

First of all, it's God's world and he makes it. God determines our reality and not us. You are NOT God! But that's the kind of thing happening in our own government today.

And speaking of Congress, an Interfaith [There is your buzzword again] School for Military Chaplains has now been dedicated. Priests, rabbis, imams, and so-called Protestant ministers came together to dedicate themselves and the nation's first joint military multi-faith [There it is again] education center.

One place this movement has been going on even longer than the military is in hospitals. I've dealt with this while pastoring in California, New York and even here in Las Vegas. One of the most difficult places to share the Gospel is in hospitals. When you go there, you'll run into all this interfaith philosophy. Hospitals in the U.S. used to have Christian chapels where families could go. They still have "chapels", but many are no longer Christian. You may notice they've even ripped out the Christian artwork. There used to be stained glass windows with a cross but now there are no crosses. Instead they have stained glass designs like fluffy flower-looking things or starbursts. It's no longer a cross as you might expect in a chapel. It has a feeling of religion with the stained glass or other things but it's now all religions. I did not follow their instructions but was told that I couldn't be preachy and needed to honor other people with different beliefs. Of course, I went ahead speaking about Jesus.

Oh, and that brings up our previous president. What was he doing in this area with his entire time in office? He went around the world saying what? It was: *'We are no longer a Christian nation.'* So, what are we then? We're a pluralistic nation of Hindus, Buddhists, Muslims, Christians, and Jews. That was his whole message. Is it any wonder that we now have schools in America that are teaching our kids the Muslim religion? Here's a quick look at what our American kids are being taught in our schools. They're learning to become a member of Islam. Remember, you can't mention Christianity and you get in trouble if you bring a Bible to school. You can't preach about Jesus, say the name of Jesus, or pray. As a teacher, if you do those things, you get fired. Children get expelled. But they apparently have no problem teaching Islam to our kids. This is going on right now and here is a list of what they are learning in the schools we pay for:

They are learning to become Muslim, fasting for Ramadan, learning about Ramadan, learning the five pillars of Islam, memorizing verses of the Quran, and adopting a Muslim name.

If that wasn't bad enough and you can check this out for yourself, school kids are being taught about:

"Staging a jihad war against non-Muslims."

That is a school exercise. Here's what one guy said about it:

"Apparently Obama has overlooked his Christian obligation and duty that he swore in public office to uphold the Constitution of the United States of America with his hand on the Christian Bible that states [in Exodus 20:3], 'You shall have no other gods before Me!'"

But the Bible's agenda is not their agenda. Their plans are to promote this pluralistic mindset that says, 'Can't we all just get along.' And of course, they're doing it even in our own government. But hey, isn't the Church holding strong? No, it is not! Let's take a look at more examples of what is going on:

"The Global Faith Forum recently kicked off in Texas. Hundreds of Christians, Muslims, Jews, Hindus, Buddhists, and atheists have convened at Northwoods Church in Texas in an effort to try to understand one another."

That for me would be the shortest meeting ever. My contribution would be:

"You are going to Hell because Jesus is the only way. Any questions?"

What do you mean we should try to understand one another? How convoluted can you make it? Again, I didn't say it. Jesus said it in John 14:6: Jesus is the way, the truth, and the life. He's the only way to the Father so no one comes to the Father except through Him. Either you believe that, or you need to! But what are the Christians involved in that event doing?! Are they witnessing to those **condemned** people? No! You're not! Well, then I'm telling you, you're going over the line! You starting that yoking thing. Here's more:

Representatives of Jewish, Catholic, Protestant, B'hai, Mormon, Sikh Vedic, Druid, and Muslims in Sacramento read scriptures from each of their religious texts, including six verses from the Quran, calling for all faiths to live in harmony. Again, and again they uttered the refrain, 'Let there Be peace on earth and let it begin with me.'

Let me translate: Let there be a One World Religion on the planet that is going to submit to the Vatican and yes, it certainly is beginning with you. But this is taking place in so-called Christian churches, who are opening their doors and getting yoked with these false teachings. They're going over the line. Here's more:

"A bishop is urging Christians to call God Allah. The Catholic leader believes it would ease the tensions between religions."

Allah is not the same as the one and only true God of the Bible. And listen to this one:

"Christians are now celebrating religious diversity..."

Diversity is another buzzword and its appeal for Christians is to be a "virtuous Christian" by allowing diversity in their accepting of lies instead of following Biblical truth.

"...on Pentecost Sunday. Christian Churches across the United States are dedicating their worship to a celebration of our [What's the buzzword?] 'interfaith' world."

Those Christians are called "Progressive Christians." They'll chastise Biblical Christians with something like,

"Hey, you're not one of those old fashioned, traditionalist Christians, are you? You're not one of those Fundamentalist Christians, are you? You need to be a Progressive Christian like me."

So, they just modified the terminology to try deflecting the truth of what's really going on there. They are literally turning "Apostate." They are skipping along down the path of this intoxicating love and tolerance that is blending everyone, including Christians, into this One World Religion. Let's continue:

"Progressive Christians thank God for religious diversity: 'We don't claim that our religion is superior to all others.'"

This is from Christians! You're right, we don't claim it, Jesus did and you as a 'Christ'-ian, which is a follower of Christ, should not be figuring out ways around that! It's scary! Here's more:

"'We can grow closer to God and deeper in compassion—and we can understand our own traditions better—through a greater awareness of the world's religions. Sponsored by the Center for Progressive Christianity—Pluralism Sunday will be promoted through churches and participating churches will be profiled in publicity releases, creating an evangelism opportunity for your congregation."

What are you evangelizing?! It's not Jesus! This is total intoxication with the togetherness stuff. Here is more:

"The number of people looking at The Center for Progressive Christianity's website is topping 40,000 per month! [They say], 'We believe Pluralism Sunday is an opportunity for progressive churches to reach some of the many people [Listen!] who were turned off by Christianity because of exclusivist claims some Christians make about it."

We didn't make those claims! Jesus did! He's the One who brings that hammer down. He is the way, the truth, and the life. No one gets to the Father except through Him. Excuse me?! It doesn't turn people off. People are shown the way out of this mess! The thinking of progressive churches is so twisted. Here are some statistics:

"Many [professing] born-again Christians are now holding universalist views."

In other words, it's working and even seducing the Church.

"One in four [professing] born-again Christians believe that all people are eventually saved or accepted by God."

So, if we have two hundred people show up on Sunday at your church, how many do not believe the Gospel? It's fifty of them, right? How can you be born-again and say that Jesus is not the only way? I know that sampling said it was of 'born-again Christians' but I've got a problem with them just assuming, with no Scripture to back it up, that all people end up with God. It gets even worse:

"A similar proportion, twenty six percent, said a person's religion doesn't matter because all faiths teach the same lessons."

This is exactly why we're going into a multi-year extensively detailed study of the World Religions, Cults & The Occult. It's because that lie about all faiths being the same is one of the most popular deceptions that is even seducing people in the Church. For us, after even a little information, let alone the amount of in-depth study we've done, now when people make the statement: "Don't you know all religions are basically the same?", we know that is one of the most ludicrous statements ever made! Yet it's seducing 25% or more of professing Christians. Even more, 40% of supposed born-again Christians said they believe Christians and Muslims worship the same God! This is a survey of the secular world. That is forty percent of those sitting in the pews in the Church!

Now where's all this coming from? Well, a lot of it is of course coming from indoctrination through our children's schools. It's this wave of intoxication that the Church is accepting, and the Church is yoking with non-believers instead of witnessing. As we saw, there is a major difference between 2000-year-old "Biblical Christianity" and this new "Progressive Christianity" with the main tenant of the latter being: "Let's all just get along." And now it's rolling down from the top, from the Christian leadership in our seminaries. This is from one so-called seminary:

"The Claremont School of Theology has launched a program to train future leaders [for the Church]. [They say] 'Not all Christians, Jews, and Muslims believe that their way is the only way.'"

Well, then you're certainly not a Christian. You can be a Jew because the Jews don't believe a person has to go through Jesus. Or you can be a Muslim, but you're not a Christian. How can you say you are a Christ follower and yet deny that Christ is the only way? It goes on to say this and remember it's from a so-called Christian seminary:

"Christians, Muslims, and Jews will now have the opportunity to take classes together to learn about each other's religious traditions, to study topics that deal specifically with interfaith issues [There's that word again], and to build bridges through coursework that assists them...[Listen! Who is it??] ***our society's future religious leaders****."*

Unless something turns around and we get serious about sharing the truth, which frankly means we need revival, then this is what's spreading throughout the Church. If you think it's bad now, wait until these new progressive-seminary-taught leaders infiltrate the entire Church. These new leaders are being trained in the intoxicating lie that all religions are basically the same thing. It's coming! It's happening right before our very eyes and not just on an individual basis, but now they're attacking the leadership and the future leadership of the Church. They are ensuring that this apostasy is going to make massive inroads and maybe dominate the future Church. Here's more on this pluralism:

Dozens of Churches are now promoting Islam, from Denver to Boise Idaho, to San Francisco, and Honolulu. They're planning to send a message, *"Both here at home and to the Arab and Muslim world about our respect for Islam with a time to read the Quran during our worship services."* The Interfaith Alliance of Human Rights First is calling on Christian clergy to read portions of the Quran during their services Sunday. In fact, Churches are now letting Muslims use their facilities. Heartsong Church near Memphis is allowing Muslims to hold Ramadan prayers in its building.

Whoa, whoa, whoa! See, now you're yoking! You are not witnessing. You're actually letting them use your facilities. When you let them use your facilities, what are you helping them propagate? Again, if you show up here and need a sandwich, I'll give you something to eat all day long. Do you have a flat tire or need some clothes because it's getting a little chilly out? Hey men, we'll get you a jacket. But I cannot be a part of anything that helps you to propagate, increase, grow, build, etc., your lie that is leading people to Hell! These churches are yoking with them. They are not witnessing. They yoked and are violating the Scripture, right?

Aldersgate United Methodist Church in Virginia allowed the Islamic Circle of North America to hold regular prayer meetings in its facility. But that's not all. We now even have Churches removing their crosses to become more inclusive. C3Exchange was formerly known as Christ Community Church and the [so-called] Reverend Ian Lawton, the Church's pastor, said the name change and removing the cross was designed to reflect the church's diverse members. He said, "Our community has really been open-minded for some years now and we've had a number of Muslim people, Jewish people, Buddhists, and atheists. We're just catching up to ourselves. We honor the cross, but [Listen!] the cross is just one symbol of our community."

Well then, it's not a Christian community. Oh, and by the way, they were so excited about tearing down the cross they videotaped it. You can watch it online. So, you get rid of your cross and you're excited about it and you change your name from a Christian name to C3Exchange. But at least after some of this study, we know what they're up to, right? Here in Las Vegas one of the largest churches, and of course size doesn't necessarily mean they're good, named Central Christian Church, changed their name to Central Church. You can go online and see it. They removed "Christian." So even here in Vegas, it's happening folks and right before our eyes.

Kenneth Copeland piped in a private message from the Pope...to his so-called Protestant Church and the Catholic bishop (Tony Palmer) stated from the **PULPIT**: "Luther's protest is over...how about yours?"

If I piped in a private message from Pope Francis and allowed a Catholic bishop to get up here and say, 'Luther's protest is over, how about yours?', what should you do to me? You need to *fire me on the spot*! Well, Kenneth Copeland is still in existence behind his pulpit and hasn't been fired. The congregation was actually cheering for that statement and then they even laughed at this remark: "Maybe we're all Catholics now."

By the way, notice that the Catholic guy made it to a Protestant pulpit. What's interesting about that is something from the Jesuit Extreme Oath of Induction. Do you remember? And I quote:

"Heretofore you have been taught to act as the dissembler; and to be a spy. Among the Reformers, to be a reformer; among other Protestants, generally to be a Protestant, obtaining their confidence to seek to even preach from their [Here it is!] ***PULPITS****, that you might be enabled to gather together all information for the benefit of your Order as a faithful soldier of the Pope." [Emphasis added]*

It's already happening!

Many of the people from the Charismatic Movement are doing the exact same thing. They're meeting with the Pope, chumming up with Pope Francis, giving him high-fives, trying to figure out how we can all get along as Protestants. No, we are not all Protestants! Catholics are not Protestants. So, the Charismatic Movement is also falling for this stuff. It's not just the false teacher, Kenneth Copeland.

We talked about this next one in our Final Countdown studies:

"Beth Moore is hanging out with the same Charismatics."

So, guess what she's starting to do. If you follow her work, you may have noticed she's starting to speak very Charismaticy. She's not mentioning what the Bible says about things as much, but she is saying Charismatic phrases like,

"The Lord told me..." and "I had a vision [or a dream], in which God communicated to me...."

Okay so now that is getting away from Scripture. We dealt with the same sort of verbiage and practices in our study of New Age. You don't want to go that route. Because of hanging out with some of these same people, Moore is also making comments like, "Catholics are our brothers and sisters." That's from Beth Moore so we better pay attention, folks. It's spilling down from the top.

Joel Osteen says he loves the Pope and is glad that the Pope has made the 'Church' more inclusive to take everybody in and that 'resonates with him.' In other words, Osteen is doing the same, so he agrees with the practice, right? Then of course we saw what is happening with a guy I characterize as the big bombshell:

Rick Warren also loves the pope and says things like 'Our Pope' and 'Us Christians', and has a picture of the Pope on his wall as a source of inspiration. His favorite way to wind down with his wife after a stressful day is, 'Mother Angelica' and 'Chaplet of Divine Mercy', Catholic shows with mindless [repeated] Catholic prayers and reciting the rosary over and over again.

And now so-called Protestant pastors are actually converting back to Roman Catholicism saying we [Christians] need to go back to the Sacraments, the Mother Church, and Mary! So now this supposed "Christian" leadership is saying, we Protestants were wrong, so Luther's protest is over. What?! And it's one thing for them to get behind a pulpit to make that statement and be allowed to make that statement, but so-called pastors are forsaking Protestantism and they're becoming Catholics. You think, "Well, how could they do that?" Scripture, in 1 John 2:19, has the answer:

"They went out from us, but they did not really belong to us. For if they had belonged to us, they would have remained with us; But their going showed that none of them belonged to us."

How could you turn from Jesus, the one and only way, and then say you're going to go along with a system that is false and a system of works? How can you do that? The Scripture says that when we're born again, we're indwelt with the Holy Spirit. We are sealed with the Holy Spirit. In Ephesians 4:30, Paul says we're sealed with the Holy Spirit for our day of redemption. We are secured and locked in. God's pledge used in Scripture is 'arrabon' in the Greek, which means God's engagement ring. When you're truly born again, God gives us his spirit. Bang! Praise God, he has sealed you so you're going to get there! However, if somebody says they were a Christian, even from behind the pulpit, and then someday later they say they've decided to give that up and go follow a false religion or whatever it is, what does the Scripture say about that? It says, "They didn't really belong to us." Isn't that a bombshell?! Think about that? How many people right now are behind the pulpit, serving on church boards, or teaching Sunday school classes even though they're not born-again?

Yet society wonders why the Church today is so powerless and ineffective. I've said it before and I'll say it again, I think the reason our Church in America is so ineffective and powerless, by and large, is because the Church is infiltrated with so many unbelievers who profess to be believers but they're not. And when they get into positions of leadership, that church goes downhill from there.

So again, there is a huge wave of intoxication that's all about: Let's all just love, tolerate, and work together! But it's going over the line. You're not witnessing and instead you're yoking together! Now you're going so far with it that you even remove the cross and change your name away from one that includes Jesus. You're not witnessing but you are allowing them to propagate their beliefs in your facility! Exactly counter to God's directive for you, you're yoking instead of witnessing.

My next question is, *"How are the Southern Baptists doing?"*

Well, this one is a massive bombshell for believing Baptists and I couldn't accept it until the facts made me realize it was completely true: Russell Moore is the President of the Southern Baptist Ethics and Religious Liberty Commission. We've already called this guy out on the carpet in our *Final Countdown* study when, a few years ago, he visited the Vatican making big waves and ruffling a lot of feathers, as it should have. He went over there for their Marriage and Family Conference. I really wonder why he would do that? Are they going to teach you practices involving marriage and family that we don't have in the Scripture already? Why are you yoking with them? I don't think you were there handing out tracts.

So that was a big concern already but now this more recent incident was all over the papers so please check it out for yourself. Again, Russell Moore is the leader of the Southern Baptist Ethics and Religious Liberty Commission that is now supporting the building of a mosque in New Jersey. In my own investigation, I found out this yoking that was already going on, has gotten worse:

"When challenged on supporting the mosque construction has said, 'As Baptists we are about soul freedom. And don't worry, we didn't spend any of the Church's money.'"

I actually, personally called the Ethics Commission when I found this out because as a Southern Baptist pastor, I wanted a direct answer. I didn't want to just read about it from articles on the Internet. After almost four weeks of calling every week, I finally got a reply. Now I get it, people are busy just as I am, but the reply was basically what now seems to be a standard answer:

"As Baptists we're about soul freedom."

That term keeps coming up. And they said, "Don't worry, we didn't spend any of the Church's money." I'm sorry but with all due respect, that's a lie. You spent your time investigating this, working on it, and supporting it. They even filed a brief and joined other folks, which I'll get to in a minute, that support the building of this Muslim mosque. So, you spent your time, your staff's time, and you also spent the time of legal counsel. Who's paying your salary, as well as staff and legal counsel compensation? Southern Baptists are paying it, so don't say you didn't spend any of the Church's money. That's a lie.

Now what about their buzzwords: "Soul Freedom." This actually came up at the last national convention when Russell Moore was called on the carpet by other pastors. Two motions were put on the floor. The first was for him to be fired. but they immediately squelched it by calling the motion out of order. Another guy named John Wolford got up and spoke. I later tracked him down and talked with him directly on the phone. Wolford called Moore out on what he was doing. Wolford said:

"Mr. Moore, do you mean to tell me, that Jesus would support Baal Worshipers building a Baal Temple?"

Moore didn't answer the question and that's when he went onto this verbiage about how Baptists are now about Soul Freedom. And what he means by that term, in his own verbiage, is that Baptists are about making sure all religions have the freedom to worship as they see fit here in America. Yeah well, as a Baptist, I'm a Christian. And as a Christian, I'm a follower of Christ. If I want to work towards soul freedom, I work at witnessing to them about Jesus being the only way. Jesus is the only way those souls are going to be free. Saying that I need to work through this political ecumenical endeavor toward everyone just getting along and having the right to worship in America, is not what Baptists are about. But that's what's being used with the term, "Soul Freedom."

In fact, let me flip it around. How would this work out if I were to make an announcement along these lines:

"Hey Sunrise Bible Church, I just want to let you know that, man I've been really busy, but there are a lot of interesting projects I've done. Now of course you know that us Christian Southern Baptists are all about soul freedom, so I've been working my tail off with a bunch of other groups from different religions here in Las Vegas. In fact, Muslims were trying to build a mosque over here. Well hey, we got together with our legal guys and a bunch of other religion's legal teams to file a brief with Las Vegas city saying the Muslims can't build. We're moving along with that effort. Oh but, by the way, don't worry because I didn't spend any of Sunrise Bible Church's money."

If I said that, what should you do? **<u>You should fire me</u>**. So why is this being allowed from the Southern Baptist Ethics Commission? And it gets even worse, if you can believe that. As we've already established, the Bible says not to be yoked with non-believers. But completely counter to the Bible, here is what Russell Moore, at the head of the Southern Baptist Ethics Committee, did:

"Russell Moore and the Ethics Commission also partnered with close to 20 'faith-based' organizations and filed an amicus brief arguing that the mosque project be approved."

And here are the non-believers he yoked with:

The American Association of Jewish Lawyers and Jurors, Baptist Joint Committee for Religious Liberty, Center for Islamic and Religious Freedom, Interfaith [There it is again!] Coalition on Mosques, and the International Mission Board of the Southern Baptist Convention.

So now the Southern Baptist Mission Board has also put their hat in the ring with those organizations! That's where the money is going, and it involves this kind of behavior. I've got a problem with it. Here are more of those organizations:

International Society for Krishna Consciousness, Muslim Bar Association of New York, National Asian Pacific American Bar Association, National Association of Evangelicals, New Jersey Muslim Lawyers Association, Queens Federation of Churches, Sikh American Legal Defense and Education Fund, Sikh Coalition, South Asian Bar Association of New Jersey, South Asian

Bar Association of New York, and the Unitarian Universalist Legislative Ministry of New Jersey.

But neither Moore nor the Southern Baptist Mission Board are witnessing to those non-believers. They are instead, yoking together with them. Again, if you're a Muslim, Sikh, New Ager, Krishna follower or anyone, and you need something to eat, I'll give you a sandwich. If you have a flat tire, I'll fix it, give you a tire pump, inflate it myself, give you a ride, or whatever. If you need some clothes, I'll give you clothes. But at each one of those opportunities, do you know what I'll also be doing? I'm witnessing to you!

However, I cannot have any part of you building a structure that is your temple that will allow people to propagate, disperse, encourage, and congregate for the furthering of your false teaching. That is denying Christ! I cannot have any of that. But it's exactly what is going on. It's not witnessing or even, "soul freedom." It is yoking and that is a violation of Scripture. Unfortunately, it continues to get worse. Here is more of what I learned from my own investigation:

"The Southern Baptist Ethics & Religious Liberty Commission is a member of the United Nations."

Now it starts to make sense, doesn't it? We can see why they're pushing this stuff, even in the Southern Baptist leadership.

"This was instituted by the previous president, Richard Land, who resigned due to some scandalous behavior, and now Russell Moore has replaced him. The problem is, being an NGO [Non-Governmental Organization] of the United Nations, one has to pledge to uphold the U.N. Agenda, which is not only to create a One World Government, but also a One World Religion."

And that is straight from the United Nation's website. The Southern Baptists' Ethics Commission is listed as an NGO at the U.N. On the U.N.'s website, they list the responsibilities of those who are NGOs of the U.N.:

"The aims and purposes of the organization shall be in conformity with the spirit, purposes, and principles of..."

Jesus Christ? Oh, I'm sorry, that's not what it says. The end of that sentence says you have to support:

"...the spirit, purposes, and principles of the Charter of the United Nations."

Secondly: "The organization shall undertake to support the work of the United Nations."

Third: "They must demonstrate that their program of work is of direct relevance to the aims and purposes of the United Nations."

So Southern Baptists are working together with twenty other faith groups to support a Muslim mosque, because all religions have a right to soul freedom. Doesn't that sound like something the United Nations would do? Yes, it does and that's because it is relevant to the United Nations purposes and aims. However, it does not agree with the Bible. So, if we wonder why this is being pushed, all we have to do is trace the trail. Oh, and remember we talked about the United Nations and its new leader? Ban Ki Moon has been replaced as Secretary General of the United Nations and the new guy is Antonio Guiterrez, who is:

"not only a Socialist [just as Hitler's National Socialist party was] and served as the President of Socialist International, but he is a Catholic."

This is the guy who's now going to be heading the United Nations. That's really weird. So, when you stir all this together, for me it brings up a question. But first let me give you the context: Push is going to come to shove and the Pope, or some world religious figure, will say we need to combine all of our religions together and work with a One World Government, which is Beast/Antichrist savior figure. Now judging from today's current leadership of the world, including the United Nations with their new Socialist Catholic leader and even the current so-called leadership of the Protestant Church, including the Southern Baptist denomination, do you think those people and organizations are going to resist? I don't think so! To me it's like the pieces are falling right into place.

Of course, we don't know the day or the hour, but we do know all this is leading to Revelation 17, which outlines the events that will take place during the Seven Year Tribulation. And wow, if the Church is already yoking to this degree with the global religion and they're already so caught up in this pluralistic movement, it has to be getting close to the time Christ comes back to get us. Isn't this wild when you stop to think about the days we live in?! It's absolutely awesome! And it shouldn't be scary. Instead, it should be motivating! Jesus is soon coming back to get us!

As a side note, I want it to be known that after our findings regarding the Southern Baptist Association, my church, Sunrise Bible Church, severed ties with the Southern Baptist Convention and became a non-denominational Bible Church, as I would encourage other Southern Baptist Churches to do as well.

In the next chapter we'll knock out the final three confirmations that need to develop, according to the writing in Revelation 17, to bring about this Woman and the Beast system she rides. Then we're going to take a look at that woman figure. There's no woman deified in Catholicism is there? Yes, of course there is. We'll take a look at that and how the world is being swept into it, as well as exploring other aspects. Then we're going to take a look at the Antichrist figure. Are there political leaders on the scene, who may not be the actual Antichrist but who are literally being called a god and worshiped as a god? And do we see any signs of global governance that will become the strong arm to punish people who don't go along with this? Yes, and we'll deal with all that next!

Chapter Six

Persecution is Coming

Anybody can look at the abundant evidence to see that Roman Catholicism is a pseudo (fake, false) Christian group. Also, they are a cult. They fit both the secular and Biblical definitions. And thirdly, they are certainly demonic, or devilish as John, Chapter 8 outlines devilish. Considering how it points out in John 8 that Jesus is the truth, how did those who disagreed with Jesus react to Him? They didn't just disagree with Him and didn't only say He was demonic; they actually said, 'We're going to kill you!' Jesus called them on the carpet for it. By the way, since Jesus is the truth, that's why we share the truth, of whom Jesus was. We saw Roman Catholicism is guilty of that same sort of devilish behavior with the Inquisitions, which by the way have not ended, even to this day. They are still in effect. The Vatican just changed the terminology for what it calls them.

The last couple chapters, we've been looking at where the whole pluralistic ecumenical unity movement is leading. What bearing does it have for us today? Well, it's leading to the last days Antichrist kingdom with the Woman riding the Antichrist Beast during the One World Religion Harlot System. And I think Catholicism certainly has some part to play in that story that is now rolling out.

As we saw when we read from Revelation 17 a couple chapters ago, there are five things that need to be happening if we're getting close. These are events, which take place during the Seven Year Tribulation. However, we are not going to be there, so get excited! We're going to be gone in the Rapture of the Church prior to the Seven Year Tribulation. Well then, what's the point for the Church? You'll hear Christians say, "I don't need to study that Bible Prophecy stuff. That tribulation thing won't affect me." Well, here's the point: We're looking at the events that take place during the Seven Year Tribulation and we are definitely seeing now, how all the major chess pieces, platforms, and machinery are being put into play to fulfill those coming events during the Seven Year Tribulation. Of course, we don't know the day, nor the hour but we can recognize the season so if all that is coming together, how close is the Rapture of the Church, which takes place prior? That realization should spur on some urgency in us! It should rid us of any procrastination and laziness. Frankly it should get us excited because if you love Jesus you long for His appearing. Amen? Don't get bogged down with this wicked world system!

So that said, Revelation 17 informs us that we're going to have to see, in my opinion, at least five things come to pass: First, you're going to need a **religious figure** who seduces and intoxicates the whole world into creating a One World Religious system. Secondly, last chapter we looked at Pluralism, which is the Ecumenical Movement seducing the people. With that we saw how it's one thing for religious figures to entice everyone to join this One World Religion movement, but does that mean people have to fall for it? Well, unfortunately that's what is happening right now. People are getting sucked into it. And this is progressing at great speed, not only in the world with our government, promoted by the media, and pushed in our school system, but it's even spreading in the Church! We're seeing major signs that all those institutions, whether they know it or not, are backing into the arms of this Roman Catholic led **pluralistic ecumenical (unity) movement**, which is striving to get all religions to come together as one.

Now in this chapter I want to finish up those five things that must come to pass. We're going to see the push for a **woman figure**, an **antichrist figure** (we're going to see proof of that, believe it or not), and an **authority figure**. For the latter, again, Revelation says she is drunk with the blood of the saints. It's one thing to say, "Hey, you need to listen to us and follow our beliefs", but 'drunk with the blood' means Christians are being martyred. They are killed! So, you're going to have to have some sort of authority on a global scale to punish those who would dare resist your system.

Let's now take a look at the woman figure. Revelation 17 is very clear that you're dealing with some sort of woman figure, who represents this One World Religion system. She is Babylon the Harlot who rides the Antichrist Beast, which is the One World Government. They work together and eventually God gives the Antichrist the ability to take the Harlot out. However, in the beginning she's riding him. She's riding the government system, which tells us she's controlling it all in the beginning. Let's take a look at Revelation 17 again. Is it really a woman figure and what could that woman figure be? What does that woman figure represent? Here are those first six verses:

"One of the seven angels who had poured out the seven bowls came over and said to me, 'Come and I will show you the punishment of the great prostitute who sits on many waters [the world]. With her the kings of the earth committed adultery and the inhabitants of the Earth were intoxicated with the wine of her adulteries.'"

Again, that intoxicating is what we saw last chapter with everybody talking about getting along, getting together, and playing nice to the point of causing this wave of exhilaration.

"Then the angel carried me in the Spirit into a desert and there I saw a woman sitting on a scarlet beast that was covered with blasphemous names and had seven heads and ten horns. The woman was dressed in purple and scarlet and was glittering with gold, precious stones, and pearls. She held a golden cup in her hand filled with abominable things and the filth of her adulteries. The titles written on her forehead:

'Mystery, Babylon the Great, The Mother of Prostitutes and of the Abominations of the Earth.'

And I saw that the woman was drunk with the blood the Saints and the blood of those who bore testimony to Jesus. When I saw her I was greatly astonished."

In that text, did you notice there were six different verses mentioning that we're dealing with some sort of female figure? It's a female icon and female representation. Now it could be just that harlot and prostitute are used similarly as when God uses the same words for Israel's idolatry in following other religions. So maybe it's just more of a euphemism for that. It could certainly be. But what's very interesting is, as we sit here, around the planet, we're seeing a large-scale extreme push to move from what's been more male patriarchal societies and religions to female matriarchal goddess worship. And believe it or not, it's even happening in the Church. So, let's take a look at that.

I don't want to go too much into the feminizing of our world, but let's explore how the Church is being feminized literally and spiritually as they move away from a male patriarchal worship. Here's some of that:

"Mary Daly, who considers herself to be a Christian feminist,"

Whoa! Stop right there. That's what is called an oxymoron. Putting Christian together with feminist is like saying icy hot, peaceful war, or yummy chicken. That's not happening! You can't be a Christian and a feminist at the same time with what the Feminist Movement believes. Here is more and remember, the woman speaking is professing to be a Christian:

Daly says this about traditional Christianity: *"To put it bluntly, I propose that Christianity itself should be castrated. The primary focus of the Christian feminist is to bring an end to what they perceive as a male dominated religion."* She continued by saying, *"I am suggesting, the idea of salvation uniquely by a male savior [Jesus] perpetuates the problem of patriarchal oppression."*

Excuse me?! Again, this is a professing Christian! Let's move on to this one:

"The website for Ebenezer Lutheran Church in San Francisco is HerChurch.org."

Last I checked, it's still there. In fact, right on their home page all the ladies are singing a song called, "Our Mother." I'll show you just the first two lines:

"Our mother, who is within us, we celebrate your many names."

So, it's this female goddess figure worship where the feminine deity can even have any number of different names so long as it's female. Don't worry about who it is you're worshiping as your god, as you are idolizing a female deity figure. That's on their website so you can go check it out for yourself. It continues with what they do on Wednesday night. At my church, we have Bible study. They, on the other hand, do this:

"On Wednesday nights they open their sanctuary for the Christian Goddess Rosary."

That's interesting. Who else has a Rosary and also a female figure in their so-called worship? It's the Catholic Church of course and we'll get to more on that in a minute. So, there's a blending going on. HerChurch.org also makes this statement:

"The exclusive emphasis of God as Father supports a domination structure that oppresses and subordinates women."

They also encourage people to pray the 'Hail Goddess Prayer' that states, 'Hail Goddess full of grace. Blessed are you and blessed are the fruits of your womb.'"

Whoa! Stop right there! What does that sound like? It's Catholic Hail Mary prayers that they have spiritualized. And again, remember their song that references the feminine deity's many names. As long as it's a female figure, they'll worship you. That's interesting, especially because this is supposed to be a Lutheran Church. It continues:

"For you are the mother of us all."

Yeah, no, it's actually the Mother of Harlots as Revelation calls it.

Jan Clanton, author of, *God, a Word for Girls and Boys* says *"Masculine God language hinders many children from establishing relationships of trust with God. In addition, calling God 'he' causes boys to commit the sin of arrogance. Calling the supreme power of the universe 'he' causes girls to commit the sin of devaluing themselves. So, for the sake of 'these little ones' we must change the way we talk about God."*

In other words, we need to feminize it all. But notice how they use the kids to tug on our heartstrings. It's the same when they appeal to people to fix society and the school system. Their solution is often, "Buy them a computer!" And that's because we all know that every time you buy a new computer it saves time, money, and hassles. Don't you love it when you get updates on your iPhone or iPad? That helps too, right? Yes, I'm joking. But they're always trying to sell you the panacea: "It will fix everything!" If you disagree at all, they come back with: "Oh, come on! Please, it's for the kids. You've got kids to think about." Whatever! It's an abomination and it's spreading in the Church. Here's another one:

One of the hottest books right now in the Church is called *The Shack*, which is openly New Age in doctrine. It actually presents God as a woman. And believe it or not, there are so-called Christian Churches that do Bible studies with this. I'm talking about Evangelical Churches promoting this even while it represents God as a woman. It was made into a movie that opened in March of 2017 and had gross sales of almost $100 million dollars. Unfortunately, over 3/4th of the audience liked it. So how many people do you suppose have, and are going to, fall for that baloney?

What you are seeing is a careful, methodical switch from male patriarchal religion worship to a female matriarchal worship. I am not interested! The future of that doctrine is grim if you judge by reading how many times a female was represented in the first six verses of Revelation 17. The road leads to the One World Religion Harlot!

So that's the feminization going on, even in the Church. And again, Catholicism has their female figure too and they do worship her. That of course is Mary. I'll give you just a quick teaser with this article from the Pope, and then you tell me if Catholics are still worshiping Mary.

Pope Francis' Twitter Feed: "The Christian who does not feel that the Virgin Mary is his or her mother, is an orphan."

One guy said this about that:

"I can't speak for anyone else but as a Christian I was extremely offended by this. Pope Francis is essentially saying that anyone who will not worship Mary as their mother, is not a real Christian. Yet there is not one Scripture that sustains this. In fact, there are tons of Scriptures that oppose it. Furthermore, who or what gives the Pope the authority to classify Christians who have placed their faith in Jesus Christ as orphans simply because they refuse to worship Mary, which by the way is idolatry. To make matters worse, in 1854 the papacy

declared Mary as sinless and in 1951 they stated that she had now ascended up into heaven where she was crowned Queen of Heaven."

"Queen of Heaven" may sound familiar to you. Queen of Heaven was the pagan goddess that God, in the Old Testament, called out Israel for worshiping. And it is the exact same title that Catholic Rome has given to Mary. Wow, that is a double abomination. It goes on:

"According to Catholicism, the Virgin Mary also now acts as our mediator between God and humanity."

But that's not what the Bible says. We have only one mediator and who is that? It's ONLY Jesus Christ, who mediates between God and man.

He continues: *"Clearly something is not right."*

That's the understatement of the year.

He continues: *"Although I find it fascinating that the Pope is bold enough to stand up in front of a crowd of thousands of people and contradict the Bible, I find it disgustingly appalling that these same crowds are blindly following what he says. The Bible says that all Christians who receive Jesus as their Lord and Savior and are led by the Spirit of God are now sons of God, despite what Pope Francis or anyone else can say--talk about dictatorial. As Christians it's important that we study God's word for ourselves. The Scriptures tell all Christians that they should study the Word of God to show ourselves approved. Catholicism is a deeply deceptive religion that disguises itself as Christianity but slowly eases its followers into idolatry and the worship of pagan gods."*

I also like what he said here, and we'll probably get into this again more later, but I want to give you a little teaser:

"One woman in the Bible tried to bless Mary."

Did you know that? And Jesus told her something that I think is significant for today. For those who say we need to say blessing to Mary. Luke 11:27-28:

"And it came to pass as Jesus spoke these things, a certain woman of the company lifted up her voice and said unto him, Blessed is the womb that bare thee and the paps which thou hast sucked."

So, she is trying to say, "Bless Mary." Jesus responded:
"Yea rather, blessed are they that hear the word of God and keep it."

That's straight from Jesus!

Yes, Mary was a great Godly woman. What a privilege she was given. But she herself even admitted in the Gospel of Luke that God was her savior. She was not sinless. She needed a savior just like the rest of us. She was just that chosen vessel. She was not sinless and didn't get assumed up into Heaven. It's just crazy! But that's part of the pagan worship that has been blended in to make up Catholicism.

So again, we're seeing that feminism movement and it's even coming into the current Church with this female deity worship where they want to switch away from that 'harsh masculine doctrine.' And then when you look at Catholicism, they have already had that sort of thing going on for centuries with the worship of Mary. But there are the same practices in Hinduism and Buddhism. With those religions, you have the Ying/Yang principle with male/female dualities. That's where we get the verbiage that has permeated our society a long time ago when people say a guy needs to get in touch with his feminine side. You've probably heard that. It's just this false Ying/Yang teaching. It's a lie! Guys are guys and girls are girls!

Hinduism worships the goddess Shiva. So, there's another female element. Environmentalism, which is so rampant today, has "Mother Earth", especially with the young millennials and on down. And man, are they militant about it. If you don't recycle, some write you off as the worst sort of person. Environmentalism has Mother Earth that is just the old-fashioned pagan worship of the goddess Gaia. That stuff is flooding back now and is promoted everywhere. There's another female deity. It's Mother Earth instead of Father God. They will only talk about Father God when it comes to insurance claims. They say, "That's an act of God", when they don't want to pay, right? But everything else good is Mother Earth. Wicca, or Witchcraft also has their goddesses who they worship.

Now when you think of the European Union and imagine the Antichrist revived Roman Empire coming together as the One World Government and then the Woman Harlot One World Religion riding that Antichrist Beast One World Government, you can see that in the new symbol the European Union has chosen. You can't make this stuff up! It's a Woman riding a Beast!

They have it in many facets of their society now. It's on their coinage, their cards, outside their government buildings, and even on their magazines. It's not some guy driving a hot rod car or a kid on a scooter. Every single one of them is this Woman on a Beast. It's almost like somebody is following a script. This is going on right now in our world. In fact, the symbol, "Europe 4 All" says, "We can all share the same star, Europe 4 All." And guess what the star is made up of? It's the symbols of all the different religions on the planet. This is what's going on in the revived Roman Empire!

So, when you look at Revelation 17, we've already seen there's a religious figure. Again, as we said before, "Hey, if the Pope isn't the False Prophet, he's working really hard to get the job." So, you have this political figure working with the Vatican to go around collecting other religion's peoples under him. Then we saw there are already people, even in the Church, that are intoxicated with this. They are getting caught up into this idea of all religions working together, holding hands, and helping each other. And now you've got female figures all over the planet in different false doctrines that are already being venerated. Wow!!

We have two more aspects that need to line up as we get to Revelation 17. The next one is an Antichrist figure. Let's take a look at that because the Bible says a woman rides the "Beast", with the latter being the Antichrist. Most everyone that studies Revelation would agree with that, so you need a female deity and then you have to have an Antichrist for her to work with. Again, she's going to be riding on him until God allows the Beast/Antichrist to destroy her. Revelation 18 talks about the destruction of the Harlot by the Antichrist.

But again, as we saw before the Antichrist is a political figure who arises on the scene and the world gets swayed by him to join him in his false utopian world that the Harlot is also going to be pushing. Then you see in Daniel 9 and Matthew 24, Daniel, Jesus, and also Paul talk about how halfway into the Seven Year Tribulation, there's this event called the "Abomination of Desolation." What is that? The Abomination of Desolation is defined in Scripture as the time when the Antichrist goes up into that temple halfway into the Seven Year Tribulation, which is the Biblical final week of Daniel's 70th week prophecy. The Antichrist goes up into their temple, declares he is God, and then, oh boy, it's all downhill from there. I mean it wasn't going well anyway, in the first half of the tribulation but then it really takes a devastating turn. So that person, the Antichrist Beast, is the political figure that people end up worshiping as a literal god.

To me, the question becomes this: Who's actually going to worship a guy as god? That's pretty strange. Well, maybe not if you really think about it. If we look at environmentalism, what's the belief? It's Pantheism, which means, "all is god." And that could be a person, a flea, a tree, or anything else. That's why whales apparently have just as much right to exist as a baby in the womb and frankly, they care more for the world than the baby in the womb. That's why it's all twisted.

How about Hinduism? What does that teach? They say all is god and we're all part of the god consciousness if we'd just realize it. New Age teaches the same thing; that we're all gods. Even in the Church we've mentioned folks like Frederick Price, Kenneth Copeland, Kenneth Hagin, Morris Cerullo, and all those other guys. What is their false teaching? They say we're little gods. So that's even in the Church. Then there is Witchcraft with Wicca where they teach about gods and goddesses. It goes on and on. There are also the supposed visions or apparitions of the Virgin Mary. That's in Catholicism. What is one of the messages from this reoccurring vision of what is really a demonic entity, or what the Bible calls a familiar spirit? One of the messages is that we're all god. We're divinity within and we just need to realize it.

How about these supposed channeled messages from space aliens? Of all things for them to say, they tell us we need to submit to a One World Ruler under a One World Government and let somebody take over the planet so they're supporting an Antichrist kingdom. They also say, as we saw in our New Age study, that Lucifer is a good guy. But we're supposedly gods, we need to acknowledge that, and that's the cosmic consciousness we need to evolve to in order to help save the planet. So, you're seeing a multitude of people out there, who are already being prepped to think that a person can become a god.

I said all that to get to this: It's one thing to say that and put a false path out there for people to believe in but it's another thing for people to fall for it and specifically for the one being praised to be a political figure. Do we see any political figure on the planet, and I'm not saying this person is the Antichrist necessarily, but do we see any evidence of political world figures literally being worshiped as a god? Yes, we are, and people are serious about it. Now in the past we've seen followers worshiping leaders like Stalin or Mao Tse Tung. Some of the communist nations put up those giant pictures and statues of their dear leaders. But it won't happen nowadays, will it? Yeah it will and you may have a good idea of whom I'm talking about. It rhymes with Obama. I had to mention that, not because I'm picking on him, but because that's what was happening. People are worshiping and have worshiped him as if he were God since even before he became president. Don't take my word for it. Listen to theirs. This is how close we're getting to what the Bible mentions about how the planet will worship a political figure, the Antichrist, as if he is God. Listen to this:

"An artist in Iowa created a picture of an inaugural parade of Barak Obama riding on a donkey, making his own triumphal entry, complete with adorers waving palm fronds..."

That was bad enough, but it gets worse. Another artist painted a Christ-like pose of Barack Obama. It was supposed to be unveiled but caused such a ruckus; I don't think they actually held the ceremony. The painting is still out there.

I don't care who it is, that's blasphemous. Then there was Newsweek. Of course, we're well aware that the media always pandered to him, but on one of their covers portraying Obama after his re-election, the caption read; "The Second Coming."

Excuse me?! Do you think that was just an arbitrary statement? No, that's deliberate verbiage. Oh, and by the way, at the top of the cover it says, "How Women Will Save Europe." That's interesting. And the media did it again with another Newsweek cover of Obama as "The God of All Things."

Now if you think that's just a coincidence and people haven't literally worshiped him as God, let me give you some snippets of evidence of people doing just that. Listen to this:

Group leader with a megaphone/bullhorn: *"We are here for the healing of the nation. With the prophet Jeremiah, we cry out: Is there no medicine in Gilead? Is there no physician here? Why then has the health of thy poor people not been restored?"*

Crowd: *"Hear our cry Obama."*

Leader: *"With the Prophet Martin Luther King Jr, we cry out: Of all the barbs of inequality, injustice in healthcare is the most shocking and inhumane."*

Crowd: *"Hear our cry Obama."*

Leader: *"From healthcare systems and industries that place profit over people."*

Crowd: *"Deliver us Obama."*

Leader: *"From lobbying efforts that block access to quality healthcare for all."*

Crowd: *"Deliver us Obama."*

Television commercial of various actors with each taking a turn saying: *"I pledge. I pledge. I pledge. I pledge. I pledge. I pledge. I pledge. I pledge. I pledge. I pledge. I pledge. I pledge. I pledge. I pledge to be of service to Barack Obama. I pledge to be a servant to our president and all mankind because together we can, together we are, and together we will be the change that we seek."*

Evan Thomas of Newsweek: *"Obama has had a really different task. What we've seen too often is the bad guys and he has a very different job from Reagan. Reagan was all about America. He talked about it. Obama is: 'We are above that now. We're not just parochial. We're not just chauvinistic. We're not just provincial. We stand for something.' I mean, in a way Obama is standing above the country and above the world as sort of God."*

Comedian Jamie Foxx: *"First of all give honor to god and our lord and savior, Barack Obama."*

Now that is blasphemous! And if you think I'm just picking on Obama again, you're missing the point. He's a world political figure, and what are people doing? This could be Canada and I'd be showing them the same thing with their political leaders. But it's here in the U.S., even in our own supposed

Christian nation. Wasn't that strange with the, "I pledge, I pledge, I pledge?" That's the stuff you see with a Hitler-type person. I mean that was a bit creepy! We're seeing a world political figure that people are not just worshiping, but out of their mouths are literally coming things like, "You're our God and our Savior. Hear our cry and deliver us." That's what the Antichrist is going to do. You need an Antichrist figure on the planet because that's who the One World Religion, the Harlot of Revelation 17 is going to ride. And that stuff is happening in our society today.

Now the fifth and final aspect that needs to ramp up for that passage of Revelation 17, is the emergence of a global authority figure. That's because the premise is this: You don't just need a female deity and an Antichrist for the female deity to work with, but you've got to have a global authority to punish those who resist this system. You say, well I'm not going to sit there and worship this guy. However, Revelation 13 says what? If you don't worship the guy, with the help of the False Prophet, you're going to die! And for those who pledge their allegiance to the Antichrist, you can't just state it publicly like those folks did about Obama…you're going to have to take a mark to show your allegiance and worship. And it's not even just taking the mark. At least three or four times in Revelation 17 it says, 'they will worship the beast.'

So, it's an attitude of worship and they take the mark but those who don't are going to die! And we know they're going to die because Revelation 13 says they're going to die. In fact, Scripture tells us these people die like flies. I'll get to that in a minute. It also says that if you don't go along with this One World Religion system, you'll end up another casualty of the Harlot, who is drunk with the blood of the saints. She's guilty of the mass slaughter of those who don't go along with this Beast and Woman system.

So, my question is: How are you going to pull off that amount of mass killing all around the planet? How are they going to find you? They have to have some sort of global structure in place to begin to disseminate information needed to attain that global order with a global army that's going to take out resisters. With the Jesuits, we already saw they are the Pope's army. Their job is to get in with the other religions and faiths. They are supposed to infiltrate them, including the Protestants, as their job in the faithful order of the Pope. And as we saw before, the United Nations is already being called upon to supposedly govern the governments and nations around the world. The U.N. is putting out orders to dictate what happens around the world like when they pass edicts about what

Israel needs to do. The U.N. is an actual entity that's been in place for decades now and it controls the governments around the world. So that's already in place.

Well, the same thing is happening right now before our very eyes in different religions. They're now calling for a "United Nations of Religions." They are saying we need a global headquarters that will control the world's religions and keep everything in tow. Let me translate that for you:

Then we'll have the global authority to get rid of the resisters.

Let me share some quotes with you from different religions:

"King Abdullah of Saudi Arabia has been planning for years to, 'Find a way to unite the world's major religions in an effort to help foster peace.' And he believes, 'A new International Organization will help make that dream a reality.'"

What about the Jewish people? You're saying, wait a second, not the Jews too. Yes, we know from Bible prophecy that they get deceived because they're the ones who actually make a peace treaty with the Antichrist for seven years. That's actually what starts the Seven Year Tribulation, so we know they're not starting out on a good spiritual note. They do wake up later after the Antichrist goes into the temple and pronounces himself as God, but by then it almost feels like it's too late. Two thirds of them die with the other third protected by God. Even the Jewish people are showing signs of this deceit where they are looking for that key figure who can help. Listen to this:

"Chief Rabbi Yona Metzger, one of the two chief rabbis of Israel said: 'We need a United Relations of Religions, which would contain representatives of the world's religions as opposed to nations.'"

What did he just say? It was basically, 'Just like we have the United Nations governing the governments around the world, we now need one for the religions.' You're seeing a call right now for this global authority over religions, even amongst the Jewish people, who are unfortunately under the temporary blindness that Paul talks about in Romans 11. Rabbi Metzger continues:

"'A Church, a mosque, a synagogue, or a holy temple must be embassies of God and we have to spread this idea to our believers.' He has suggested that the

Dalai Lama could lead the assembly. 'Muslim figure Adnan Oktar met with three representatives from the reestablished Jewish Sanhedrin, to discuss how religious Muslims, Jews, and Christians can work together on rebuilding [What?] the Temple.' An official statement about the meeting was published on the Sanhedrin's website where they stated, 'We are all the sons of one father, the descendants of Adam, and all humanity is but one single family. Peace among nations will be achieved through building the house of God where all peoples will serve.'"

And could that be the very temple that will be in existence for the Antichrist to go up into to commit the Abomination of Desolation? Maybe it will be more of a universal temple that gets built. The Jewish people would get to go there too but maybe it will be for all the people. Then halfway into that Seven Year Tribulation time frame, the Antichrist goes up into the temple and tells everyone they no longer get to worship who they want. He'll say, "Now worship me." We're seeing people call for this right now from different religions. Would you ever have thought Muslims or Jewish people would go along with this new conglomeration? It's happening before our eyes and they are actually calling for the temple to be built. In fact, listen to what the Muslim guy, Oktar added:

"The temple will be rebuilt, and all believers will worship there in tranquility. The Temple could be rebuilt in one year."

Wow! Very interesting. Oh, and here's another interesting one:

"Shimon Peres, the former President of Israel, met with Pope Francis to discuss the idea of creating a U.N.-like organization that he called 'The United Religions.'"

Wait a second. Of all people he could be meeting with, it's the Pope and Catholic Church. He's meeting with them to discuss what? It's about how to get somebody in charge of all the religions. Why would you be talking to and thinking about the Pope unless of course maybe you want to get a key religious figure to fulfill the Biblical role we've been looking at. And that's the actual picture. Shimon Peres also said the following:

"This will bring an end to the wars raging in the Middle East and around the world."

So right now, we're seeing a call for a global authority to govern, not just the nations because that's already in place, but to govern the religions. And if you don't think they're going to ultimately turn on people who dare not go along with that, we know it will because it's already happening. For an in-depth look at the Jewish People and their future relationship with the Antichrist, I suggest you get the *Tribulation Rising: The Jewish People & the Antichrist* book and/or DVD set that was recently released on our website.

Let me just show you a verse about the first half of the Seven Year Tribulation and it's not referring to the Church. These are the tribulation saints which are those who will get saved after the Seven Year Tribulation starts. Listen to what is happening to those people in Revelation 6:9-11:

"When he opened the fifth seal, I saw under the altar the souls of those who had been slain because of the Word of God and the testimony they maintained. They called out in a loud voice, 'How long Sovereign Lord, holy and true, until you judge the inhabitants of the earth and avenge our blood?' Then each of them was given a white robe, and they were told to wait a little longer until the number of their fellow servants or brothers, who were to be killed as they had been, was completed."

This is not a preservation of the Church as some people say who want to put the Church in the Seven Year Tribulation. They say God will preserve the Church during that time. There is no preserving going on there. It's a horrible slaughter. The whole Seven Year Tribulation is full of God's wrath and the Bible is extremely clear that Christians through Jesus Christ are not appointed unto wrath. We are saved and rescued from God's wrath. That includes being saved from living through the whole Seven Year Tribulation. These souls are people who got saved after the Church is taken up to Jesus at the Rapture.

The Bible tells us that people can still be saved during the Seven Year Tribulation. We see that the Gospel still goes forward. We certainly see this with the 144,000 male Jewish evangelists mentioned in Revelation 7, along with all those in white robes saved out of the tribulation. We also know about the two witnesses as well as the angel that flies around the world declaring the eternal Gospel. So, God's mercy is still there in the midst of His judgment, but of course the point is to get saved now because these people are going to be slaughtered like flies.

The Book of Revelation tells us the One World Religion is going to be drunk with their blood. And secondly, if you decide to pass on worshiping the Antichrist, you'll die because of that too. If you don't take the mark, you're going to die. It is horrible. Revelation also tells us that people will have their heads chopped off. It's not going to be good! You need to get saved now and that's the point.

Notice that those martyred souls taken to Heaven had maintained their testimony and kept the Word of God. That's why they were killed. I believe we're seeing signs of that happening already. For a long time, society disagreed with us. But now with what's happening with the verbiage and even with the legal rulings, it is getting so it's not enough to disagree about beliefs, even including moral beliefs. Step one is where they are now saying we are guilty of hate crimes. That's already gone on now for twenty years, so step two is when they say society needs to round up and take care of those hate crime folks. And they're doing that with two issues we'll talk about as their excuse. I think this is all part of getting our world prepped to not just disagree, but specifically to get to that next stage where they can get rid of the resisters. They want to get rid of those who maintain the Word of God. And right now, it's being based on a moral issue and a spiritual issue. Let's look at what they're doing, and you need to pay attention. But again, we in the Church are not going into the Seven Year Tribulation though we're seeing these events lead up to a global slaughter of those who hold to the Word of God.

The first reason they'll use is the moral issue of homosexuality. It used to be you could just disagree on that one and move on. Now because of the court system (Europe is further along but we are close on their heels), you're seeing that it is not just a hate crime, but people are actually losing their businesses. It's not even just being fined. People are being ostracized, not allowed to go into universities, having their university degrees taken away, and there are certain areas in the military you cannot serve, and other things of that nature. It's all because of the moral issue where they say you're guilty of a hate crime and for that you will be punished. So, the homosexuality disagreement is the moral issue excuse to round up the resisters right now as you read this.

The second thing they'll use is what I call a spiritual issue, which is the ecumenical (unity) issue we've already discussed. The underlying lies are that you and I must agree all religions are basically the same, we need to all just learn to get along, and we must stop saying that our way is the only way, even though that's what Jesus said. For that attitude they are using the same persecuting and punishing verbiage against Biblical Christianity as the moral issue about homosexuality. Christians are being called exclusivist and that too is now being labeled a hate crime. In fact, there's a pastor in Ireland, speaking in his own church (You'd think there would be some freedom there) who spoke out against Islam and was then jailed because his public discourse was labeled a hate crime. What he said was, Jesus is the only way and Islam is a false path that leads people to Hell. So, this persecution for standing on the Word of god is happening now because of this spiritual issue, which is the issue of the ecumenical movement.

To me these are birth pains. They're signs that we're getting close to the excuses that a global entity will use to round up those who maintain God's testimony. If you disagree morally with what those in authority think should be accepted and tolerated, and you have the audacity to keep speaking out by saying your way is the only way, you will be rounded up and taken care of. You will be punished and persecuted because of those two crucial issues, the moral issue of homosexuality and the spiritual issue of the pluralist ecumenical unity movement (can't we all just shut up and get along), are ideas that Biblical Christians can't go along with.

The important point is that this kind of behavior is already happening to the Church around the world. It's this rising attitude for rounding up Christians and slaughtering them. In fact, it's been one of the most despicable egregious crimes and it involves at least fifty countries of the world while the Obama administration spent eight years ignoring it. There's been a new holocaust going on. I will use that word because even Jewish people have referred to this Christian massacre as a modern-day holocaust so I'm not saying this lightly or just for effect: There's a new slaughter going on against a specific faction of peoples in many places around the world. It's been going on for a while but in the last eight years, with the previous administration, there has been zero said about it.

Let me share some information with you and remember, these are Christians who are holding to the Word of God. So, what is happening and why is it acceptable that non-believers are rounding up Christians, getting rid of them, and killing them. Here are some statistics:

Right now, there are over 250 million Christians worldwide under the threat of persecution. Right now, our fellow brothers and sisters in Christ are being beaten, tortured, imprisoned, and murdered. Why? Because they refuse to compromise God's truth and go along with an Ecumenical Movement promoted by this One World Religion. In fact, in one year alone, there were 310,000 Christians slaughtered. Again, that was in just one year! Why isn't the news talking about this?

More Christians have died for their faith in the last century alone than in the previous nineteen centuries combined. And it's getting worse. North Korea remains the worst country in the world to be a Christian because it's a behavior that's punishable by death or life in prison. There are an estimated 70,000 Christians in prison there, in camps, just like the Jews in Nazi Germany and it's a sentence that's not just for the individual believer but for three generations of their family; Their parents, their children, and the grandchildren. In fact, recently North Korea passed a law that says possessing a Bible is punishable by death.

Right now, today, in North Korea, 70,000 Christians are in camps. I think that figure is much higher as some others would say but can you imagine 70,000 Muslims being held in a camp? Do you think the news would cover it? And what if the government of the country said they'd kill anyone, who brought in a Quran? Would it get more notice than these poor Christians are seeing? Why do you suppose it's okay to do this to Christians? The answer is because Christians are the ones who do what? We hold to the Word of God. We do not budge. As a consequence, Christians are the people who will be slaughtered like flies in this system.

In Syria they're using the current war as an excuse to get rid of Christians in their country. Why is that not making the news?! All the media mentions about Syria is concerning Assad, Russia's Putin, and Iran coming in. What about the Christians over there? It's the same for North Korea with news being about Kim Jong-un, the missiles, and nuclear bombs. What about the Christians over there? Why don't you talk about that?! Now listen to this and again, I'm not making it up; you can check it out for yourself:

There are forced conversions or killings by those who do not convert to Islam and 41 of the top 50 countries persecuting and killing Christians right now around the world are Muslims. Thousands of Christians are being slaughtered right now for their faith in India, Burma, Nigeria, Afghanistan, Egypt, Saudi

Arabia, Turkey, Belarus, Sudan, and on and on it goes. In fact, Christians are being persecuted so bad that their assailants are killing them, draining their blood, and selling it for profit, weapons, and to (supposedly) go to Heaven.

Let me explain that last gruesome Muslim practice. Christians are saying that the Muslims over there are actually draining the blood of our fellow brothers and sisters in Christ to put into vials for sale. One figure was $100,000 per vial because there's a belief going around in the Muslim communities, with that works-based religion, that this Christian blood can ensure them getting to "Heaven." As you probably know, they believe one of the only ways to be sure you get to Heaven is to blow non-Muslims up as part of a jihad. Well now a rumor is going around that the same is true if you drink the Christian's blood, so people are paying big bucks for it and those selling the Christian blood are using the ill-gotten gains for buying more weapons to continue killing Christians. This is going on right now! Why is that not in the news?! No one is talking about it! It's sickening!

It's not just sick, it's exactly what the Bible says the One World Religion Harlot will do in the last days. She will be 'drunk with the blood of the saints.'

That is absolutely wild! Let's take a look at that again in Revelation 17:6:

"I saw that the woman was drunk with the blood the saints, the blood of those who [What?] bore testimony to Jesus. When I saw her, I was astonished."

It gets even worse:

Apparently, that's why a new research study from the Pew Research Center said, "Christians and Christianity are now the most persecuted religion on the planet." And yet, the last United States Presidential Administration kept their mouth shut about the horror of what has been, and is still happening, with the most persecuted religion on the planet. Right now, as you read this:

"A Christian is being killed every 11 minutes, Christian persecution is turning into Christian extinction, and it's the biggest story in the world that's never been told."

Those are their words, not mine. So, what's the point as far as our study? It is that in the Seven Year Tribulation, those who hold to the Word of God are going to be slaughtered like flies. You think, "Oh, come on. It can't get that bad. People would speak up." I believe we are seeing the groundwork being put in place so that the populations of the world will get so calloused, specifically towards the Christian, that when Christians are slaughtered in the tribulation, it's going to be a gleeful event. In fact, Revelation 11 gives us a confirmation of this with the account of the two witnesses' deaths. Those witnesses are declaring God's righteousness throughout the first half of the Seven Year Tribulation from Jerusalem. What will be the reaction of the world when they are killed? The Bible tells us people around the world not only send gifts to each other, but they will hold great celebrations. All that will be because of the murder of two righteous men, who are declaring God's Word. It's crazy folks but we're heading towards that time quickly. This is why one evangelist in Europe is now warning,

"The fate of Christianity in the U.S. is not far from what's happened to Christianity in Europe. The Church is sleeping and dying out."

We're more worried about what time the game is going to start, when the economy is going to pick back up, or getting in another quick round of Candy Crush on the iPhone. The Church is sleeping and dying out while all this is going on. Each week, fifty to seventy-five churches are closing their doors in America, in the Western Hemisphere. So that's the first reason Christians are headed for ramped up persecution and he continues with reason number two:

"The homosexuals are stamping out Christianity and the Bible."

After the Supreme Court decision on gay marriage, you may have seen our study called, *A Christian Response to the Supreme Court Decision*, we dealt with that for four weeks and four total hours of Biblical information. I was really excited about all four messages to get us equipped in our country on that issue so we can lovingly give a Word-of-God response to that issue. But I was especially excited about the last one, which is on the apologetics of the issue. In that study, there are answers to fifteen objections people throw out against Christians about that issue. It's all the information needed to Biblically, lovingly, philosophically, and logically speak to the objections. What a great resource, right? Now I'm not trying to boast by saying we put out the best information since sliced bread, but hey, at least it's a resource available on this massive issue for our lifetime. We sent this resource out to around 40 ministries in the United States and Canada. We wanted to help churches and ministries get the word out and get equipped on this subject. Again, it was right after that Supreme Court decision. In the U.S.

and Canada, how many do you think responded? Only two even responded, but then just <u>*one*</u> ran with it. At that point I thought, "We're toast."

So, what the European guy said about the Church sleeping, dying out, and being attacked by homosexuals is, we're being chickens. We're afraid to speak up. We have been boxed into a corner and conditioned with the attitude of society that says: "Keep your mouth shut or we're coming after you." We've lost our boldness even though sharing God's truth is the greatest act of love because God's truth is what sets people free. Sin hurts, harms, and destroys. If you keep it up and still don't receive the truth that Jesus is the only way, you're going to Hell. I've said it before and I'll say it again: I'd rather have someone hate me and go to Heaven, then love me and go straight to Hell. I wouldn't want the kind of friend who would remain silent and allow me to go to Hell. That's not a friend.

Here's the third reason he says Christianity is on the same scary decline that England saw years earlier:

"Atheism is not being debated, just denounced."

What is he saying? Let me translate that for you with what I feel Christians are thinking and saying:

"Oh, we don't need to study Atheism. That's those people and we don't believe it, so we don't need to know anything about it."

That goes right to the reason why this ministry, *Get A Life Ministries*, does so much apologetics. In fact, this fellow mentions apologetics in his fourth point:

"The role of apologetics is being downplayed to reach the skeptics."

That's right. Historically, in all the places I've ever pastored, the two biggest topics I have gotten the most flak from the Church about, have been whenever I talk about "Creation versus Evolution" and when I teach on "Bible Prophecy." They either flat out don't want it taught or they'll say, "Well, if you have to, then at least relegate it to a Sunday School class." But I think, "No, I want to give that information from the pulpit because as it is, I only get a very small portion of the sheep and we all need to know this stuff!" So that's what he's saying: Apologetics is not being taught! Churches aren't teaching it, so the

Christian response is something lame like, "Oh, you're wrong and you're a bunch of goobers." But because that response is so uninformed and reactionary, people look at Christians who use it like we're the goobers since we have no substantive response. The problem is that the Church hasn't been equipped with apologetics training so we can give answers.

The fifth point he mentions is this:

"People continue to think it can never happen in the United States."

But frankly, it can and is happening! We're living in La La Land. And that's why it's coming to the United States a lot quicker than it would have. It's already begun. Now I'm going to share some headlines about what is happening now in our country:

"Christian songs have been disqualified from the Oscars and Hollywood is portraying Christians as dangerous terrorists in the movies."

They're also portraying Christians as duped idiots.

"Bibles are being banned from hotels. Home Bible studies are being declared illegal. The IRS is specifically targeting Conservative Christian Groups. Amazon and PayPal are being pushed to blacklist Conservative Christian Websites."

Of course, the latter few examples there encompass a huge portion of what we 'buy and sell', as Revelation warns us about.

"Police are investigating a Church that had a poster suggesting non-believers would burn in Hell. It was turned in by a passerby as a hate incident."

What?! That's just a sign out front. But now it's considered a hate incident, or a hate crime.

"Military troops are being banned from guest speaking at Vacation Bible School. Teachers are telling students, 'Jesus is not allowed in school.' Colleges are rejecting applications from Christians because of their Christian faith. Schools are banning Christian Clubs. Schools are banning books from Christian authors."

And if you start to add this up and look at the history, it's the exact same path Hitler took to his final ultimate solution to exterminate the Jews. Below is what he did in a well-planned chronological order. In his first year there in Germany, he didn't immediately announce German plans to exterminate the Jews. Instead, slowly but surely, he turned the Jewish people into the bad guy. And then it progressed until it became, 'Off to the death camps.' Now with the information in mind about the persecution happening to Christians around the world today, here is the order of events Hitler used to sneak up on the Jewish people in a way that got society to go along with it:

1. Public burning of books by Jews.

People say, *"Well, that's freedom of expression. We can do that. People deface the Christian Bible, make fun of Christian authors, and even burn Christian books, but that's okay because we have freedom of expression."* But that's where Hitler started and we're already there.

2. Random attacks on Jews and Jewish property.
(That's already here against Christians.)
3. Police and the courts no longer protect Jews.

4. Boycotts of Jewish shops.

5. Jewish practices banned.

6. Jewish students excluded from exams in medicine, dentistry, pharmacy, and law. (That's already happening to Christians in certain areas of our educational system.)

7. Jews excluded from military service.

8. Laws denied Jews many basic civil rights.

9. Jews no longer allowed to vote, and they lose German citizenship.

10. Jews banned from parks, restaurants, and swimming pools.

11. Jews banned from communication devices and transportation.

12. Special identity cards issued to the Jews.

13. Jews rounded up and arrested.

14. All schools closed to Jewish children.

15. Jews sent off to the death camps.

Where are we in that order? Not that far off, folks.

So, if you put it all together, we Christians are on the exact same path. In fact, one guy said, "It's coming to America much sooner than you think, and you better get ready!"

Now listen to this excellent analysis of the situation Christians now face in our world today:

"The Church in America is going to suffer so terribly, and we laugh now but they will come after us. They will come after our children. They will close the net around us while we are playing soccer mom and soccer dad. While we're arguing over so many little things and mesmerized by so many trinkets, the net even now is closing around you and your children and your grandchildren, and it does not cause you to fear.

You will be isolated from society as has already happened. Anyone who tries to run for office, who actually believes the Bible will be considered a lunatic, until finally we are silenced. We will be called things that we're not, and persecuted, not for being followers of Christ but for being radical fundamentalists who do not know the true way of Christ, which of course is love and tolerance. You'll go down as the greatest bigots and haters of mankind in history.

They've already come after your children and for most of you they got them. They got them through the public schools and indoctrination in the university and other indoctrination and then you wonder why your children come out not serving the Lord. It's because you fed them right into the Devil's mouth.

So little by little the net is closing around and then it's not little by little. Look how fast things are going downhill just in a matter of weeks...a matter of weeks. But at the same time know this: Persecution is always meant for evil, but God always means it for good. And is it not better to suffer in this life, to have an extra weight of glory in Heaven?

You must settle this in your mind. This is the one thing I want to say over and over; ...Down through history you have a wrong idea of martyrdom and persecution. You think that these men were persecuted and martyred for their sincere faith in Jesus Christ. That was the real reason, but no one heard that publicly. They were martyred and they were persecuted as enemies of the state, as child molesters, as bigots, as narrow-minded stupid people who had fallen for a ruse and can contribute nothing to society. Your suffering will not be noble. So, your mind must be filled with the Word of God when all people persecute you and turn on you. And then the Spirit of God and common grace pulls back, and you see even your children and your grandchildren tossing in the lot that you should die. This is no game.

You want revival and awakening but know this: for the most part, great awakenings have come only preceding great national catastrophes or the persecution of the Church. I believe God is bringing a great awakening but I believe that he is raising up young men who are strong in trust in the providence of God to be able to wade through the hell that's going to break loose on us, and it will be on us before we even recognize it-- unless in God's providence, he is not done--he is not done. And note, this is not silly talk. Apart from a great awakening, these things are going to come upon you. Be ready to lose your homes, your cars, and everything."

That's in America because we have been asleep at the wheel and we are chickens. We have lost our boldness for Christ to stand for His truth no matter what people threaten us with and no matter how popular it is. I love his words: "This is not silly talk." This is happening as you read right now. It's why, after the presidential election of 2016, this was on my heart as a Christian and as a Pastor:

Maybe we're being given a reprieve, though I don't know, it could be a multilayered ruse where we'll figure out that we've been snookered. But if in fact we're being given a reprieve, especially after the previous eight years of the most anti-God and anti-Christian administration in all of American history, we know it's not going to last forever. That's because the Bible is very clear about what is coming. Either way, we better not go back to sleep again! We must use this time and use it wisely to speak up and do our best job to hold the line for God's Word and store up as much treasures as we can in Heaven because one day, the hammer is going to come down on Christians. That's my fear; that we will go back to sleep. And as the man from Europe said, it's because we've been sleeping that we're in this mess. If in fact we've been given a reprieve and still fall back asleep, we deserve a spanking. Let's not go to sleep! Amen?

Chapter Seven

Doctrines of Demons

Now we're going to further develop the character of Roman Catholicism. We know they are a pseudo-Christian group that is a cult by definition and they are demonic, or devilish. All that is leading Catholicism to play a large part in fulfillment of the last days Antichrist Kingdom, the one world religion, and the Harlot riding the Beast. Now here is the question I had that lead to all this research: "Why is Catholicism so messed up?!"

Why is Roman Catholicism a pseudo-Christian group? Why are they defined as a cult on both sides of the coin with either the Biblical or secular definition? Why are they so demonic and devilish? Why are they the ones leading this charge to the fulfillment of Revelation 17? We can answer those questions with the whole theme of the next few chapters and it's basically that they veered off Scripture. That's it! Whether a group has detoured from God's word, is one of the absolute easiest ways to identify them as a cult and that's what Roman Catholicism does over and over. Let's take a look at how one guy explains it:

"Remember that all false philosophies; religious, psychological, etc., are Satan's creation."

Who is the father of lies? Jesus, in John Chapter 8 says Satan is the father of all lies so any distortion of the true Gospel is the work of Satan and his aim is to deceive people into thinking they're on a path to be rewarded with Heaven upon their death. But where is their path actually leading them? It's in the opposite direction. They're going to Hell. This is salvation by works which is a doctrine of doing good things and not doing bad things. Many times, even in the Church, you hear the following sort of false hopes:

"Well, I'm trying to be a good person."
"I am a good person and I'm a Christian."
"I'm American, I don't kick my dog too much, I believe in the Ten Commandments, and I try not to cheat too much."

So that makes you a Christian? What are you talking about? No, it doesn't. But again, it's that mentality where people think they're not that bad of a person and their good stuff outweighs the bad. That frame of mind is satanic. Only 1% of that attitude or even 0.0001% of that belief makes it satanic. That's a false way because being a Christian is not based on any of our works. And of course, what we're going to see with Roman Catholicism, is that works is a core issue. He continues:

"If one carefully studies the various religions and cults of the world, he will soon discover, without exception..."

So, he is going to present a universal rule for how to know if an entity or group, who's spouting off their views and maybe even claiming to be Christian, is actually, without exception, a cult. Here's what he says:

"Cults are founded on some form of human effort and works righteousness."

But what does the Scripture say? Isaiah says our righteousness is as filthy rags before God so one sign of a cult is any philosophy that says mankind is going to aid in helping a person get to Heaven.

"Only Grace-centered Biblical Christianity is from God. Every other form of religion is from Satan."

Why? It's because it's a lie and Satan is the father of lies.

"It's inspired by his demon spirit, promoted by his lying agents, and centered in works righteousness."

In other words, satanic doctrines teach that salvation is up to you. So, for the sake of effect but also to get to the truth, let's reword that with a couple of specifics: Every false teaching of Roman Catholicism is from Satan, inspired by Satan's demon spirit, and promoted by his lying human agents. You could say the same thing with Mormonism, Jehovah's Witnesses, Hinduism, Buddhism, Islam, and all the other false religions. This is a serious issue! It's not that what we believe and what they believe are similar, but these are just side issues. No! Anything other than salvation through Jesus Christ is ultimately satanic in its source. Those are strong words but that's the reality of what we're dealing with here.

Let's take a deeper look into the origins of Roman Catholicism.

"To categorize Roman Catholicism is somewhat challenging. Other groups like Mormons or Jehovah's Witnesses are easy to classify as a Christian cult because they have distinctly aberrant beliefs."

Mormons tell us that Jesus is the spirit-brother of Lucifer and the Jehovah's Witnesses say that Jesus is merely the Archangel Michael. But of course, neither is true. He continues about why religions like Mormonism and Jehovah's Witnesses are easier to classify then Catholicism:

"Also, because they began at a point of time relatively recent in Church history, claiming new unbiblical revelation from God."

Wait a second! Who else in the Church unfortunately also claims to receive new unbiblical revelation from God? That's a huge massive chunk of charismatic theology! It's not just the Bible they point to. It's the Bible and 'God told me' or 'God gave me a word' or 'I'm a prophet or prophetess' or 'It's a new word.' With all that "new revelation" coming out, we have to ask: Well, why aren't we writing a brand new, New Testament? If those messages you folks keep getting are genuinely from God, you're doing a disservice to the Church by not promoting the need to add them to the New Testament.

But of course, it is not from God! New revelation stopped with the Bible. Plus, with all due respect, Mr. or Mrs. Charismatic, if you're going to go down that route, then how can you witness to a Mormon because new revelation is the basis of what Joseph Smith believed and taught as Mormonism. He also got a lot of supposedly divine new information as he was staring at that rock in his hat.

Basically, saying those groups like Mormons and Jehovah's Witnesses are relatively recent and they've got some really weird doctrine is why they're *easily* recognized as cults. He continues about cults like Mormonism and Jehovah's Witnesses:

"These groups have always been referred to, by historic Christianity, as cults and this labeling serves to highlight their aberrant beliefs. But Catholicism on the other hand, is a historically 'Pseudo-Christian' group, meaning that it did not begin at a certain time but developed slowly into what it is today."

So, the point is, Catholicism has been around many centuries longer than the Mormons or Jehovah's Witnesses and as we understand from this study of Catholicism, maybe we can't know the exact date it started, but we know Catholicism began right after the time of Constantine. His time started the whole environment that fostered the birth of it and then shortly after him was the establishment of the first pope so we know the general timeframe, but I see what this fellow is saying. When it comes to Roman Catholicism, people see them as being around forever and sometimes when Church history is being spoken about, Catholicism gets thrown in there as if it is Christian.

Christendom, which is what's used in Church history, is not necessarily Biblical Christianity. It might be Roman Catholicism that was happening in Western Europe but that doesn't mean it was Christianity.

So, he's saying it's hard to get the straight Biblical Christian history because people have looked at Catholic history and lumped it in as just another aspect of Biblical Christianity even though it is not! Now here's the question: When we say Catholicism is a cult, satanic, demonic, devilish, and pseudo-Christian, why do people respond with: Oh, come on now. You could say that to the Mormons and Jehovah's Witnesses but come on, isn't that harsh to the Roman Catholics? Well first, people have that feeling because Catholicism has been around for a long time so they think it must be Christian, and secondly, Catholicism does have some doctrines we would consider orthodox. However, that doesn't make the rest of what they teach correct. And there's the problem.

Let's first look at some of those ways Roman Catholicism has been said to conform to orthodox Christianity. Number one is the idea of the Inerrancy of the Bible. (But that's a tricky example because as we're going to see in just a minute, their Bible is not the same as the Christian Bible and they don't even stick with the Bible.) Number two is the Trinitarian Nature of God. Third is the Deity of Jesus Christ and number four is some aspects of Christ like the virgin birth, sinless life, the crucifixion, and the resurrection. So, people look at those and say, "Well, see. It's the same thing as Biblical Christianity." Excuse me?! You need to keep looking!

As I've mentioned before, when you have a Mormon or Jehovah's Witness come knocking at your door, what is the first thing you might say? It may be something similar to this: "Oh, hey listen, I know who you are because I can see your white shirt, the little tie, and you rolled up here on a bicycle. But with all due respect, I'm a Christian. I believe in Jesus." What do they say? It's usually this: "We do too!" So, because they claim to believe in the same Jesus, what should you do? You have to go behind their general statement of a belief in Jesus and ask some investigative questions. Then when you get to know who their Jesus is, you find out He's not the same and that is amongst many other issues.

With Roman Catholicism, when you explore it with them, they may say they believe in the inerrancy of Scripture but is it really the same, as we believe? No, it's not! Again, we'll get to that. Also, they may say they believe in the Trinity and maybe they do, but when you explore further, there are non-biblical Trinity issues in their doctrine. Again, you have to go behind the veneer, including with Roman Catholicism. That's why it can be tricky:

*"The cult label may be considered inflammatory by some when applied to Roman Catholics, perhaps unnecessarily limiting witnessing opportunities. With this said, the Roman Catholic Church has several doctrines that would place them into the cult category. There are many doctrines we can highlight that distort the true Gospel. Errors in the Roman Catholic doctrine are present in **almost every major area of doctrine**."*

And we're going to get into a lot of them. We'll go down the list of all the false teachings mentioned and promoted by this entity called Roman Catholicism. Their false doctrines are not just that they like wearing robes and we don't wear robes, those are secondary issues. We are talking about almost every major area of doctrine. Maybe they got the Trinity of the Godhead correct but in almost every major area of theology, they get it wrong just like any cult does, so we are not just being harsh.

Now we could spend a great deal of time investigating each one of these numerous deviations from Scripture but for this study, we're going to focus on five areas that define an organization as a cult.

The first one we're going to deal with is their **Source of Authority**. The question is, "Where are they getting all this stuff?" Because Catholicism says they believe in the Bible, we must agree on all the doctrines, right? No, that's the problem! Cults like Catholicism have a different source of authority. Mormons say they believe in the Bible but then point you to the writings of Joseph Smith. That messes it all up! Jehovah's Witnesses also say they follow the "bible" but theirs is a perverted twisted Bible. And their so-called Greek and Hebrew scholars were neither Greek nor Hebrew scholars. In fact, one guy was a short order cook from Ohio. Later we'll take a look at that ridiculous lunacy. In their desire to control a population of followers, they twisted and perverted God's word.

Again, that brings us back to the Charismatic issue in the Church. I'm trying not to pick on that too much but as a Charismatic they duplicate the mistakes of Mormonism, Jehovah's Witnesses, and Catholicism as they say they believe in the Bible, but then go on their own experiences, feelings, and supposed new revelations. Charismatics are adding to the Word of God! Their source of authority is not the same and that's why everything's all messed up!

Besides the S**ource of Authority**, in the chapters ahead we're going to look at the Catholic view of the **Nature of God, including the Trinity**, the **Person and Work of Jesus Christ**, the **Nature of Man**, and the **Means of Salvation**. If you get even one of those five things wrong, you are a cult. Now you can like it or not, or say it's too harsh and inflammatory, but I'm sorry, you are a cult. And when it comes to Roman Catholicism, they get those things wrong.

Let's look at Roman Catholicism as far as their source of authority:

"To understand Catholic teaching concerning authority, we can look at the Catechism of the Catholic Church."

What is a catechism? Catechism is a Catholic word and based on the Greek word "katichisi", meaning; *to teach orally or by word of mouth*. Basically, their Catechism is, if you will, the Catholic Word, which means it's their manual for teaching their doctrine so unfortunately, it is their false doctrine. Again, the Catholic Catechism is their official teaching manual laying out their Catholic doctrine.

What we'll see in this chapter is quoted directly from their own words in their own catechism. I'll try not to say it too much but just so we're clear, I'm not just making these claims up. As you read, you may think, "I can't believe that! They don't teach that!" But I will be quoting straight from their catechism that is their manual of official religious doctrine.

With that in mind, let's continue on with their Latin catechism published in 1997:

"The Catholic Church Catechism, or C.C.C., is a summary of all essential and basic teachings of Catholicism."

And of course, there's nothing wrong with having a manual for teaching. At my church, we as a Christian Church have an official doctrinal statement, bylaws, and a constitution. We have all kinds of nifty stuff we follow. But the problem Catholicism has is that they don't just stick to the Bible. Where they derive their catechism, which again, is their belief system and official doctrine, comes from all over the place. Let's take a look:

Number one, they have their own **Catholic Bible** and that's not good! The Catholic Bible has the sixty-six books of the Protestant Bible *plus* the Apocrypha. We'll get into the Apocrypha more later but to give you an idea; Apocrypha means secret or hidden things so it's the hidden books with secret knowledge. As far as the Apocrypha, we've probably all heard someone claim there are "lost books of the Bible." Well, believe or not, there were reasons why these ancient writings were rejected as possible additions to the Bible but with Catholicism's decisions to add some of them, by exploring which ones they choose to add and the others they didn't, it reveals their unfortunate motives. Their choices really make them look bad! So, Catholicism says they believe in the Bible but it's the Catholic Bible, which is not the same as the Christian Bible and it contains books with false teaching.

The second place from where they derive their catechism is, *"the decrees of* ***twenty-one Ecumenical Councils****, out of which three are the most referenced but technically there have been twenty-one. The top three are The Council of*

Trent, The First Vatican Council, and The Second Vatican Council, with the latter being as recent as 1965."

That's their source of truth. This is where they're getting their official doctrines. Of course, there is nothing wrong with have a council or a conference, but the problem is that a meeting would not produce a consensus opinion on par with Scripture. At the end of our meetings, we're not going to say our final decisions should be stamped with, "Thus saith the Lord!" Would we put man's meetings on par with the decrees of God? Well, that's what the Roman Catholic Church does. That's where they derive doctrine.

And it gets worse. The third place they get their Catholic doctrine is from **the writings of the popes**. So, you mean to tell me that whatever one guy says or does is supposed to be on par with Scripture?! I mean listen, I work hard to put out information that is correct and truthful, but I would never say everything I've ever taught is equal to the Holy Spirit breathed Bible. I try my best to line up with Scripture and be scriptural, but I think it would be the height of arrogance to say that whatever I've ever taught, said, or written down is on par with the Scripture. But that is exactly what Catholicism does with their popes. It makes you want to ask them, "What in the world are you doing?!" Again, this is another of their sources of authority. This is where Catholic leadership derives its catechism, which is their official manual of religious doctrine.

Other places Roman Catholicism gets their doctrine is their **Code of Canon Law that is 1,752 laws**, which govern the Roman Catholic Church. So, you have to throw those in the mix as well. It's just more supposed truth they put on par with the Bible. There is also **church liturgy**, which is the public worship and practice. That is the traditions like standing at appropriate times, sitting at others, and kneeling when called upon, as well as the order of services and much more. We'll get into the traditions a bit later. There is the **Catechism of the Council of Trent**, which is the guide to the Roman Catholic faith published in 1566 by Pope Pius IV. Another individual guy who added doctrine other than the popes was **Thomas Aquinas with his Summa Theology work**.

So how many is that? Just right there we've listed **seven different sources of truth**. No wonder it's messed up! And even the one that is supposed to be the Bible isn't the same as the Christian Bible. So really, do they have any source that is pure? No! There is not one! They have none. No wonder there is so much false teaching. Since that is what they derive their authority from, it's not shocking at all.

"According to Catholic teaching, the source of authority does not rest with Scripture alone."

With that statement, of course we're going to hear things like, *"What?? That's a serious charge. How could you say that? You're just being a Christian fundamentalist."* But we're only quoting what they say. I didn't say that. They said it. So, in reference to the authority of Scripture, listen to this:

"According to Catholic teaching, the source of authority does not rest with Scripture alone but with Scripture, Tradition, and the pope; each with equal authority."

What?! They are really saying that all that random instruction from fallen men carries equal authority with the Bible?! No wonder they've got their philosophy all messed up.

Now let's start quoting from their official doctrine, their Catechism:

"Sacred Tradition and Sacred Scripture then, are bound closely together and communicate one with the other. For both of them, flowing out of the same divine wellspring,"

So, your manmade tradition is supposedly divine?! And you're saying it's not just divine, but you are putting that manmade tradition you created of various meetings of church leaders, on par with the Scripture? Okay, that makes the corruption of doctrine pretty clear. Again, I didn't say that. They did. Continuing now in their catechism:

"...flowing out of the same divine wellspring, come together in some fashion to form one thing and move towards the same goal. Each of them makes present and fruitful in the Church the mystery of Christ, who promised to remain with his own 'always to the close of the age.'"

Now here's a second quote from the Catholic Catechism:

"Sacred Scripture is the speech of God as it is put down in writing under the breath of the Holy Spirit..."

If they would have stopped right there, that sounds pretty good. Unfortunately, they kept going, and listen to what they said:

"...and Holy Tradition transmits in its entirety the word of God, which has been entrusted to the apostles by Christ the Lord and the Holy Spirit. It transmits it to the successors of the apostles so that, enlightened by the Spirit of truth, they may faithfully preserve, expound, and spread it by their preaching."

Here's a third quote: *"As a result, the Catholic Church, to whom the transmission and interpretation of Revelation is entrusted,"*

What?! You mean to tell me you're the only one who can interpret that? Yes, it's what they call their Magisterium and we'll get to that in a minute.

"...the Catholic Church does not derive her certainty about all revealed truths from the Holy Scriptures alone."

So, they admit it again! They rely on both their version of Scripture and their traditions.

"Both Scripture and Tradition must be accepted and honored with equal sentiments of devotion and reverence."

Excuse me?! So, in one or more of your meetings, you decided that I have to revere and obey your manmade traditions as much as the literal Holy Spirit-breathed Word of God!

Isn't Catholicism starting to sound like the group Jesus confronted in the New Testament that rhymes with Pharisees? Hey, that's right. It's the Pharisees. We continue in their catechism:

"It is clear therefore that, in this supremely wise arrangement of God, Sacred Tradition, Sacred Scripture, and the Magisterium of the Church are so connected and associated that one of them cannot stand without the others."

Whoa! Now you've slipped a third thing in there. First you said Scripture is your source of authority although your scripture isn't the same as Christian Scripture. Even if you want to give them the benefit of the doubt on their bible, they clearly said that tradition and the Catholic Magisterium are on par with the Bible.

The Magisterium of the Catholic Church is basically a group of men made up of the popes and bishops. It's Catholicism's belief that these ever-changing members of this group of men are the ones in charge of interpreting Scripture for us, so unless they say something is so, good Catholics are not supposed to believe it. Actually, I can't believe they have the nerve to say you can't believe anything without their stamp of approval on the interpretation. Maybe if you wait long enough, as the members change, someday they'll come around to believing as you believe.

In other words, we don't have the right to interpret Scripture on our own. Well, let's look at what Scripture says about that. Who is considered noble according to the Bible? Even when the Apostle Paul, who probably wrote thirteen of the Epistles under the inspiration of the Holy Spirit with a direct revelation from Jesus Christ, preached to the Bereans that they need to search the Scriptures to be sure what Paul was saying was correct and Biblical. It's the same caution I give when I'm preaching. Whenever we begin the opening text I always try to say, "Don't take my word for it. Let's listen to God. Open your Bible." So, I encourage all Christians to exercise the liberty we have to open the Bible and read it for ourselves.

Why were the reformers murdered, strangled, drowned, and even after they were dead, their bones were dug up and burned, after which their ashes were chucked away? Why were they treated as an anathema and cursed? Their only offense to Catholicism was that they translated the Bible so that anyone could read it. They violated a teaching of the Catholic Magisterium that says only the Magisterium has the right and ability to explain the Scriptures. They say individuals have no right to interpret the Bible for themselves. They put their Magisterium on par with their version of the Bible.

Now let's continue in the Catholic Catechism where they talk about how God, sacred Tradition, [Catholic] Scripture, and the Magisterium combine to give us salvation:

"Working together, each in its own way, under the action of one Holy Spirit, they all contribute effectively to the salvation of souls."

Wow! That is in their words!

Now one important phrase I want to point out is, "Supreme Pontiff", which is what Catholicism uses to refer to the pope. Still to this day they call him the "Vicar of Christ" and the "Supreme Pontiff." I decided to find out where Supreme Pontiff came from. Even a search of the secular definition brings up the same:

*"**Supreme Pontiff** is the former title of the **Pagan High Priest** at Rome."*

You can go look it up! That explains some things, right? Doesn't that make sense when you know how Roman Catholicism started? The Roman Empire under Constantine blended Christianity and Paganism together so much so that even that title for the pope was taken from the pagan high priest of the time. It's just crazy!

*"The Supreme Pontiff, in virtue of his office, possesses **infallible**..."*

What's does infallible mean? It is saying all popes are without error, just as Jesus was. They want us to believe every pope ever elected by a group of guys at the Vatican, lives without making errors. They would have you believe their popes are always right 100% of the time.

"...possesses infallible teaching authority when, as supreme pastor and teacher of all the faithful, he proclaims with a definitive act that a doctrine of faith or morals is to be held as such."

What?! So, a guy on the planet born with a sinful nature like the rest of us is now infallible and on par with the Scripture, just for being chosen to lead his group by his peers. Again, even that Catholic Scripture is not entirely the same as our Scripture. Now continuing in the Catholic Catechism:

"The task of interpreting the Word of God authentically has been entrusted solely to the Magisterium of the Church,"

So that clearly takes issue with you and I having the supposed audacity to open the Bible and read it for ourselves. And if you don't think they take you interpreting the Bible for yourself as a serious charge, you need to look back at how the Catholic Church, over and over by the thousands, killed the Protestant reformers. They were murdered, not just because they disagreed with Catholicism, but because Catholicism claimed the reformers really went over the edge when they let people read the Bible in their own language. The Vatican, with popes who willingly take the same title as the old pagan high priests, killed them for it. Those leaders and the Catholic Church massacred the reformers.

That's what the Catholic Church teaches. They are supposedly the only ones who had the ability to tell us which interpretation to believe from their corrupted version of the Scripture. So again, they say interpretation is,

"...entrusted solely to the Magisterium of the Church, that is, to the Pope and to the bishops in communion with the Pope."

So, it all still goes back to whatever the Pope says.

Here's a helpful Christian analysis of the Christian Bible versus Catholicism's Bible:

"We agree with Catholicism that Scripture is authoritative, though only the sixty-six books that were recognized before the Council of Trent."

The Council of Trent was of course the Catholic Church council held in Trent, Italy from 1545 to 1563. The Council of Trent was the Catholic reaction to the Protestant Movement because Catholicism had lost control. So before then, they only had the sixty-six books of the Bible, but during that 18 years, they basically came up with those ideas and teachings they wanted to add to the Bible to accomplish the ends and control they desired so they added information called the Apocrypha just to distance themselves from the Christian Bible.

Let's take a look at the Apocryphal writing they include in their version of the Bible so we can see that it needs to be rejected. Remember, we're still looking at their sources of authority and Catholicism has about seven different sources of authority while even their version of the Bible is not the same as the Christian Bible. Again, it's no wonder Roman Catholicism is so messed up.

As was mentioned earlier, in their version of the Bible, they add these writings called the Apocrypha. Apocrypha means "things that are hidden or secret." The Apocrypha books, or "Deuterocanonical" books, which basically means "second canon books", consists of a set of books written between approximately 400 BC and the time of Christ. The Old Testament Apocrypha includes the following books:

"The Wisdom of Solomon, Ecclesiasticus [this is not the Christian Bible's Ecclesiastes], also Sirach, Tobit [wait until you hear what's in that thing], Judith, 1 and 2, Maccabees [which is where they get their false teaching of Purgatory, amongst other false teachings], Prayer of Azariah, Susanna, Bel and the Dragon, Baruch, Letter to Jeremiah, Additions to Esther, 1 and 2, Esdras, and Prayer of Manasseh."

That group of books is classically defined as the Apocrypha. Catholicism doesn't add every one of those, but they do add 11 of the 15. These Apocryphal writings came on the scene during that 400 years from 400 BC to the time of Christ, but the early church rejected them. Why were they rejected? Was it because these early Church fathers made some arbitrary decisions though they had no authority and instead they should have submitted to a Catholic Magisterium or some similar council to help them understand what was appropriate to include? No! There were good and commonsense reasons why these books were rejected and not considered on par with Scripture. But even with that rejection of the Apocrypha books by the early Church fathers, Catholicism decided to add them to their Scripture/Bible. So now Catholicism considers these rejected texts as "Thus saith the Lord", which means they consider them divinely inspired just as the Christian Bible.

Those books were rejected for important reasons including various high standards. I'll give you a quick idea of why books were rejected. Common sense cannon-filtering questions were asked and if any book did not meet these standards, it was thrown aside. One standard was whether the author of the book was an Apostle. Another asked whether a particular book agrees with the rest of Scripture. Why? It's because God doesn't lie so if it really came from God, it won't contradict the rest of the Bible. A third criterion was whether the early Church accepted, circulated, and quoted from it. Fourth, they determined if it came with the power of God or not.

Now let's talk about some books from ancient times that were rejected for inclusion in our Christian Bible. You've heard claims about these kinds of "mystery books." They are usually introduced with something like, "The lost books of the Bible!" But of course, these "lost" books somehow keep resurfacing every 15 years or so, which is about the time it takes the television audience to forget about them. For example, they keep being recycled on programs broadcast by the "Hysterical Channel", or History Channel, or whatever you want to call it. We should call it by the most appropriate name, which is the Anti-Christianity Channel. But hey, I'm sure it's just a coincidence that every Christmas and Resurrection Sunday, the Hysterical Channel puts out their stories asking questions like, "Did Jesus really rise from the dead or is there a secret theory to explain the event?" Whatever! But you can tell I'm not bitter about it, right? Well, maybe a little. Let's just move on.

Let me give you some examples of these rejected texts. "The Judas Gospel" was rejected because . . . there is a conspiracy to keep it out of people hands, right?! No! Let me give you just one excellent reason it was thrown out. It portrayed the Apostle Judas, who betrayed Jesus, as some sort of a hero. That got tossed out the window and rightly so. Give me a break!

The "Letter to Herod" was a rejected early writing and a pretty hilarious forgery because the person creating it pretended to write as King Herod but forgot that the Herod, at the time of Jesus birth was not the same Herod at Jesus' trial and crucifixion. As one guy said:

"Whoops! Get your history right if you're going to do a good bit of forgery."

The "Gospel of Thomas" was also rejected. This one actually came up when I first got saved in 1993. That book was big back then. We discussed it in our college and career group. The group talked about how maybe it really has some secret knowledge not found in the Bible. The so-called Gospel of Thomas reports supposed secret details about Jesus' early childhood years by making wild claims of events like this one:
"As Jesus was playing, a child bumps into him and Jesus strikes him dead."

Uhmm, that's not consistent with the Jesus from the rest of the Bible.

The "Acts of John" must have come from the Apostle John because the book says it's him. Excuse me?! This crazy book tells about how John supposedly checks into an inn for the night and there are bedbugs in the bed. So, John commands the bedbugs to leave. They obey as they get out of bed and march in line right out of the room. Maybe the hiding of that book for all these centuries has been a conspiracy to keep bedbug truth away from us. Understandably, the supposed bedbug events involving John were rejected.

The "Acts of Paul" had to be from the Apostle Paul, right? No. In this supposed real-life epic tale, Paul baptizes a lion and later this same lion returns the favor by saving Paul from a martyr's death in the Roman amphitheater. But doesn't that story make sense because of course Christians are taught to baptize animals, right? No! That one too was kicked to the curb.

The "Protoevangelium of James" is a very cool name and so dramatic that it's got to be true. Hey, I couldn't even write the word without spell-check. It was written to "perpetuate the perpetual virginity of Mary and says that she was placed in the temple at age 3 where angels fed her." Excuse me?!

Give me a break. With the books included in our Christian Bible, there was no conspiracy to leave out important truth. The books just mentioned, as well as the Apocryphal books, were rejected because of these sorts of issues. There was no conspiracy to hide information or knowledge from the public, but the Catholic Church decided to include the Apocryphal books in their Scripture, so still to this day, those erroneously included books are there as part of their so-called divinely inspired knowledge while the books themselves are full of false teaching.

Catholicism rejected a few of the Apocryphal books. Of course, my inquiring mind wanted to know why so I took a look at that and here is the result:

"The Roman Catholic Council of Trent accepted all the Old Testament Apocrypha as canonical [worthy of the inclusion in the Bible] in 1546 with the exception of 1 and 2 Esdras and the Prayer of Manasseh. While there are fifteen total books in the Apocrypha, Roman Catholic Bibles count only eleven because they combine the Letter of Jeremiah with Baruch and they omit 1 and 2 Esdras and the Prayer of Manasseh."

To find out why the Catholic Council of Trent rejected only those couple books of the Apocrypha, we can easily look up what these books teach. Remember, these books are historically interesting reading but they're not to be trusted on par with the Scripture and they do have false teachings, so we need to stay away from building any doctrine from them.

"The teaching in 2 Esdra 7:105 is in opposition to the prayer for the dead and this may have led to the exclusion of it by the Roman Catholic Church."

Of course, the Catholic Church would say their Magisterium prayed over the issue of including 2 Esdra and made an intelligent decision that the book shows no signs of authenticity, so the Magisterium decided not to include it. The more likely reason is that the 2 Esdra book, which again, does have false teachings, contradicted one of Catholicism's own false teachings so they couldn't have that. Let me quote from 2 Esdra while you keep in mind that the context in this part of the book is the Day of Judgment and how there is no intercession for the dead. Verse 7:105 specifically says,

"So no one shall ever pray for another. On that day all shall bear their own unrighteousness."

The Catholic Church can't allow that in their Bible because it messes up what they want to hold on to in their tradition. That's interesting but let's continue on with more about their affinity for the Apocrypha books because their explanation of it unfortunately gets worse.

Catholicism suggests that these extracanonical Old Testament books are good stuff. In fact, they're just as good as Scripture except for those three just mentioned above, which they do not feel the same about. Here is the Roman Catholic rationale for including these books as on par with the Bible: Catholicism says 'some' early Church fathers accepted the Apocrypha books as did the Syriac Church in the 4th century. The latter is actually not totally true, and we'll get to that in a minute, but even if it was totally true, I'm not sure any Christians have staked their doctrine on the foundation of "Sola Syriac Churchicus!" Is that what we as Protestants should stand upon? Is whatever they said something we need to bind ourselves to? So, what?! It can also be said that, "the Eastern Orthodox Church accepts them." Well, two wrongs do not make a right or as our mom or dad asked us: "If your friends jumped off a bridge would you do the same?" Catholicism is trying to make it right by pointing out others who accepted the Apocrypha. We can't care what a particular group thought about certain texts being able to help us decipher truth because that is putting our faith in the lap of man.

Roman Catholicism didn't proclaim the Apocrypha books as canonical until their Council of Trent in 1546. Catholicism points out that the Apocrypha books are included in some Protestant Bibles, including the original King James Version from 1611. However, those books are not in the King James Version now and it still doesn't make it right even if another Bible version did include them.

Catholicism also points to the fact that some of the Old Testament Apocrypha were among other Old Testament books found in the Dead Sea Scrolls. But isn't that just a guilt by association argument? In fact, I similarly have a lot of different Bibles in my office collection, as well as a huge array of other books so does that mean I believe every book in my office is on par with the Bible? No, of course not. I have books in my office for research purposes that are completely unbiblical. They are New Age, occult writings, and whatever else I need for opposition research. I don't recommend any of it. Because these books are in my library, just as some Apocrypha books were in there with the Dead Sea Scrolls, does not put them on par with the Bible. It's crazy to make that connection but it's what Catholicism tries to do.

"There is abundant and compelling evidence for ***rejecting*** *the Apocrypha as inspired by God. While these books may be of historical value and in some way supplement God's truth, they are not canonical for the following reasons:*

1. Jesus and the Apostles did not accept these books as part of the Scripture. [If these Apocrypha books were important, they would have talked about them, but they did not.]

2. There are no New Testament references to any Apocrypha as being authoritative in any way and the New Testament writers quote not one part of the Apocrypha.

3. Judaism has never accepted these books as part of the Scriptures and ancient Jewish leaders specifically rejected the Apocrypha.

[In my office are some big guns of Judaism, including the books of Josephus and Philo. If you ever feel like a really large read, those are a good option.]

4. While a few early Church leaders may appear to take some material from the Apocrypha, most were opposed to the inclusion of the Apocrypha in the canon of

Scripture. Furthermore, ***no Church council*** *for the entire Church accepted these books as Scripture.*

5. The Apocrypha itself recognizes our Old Testament Canon as the distinct twenty-four books, which corresponds to the Hebrew Bibles known today. In 2 Esdra's 14, 70 books are distinguished from the 94, leaving 24, which is the exact number of Hebrew Cannon, which became the 39 Old Testament books. Not only does the Apocrypha not claim inspiration for itself; it actually disclaims it when 1 Maccabees 9:27 [one of the Apocryphal books], *describes an existing cessation of prophecy."*

That last part means the Apocrypha itself attests to the absence of any prophets during its own time. So that period is from the time of the Apostles up until about 400 A.D. but Catholicism includes the Apocrypha in their version of Scripture, which means Roman Catholicism is saying the Apocrypha books they included were inspired by God just like the rest of the Scripture. However, these actual Apocrypha books themselves say differently. Therefore, Catholicism can't say these books are Scripture worthy when the books themselves say they are not. You can't have it both ways.

"The Apocrypha includes unbiblical teaching including prayers for the dead..."

Again, they get prayers for the dead and purgatory from 2 Maccabees.

"..and also salvation by works."

Salvation by works is taught in the unbiblical Book of Tobit, which ended up in the Catholic Bible. I want to give you Tobit 12:9 because it's not just salvation by works but something you probably remember that we started with in this study of Catholicism. Tobit also mentions penance, which again, is all the things you can do to shave off your sins, including payments in cash to purchase indulgences. Well, it's interesting to see how Catholicism liked and included the book of Tobit most likely because it's not just salvation by works but there is a specific and lucrative work mentioned and that is money.

So, wait a second. During your Council of Trent meetings, you got rid of the 2 Esdra book because it happened to contradict your prayers to the dead. But oh boy, you clung to the Tobit book and I can see the huge gain you got from it.

Let me quote to you from this Tobit book, which they decided to like. Here is Tobit 12:9:

"For alms giving saves from death and purges all sin. Those who give alms will enjoy a full life."

You kept that book, didn't you? Because it works well for you, right? And it especially comes in handy when you need to build a new cathedral. Any project only needs the right campaign so maybe with the backing of your false-teaching Apocryphal books, you put together something similar to this:

"Hey, we're running a special! Jump on it today because it may not last! Remember, 'as a coin in the coffer rings, a soul from purgatory springs.' Do you want your sins forgiven or not?! Well, then come here and cough up the cash. This week only! Have you slept with a prostitute? Complete forgiveness of that is now only $2.50. Come over here and let me see how much is in your pockets!"

You think I'm kidding but remember; this is what Catholicism did to get money out of people. It was not just getting you to do certain works, they also wanted your hard-earned assets, your income, and/or your savings. So, it is convenient that Catholicism kept that book, but it wasn't until the Protestant Reformation challenged their power and the Catholic Church was forced to answer back at the reformers. That response came from their big meeting and here is the outcome of that get-together:

"The first official adoption of the Apocrypha by the Roman Catholic Church came at the Council of Trent in 1546, over 1,500 YEARS after the books were written."

Seriously?! If these books were truly inspiring, you'd think you would have figured it out earlier than 1,500 years.

"This was part of the reaction by Catholicism to the Protestant Reformation and if anyone did not accept these books, they were considered accursed."

How dare we disagree with the all-seeing Wizard of Oz...I mean, Magisterium? Excuse me?! So, you're saying I'm accursed if I don't accept these false-teaching books as authoritative Scripture from God? Well, let's look at what the Bible tells us about that. Paul said this in Galatians 1:8:

"But even if we or an angel from heaven should preach to you another gospel, let him be accursed!"

So, Paul actually says, it's you who are accursed because these books you say I have to accept, or be accursed, are actually pointing out that you're the one accursed and it's because you're leading people to Hell. These books are false teachings and you've glommed onto them. You've decided to go along with Tobit so you can take cash to supposedly purge sins! Paul says, "Let you be cursed!" But let's continue on:

"When the Apocrypha appeared in Protestant Bibles, it was normally placed in a separate section since it was not considered of equal authority. When Greek manuscripts do include books of the Apocrypha, they do not do so completely. In fact, no Greek manuscript contains the exact collection of books of the Apocrypha as was accepted by the Council of Trent. While the Syrian Church accepted the Apocrypha in the fourth century, the translation of the Bible into Syrian in the second century did not even include it."

So even if you thought the Apocrypha was supposed to be condoned by the Syrian Church, again it all falls apart. The Dead Sea Scrolls found in Qumran don't lend any credibility to the Apocrypha either. Listen to this:

"The Qumran community had hundreds of books in its library beyond the Scripture."

Again, just because you find a library containing books other than Scripture, it does not mean the library's owners thought all the books in their collection were divinely inspired.

"While the [Qumran] library had some of the Apocrypha, it did not have commentaries on the Apocrypha as it did with [the Bible's] Old Testament books. The Old Testament books had special script and parchment unlike the Apocrypha. The Qumran community clearly considered the Apocrypha as different from Scripture."

The Apocrypha books might have been historical books they had around as part of their library, but those books were treated differently because they were not considered Scripture.

"Up until the [Catholic] Council of Trent established the Apocrypha as [Catholic] Scripture... different people viewed it with different degrees of value. Very few considered it to be Scripture and if so, it was for flawed reasons. We should not consider people who view the Apocrypha highly as necessarily supporting it as authoritative Scripture."

We have to understand what was happening in this early time of the Church. Early Christians were getting out there sharing the Gospel and of course they were already seeing signs of false teachings creeping into the Church. Satan had lost, Jesus rose from the grave, the Church was born, and Jew along with Gentile was now all one in Christ. Satan is defeated big time and can't stop the fact that Jesus will be coming back to set up the Millennial Kingdom and chuck the False Prophet and Antichrist into the Lake of Fire. Satan gets to have one more final rebellion at the end of the Millennial Kingdom that Jesus sets up on Earth. After that, Loser-fer [Lucifer] is going into the Lake of Fire forever and ever and ever. He knows his gig is up because he lost.

So, because of all that, Satan decided to leave us alone, right? No. What did he do? He began to cloud the truth to get people away from it. How so? It was then, and still continues to be today, by false teachings. Paul was already dealing with false teachers who wanted to say, "Oh yes, it's Jesus but it is also the law." Those were called Judaizers. And John was dealing with Gnosticism, which is kind of like a warmed-over New Age type teaching with a little sprinkle of Jehovah's Witnesses stuff.

They had false teaching going on back then, even in the early Church, so they designated the false teachings as being outside the Scripture since they'd already seen an influx of that corruption. It continued on from there with random people showing up with things like, "Hey, we have the Protoevangelium of James!" Ah ha! But of course, a fancy name doesn't mean it came from the Apostle James. And that's what a lot of these con artists did. They wrote a book and put a famous and respectable person's name on it. It's like the Gospel of Thomas. The name they slapped on their false teaching doesn't mean it came from the Apostle Thomas.

Now let's talk about a hot book being much discussed today: The Book of Enoch. It's an interesting book with interesting material in it and it's a historical writing so I'm not even saying it isn't an interesting read because it really is but here's the problem: You cannot build a doctrine from it as

Catholicism does with other books outside Scripture. That is called false doctrine and you can't do it. Here's some explanation of this Enoch material:

"The book of Enoch is one of several pseudepigraphal books."

That big word means it is "falsely attributed" to a person. In other words, it did not really come from Enoch. Enoch was the great grandfather of Noah so first of all, he was not even around anymore. Secondly, people get confused about the book of Enoch because it is mentioned in the writings of Jude, which actually is inspired and part of the Bible. The Biblical book of Jude quotes from the book of Enoch in verses 14 and 15:

"Enoch, the seventh from Adam prophesied about these men: 'See, the Lord is coming with thousands upon thousands of His holy ones to judge everyone and to convict all the ungodly of all the ungodly acts they have done in the ungodly way and of all the harsh words ungodly sinners have spoken against him.'"

One guy says this about that: *"But, this does not mean the book of Enoch is inspired by God and should be in the Bible. First, Jude's quote is not the only quote in the Bible from a non-biblical source."*

Let me explain and give evidence for that last sentence: Paul actually quotes at least two secular philosophers. One of them is a philosopher named Epimenides who is mentioned in Titus 1:12 when Paul says this about Epimenides:

"Even one of their own men, a prophet from Crete, has said about them, 'The people of Crete are liars, cruel animals, and lazy gluttons.'"

Paul is quoting Epimenides even though Epimenides is a secular person. However, Paul doesn't mean for you to think that everything Epimenides wrote is true.

It's the same with a quote from a Greek poet named Menander that Paul mentions in 1 Corinthians 15:33: *"Bad company corrupts good character."* Menander is another secular source but because Paul quoted him, does that mean Paul agrees with everything Menander had ever said? Let me give you an analogy: If I'm explaining God's truth and in doing so, I mention something Paul Harvey said, which was true, does that mean I think everything Paul Harvey says must be the same as God's truth? No. I'm just quoting one thing he said. It's the same with Jude quoting Enoch in Jude 14 and 15. Here is more analysis of that:

"Jude is quoting from the book of Enoch but it does not indicate that the entire book is inspired or even true. All it means is, that particular quote he uses, that piece, is considered by God to be true. No scholars believe the book of Enoch is truly written by Enoch...period. We should treat the book of Enoch and the other books like it in the same manner as the Apocryphal books. Some of what the Apocrypha says is true and correct but at the same time, much of it is false and historically inaccurate. If you read these books, you have to treat them as interesting but fallible historical documents; not as the inspired or authoritative Word of God."

And yet that's what people are doing. They are literally building doctrines on those books. Whole theologies about angels are being built out of Enoch. Now the book does mention a lot about angels, but you can't build doctrine from the information. If you want to have an interesting conversation, Enoch is great for that, but you can't build a doctrine from it. Again though, that is exactly what the Catholic Church has done. Much later than Catholicism's founding, all of a sudden, these long-known books supposedly jumped into the divinely inspired category for Catholicism when they decided during a long council meeting, to squish all these kind of books into their Bible because it would differentiate Catholicism from the Protestants. And man, that addition of the Apocrypha books really caused their doctrine to spin out of control. It was bad enough before those false teachings were lumped in but with the huge does of corrupted literature, it became a complete mess!

The second area where Catholicism got it wrong is with their **Tradition**. We're going to see evidence for the need to reject tradition in the way that it corrupts Biblical Christianity. And again, notice that with these five aspects we will cover, like their source of authority with the Apocrypha and their reliance on Tradition, they believe each is on par with the Scripture. They teach that each is just as good as the Bible. Now let's explore their focus on their traditions, which lead to more false teaching:

"Tradition, used thirteen times in the New Testament means that which was delivered teaching. It's used negatively and positively. Tradition means that which is passed along by teaching. It's used in a negative way in the New Testament referring to manmade ideas or practices."

The negative use of tradition in the Bible is about certain practices like those of the Pharisees. Jesus had very strong words against the Pharisees' teachings (traditions). We'll see that in a minute.

"But tradition is also applied to divinely revealed teaching. Paul talks about inspired apostolic teaching in the Corinthians and encouraged the Corinthians to hold to it firmly."

We'll look at that in the context. You'll see that it wasn't just a case where Paul had some really cool tradition he came up with one day and expected the whole Church to uphold it. It wasn't like Paul started a tradition with something like how we should tie our shoelaces. He didn't teach that we need to first start with one bunny ear, then get yourself a second bunny ear from the other lace, and finally you loop one around the other counter-clockwise. And so, to this day, that is how every Christian needs to tie their shoes. No! That would be a manmade tradition. What Paul promotes is tradition inspired by God. Paul is talking about conduct and behavior. It's not just the sort of tradition where we are told to stand up, sit down, do this, here's what I think, or whatever. There's a major difference. Let's take a look at those opposing types of tradition:

"Negatively, we should refer to manmade doctrines, teaching, or rules, which take the place of Scripture."

So, it's not just manmade tradition but specifically tradition that is used to take the place of Scripture.

"In fact, these traditions invalidate the Word of God."

"Invalidate", is actually the exact word used in Scripture to speak against manmade traditions like from the Pharisees and the Scribes.

"Invalidate is the Greek word, 'Akuroo.' It means to 'render void' or 'deprive by force or authority.'"

"Akuroo", or "invalidate", is the same word used against the Pharisees when the Pharisees ask Jesus why His disciples don't follow the Pharisee's traditions about how believers should wash their hands before they eat. The word that's used in the Scriptures is "akuroo", so the Bible is saying the Pharisees are "negating the Word of God with force and authority." Of course, the Pharisees want to reply to Jesus with something like this:

"Oh, you are toast now! You're doomed straight to Hell for that. How dare you disagree with us Pharisees? We are the ruling elite and the masters of the Scripture. We know what's right."

Does that sound familiar? Again, that word, 'invalidate' or 'akuroo' in the Greek, means 'with force or authority', so it's the same thing we see with Catholicism. If you don't do what the Roman Catholic Church commands or if you don't believe what they say, you are supposedly accursed by Catholicism. To the Protestant reformers, Catholicism basically said, "How dare you challenge what we say! If you don't do what we tell you and stop your protest, you will die, and we will condemn your soul to Hell."

It's the same thing Jesus confronted the Pharisees with in Matthew 15:2. Let's take a look at that with Jesus speaking to the Pharisees about the negative aspect of tradition that is on display when the Pharisees teach and follow their own traditions as if those traditions are more important than Scripture:

"Why do you yourselves transgress the commandment of God for the sake of your tradition? For God said, 'Honor your father and mother,' and, He who speaks evil of this father and mother will be put to death.' But you say that if anyone declares that what might have been used to help their father or mother is 'devoted to God,' they are not to 'honor their father and mother' with it. And by this you <u>*invalidated*</u> *the Word of God for the sake of your tradition."*

There's that word: Invalidated. He is saying they have rendered Scripture void by putting their tradition above the Scripture and that they are doing so by force with authority.

Jesus is also talking with the Pharisees in Mark 7:5:

"The Pharisees and scribes asked him: 'Why do your disciples not walk according to the tradition of the elders, but eat bread with impure hands?' And he said to them, 'Rightly did Isaiah prophecy of you hypocrites, as is written': 'these people honor Me with their lips, but their hearts are far from Me. But in vain do they worship Me."'

What is Jesus issue with them? He's saying they are teaching doctrines, precepts, or traditions of man. Jesus continues:

" 'Neglecting the commandment of God, you hold to the tradition of men.' He went on to say to them, 'You are experts at setting aside the commandment of God in order to keep your tradition.' "

And now Jesus again is going to quote what the Pharisees say concerning the mother and father. Jesus compares what the Bible says versus what the Pharisees do. Mark 7:11 is Jesus speaking:

"You say that if a man says to his father or mother, 'Whatever I have to help you is Corban [which means, given over to God], *you no longer permit him to do anything for his father and his mother, thus <u>invalidating</u> the word of God by your <u>tradition</u>, which you've handed down. And you do many things such as that."*

So, what was the problem with the Pharisees and how did they become corrupted? If you do the research, back before there were Pharisees, the Jews were becoming "Hellenized", which is basically becoming like the Greek or Roman people of the time. They were becoming worldly just as happens to people in the Church today. So, the Pharisees were a reactionary movement against these worldly inclinations of the Jewish people. From a Jewish sense, not necessarily a Biblical sense, the Pharisees became very zealous for the law because they saw the Hellenization of the Jewish people happening all around them. The Jewish people were walking away from traditions, so the Pharisees rose up and told them to get back to the law, which was in their Old Testament Bible. That wasn't necessarily a bad thing until the Pharisees grew all high and mighty from it. The Pharisees became the Jewish version of Catholicism's "magisterium" where the Pharisees came to see themselves as the only people competent enough to interpret God's word. Jesus saw right through them and basically called them on the carpet with things like this:

You guys may have started out well but now it's just a bunch of traditions. You don't love me. Your hearts are far from me. You sit there with your robes and tassels while you have that fancy look and do all your very religious traditions. And when you pray, everybody knows it because you are out in the public with your highbrow language: You gesticulate and groan deeply saying things like: "OH LORD...THEE...THY...THOU..." When you fast, you put white powder on your face to falsely portray yourself as not having eaten in weeks. You're so spiritual.

But hey, do we play those games in the Church today? Do we run into Church people who dress, talk, and act just right to attempt to portray themselves as the perfect Christian? Sometimes they even put their fist on their chin when they speak, right? Just look at them. They've got to be Christian! But no, it's all tradition they are practicing.

Let me mention something I've noticed about how people, even in the Protestant Church, stick to tradition at the expense of truth. Have you ever seen a Church try to tweak things with the service? People get weird about that. Also, folks play favorites with denominations like when you try to confront people with the truth, you hear: "Well that's not what my pastor says." What is the best response and most important source of truth? What we should always say and hear first is this: "What does the Scripture say?" Now I'm not saying to be mean and nasty to your pastor, but we know, and he knows that the Bible comes first. You need to be a Berean. I don't care what anybody says. I'm going to support the word of God because that's what I align with. If you get out of alignment with the Bible, you're the one in trouble. It's not me. The issue negatively affecting Christianity is when we put tradition above the word of God. If we're not careful, it's easy to do for any of us. Okay, let's continue on in Colossians 2:8:

"See to it that no one takes you captive through philosophy and into deception, according to the <u>tradition of men</u> and the elementary principles of the world, rather than according to Christ."

So, all that spoke of tradition negatively but how is it mentioned positively in the Bible? Paul mentions positive tradition as it is inspired apostolic teaching. That means Scriptural tradition. When Paul says to follow traditions and do as he says with the pattern he has set before them, it wasn't pertaining to some helpful technique he learned from a shoe maker about the best way to tie shoe laces. Paul didn't give a suggestion to eat soup with the larger spoon and never a fork. Paul wrote and was advocating tradition that actually passed the test to become Scripture. Why? It was because what he said was the inspired Word of God. Paul says this in 2 Thessalonians 2:15:

"So then, brethren, stand firm and hold to the _traditions_ *which you were taught, whether by word of mouth or by letter from us."*

Is Paul telling us to comply if the tradition of your Church directs those who pray from the pulpit to do so on one leg while wearing a purple shirt? He said right there that we need to follow and honor our traditions, right? That is NOT what he's talking about! That interpretation would be out of context. Now there is nothing wrong with man's traditions if they are godly traditions; if they agree with Scripture. I'm not against tradition because there is a certain value in tradition. There are helpful benefits of tradition. Sometimes we forget our history if we don't have traditions so I'm not against tradition, but that said, when tradition supersedes Scripture, you have a problem! Continuing, Paul says this in 2 Thessalonians 3:6:

"Now we command you, brethren, in the name the Lord Jesus Christ, that you keep away from every brother who leads an unruly life and not according to the tradition, which you received from us."

What tradition is that? Paul is standing behind the traditional Christian behavior that is recorded for us in the Scripture. It's not just tradition for tradition's sake. The context is that he's talking about Godly behavior. In 1 Corinthians 11:2, Paul says this:

"Now I praise you because you remember me in everything and hold firmly in the traditions, just as I delivered them to you."

Is Paul saying we've got to follow every tradition that's ever delivered down to us? No! What's the context of that passage? What follows next in 1 Corinthians 11? It's communion, and communion is a tradition in the Church. Is that a bad thing? No. Now if you want to say communion is something that helps you earn merit with God, that would be wrong because it supersedes Scripture so there are positive and negative aspects of historical tradition. Unfortunately, the traditions of the Roman Catholic Church are negative. It's basically a newer generation of the Pharisees, who Jesus confronted. Let's finish up:

"In addition, only Scripture is referred to as being written by men moved by the Holy Spirit of God. From these passages it's clear; tradition is acceptable if it does not invalidate the Word of God. Scripture has the final authority. We must not exceed what is written."

In 1 Corinthians 4:6 Paul says this:

"Know these things, brethren, I have figuratively applied to myself and Apollos for your sake, so that in us you may learn not to exceed what is written."

What is he saying? It's this: Stick to the Bible! Don't you dare go outside the Scripture! I don't care who it is. It could be your most trusted family member, friend, or dignitary. It may be a book from one of the most revered people of all time. I don't care who it is! Do not go outside the Bible!

Why are there so many different denominations today? Catholicism says it's because we are not listening to the Magisterium of the Roman Catholic Church. That's one of their biggest justifications for why we should not interpret the Scripture. They say we need to leave it in the hands of this ruling religious elite and they'll tell you to just look at what has happened in order to know it's true. There are so many different denominations instead of one true church, which they think is Catholicism.

However, we do know that two wrongs don't make a right. The mess with all these unbiblical religions, doctrines, and practices isn't from individuals being able to read the word of God, Scripture has never been the obstacle. The problem is how people approach and interpret the Bible. The issue isn't with people being able to read the Scripture for themselves, the problem is people being inconsistent in how they apply Scripture but that doesn't negate the liberty we should have to read the Bible. Proverbs 30:5 says this:

"Every word of God is tested. He is a shield to those who take refuge in him. Do not add to His words or he will reprove you and you will be proved a liar."

One of the last four verses of the Bible, Revelation 22:18, issues a warning about the same. What does it say is going to happen if anyone adds to the words of this book? It says you will get the plagues that are mentioned in the book! So, don't do it! Don't add to God's word. I don't care if it's tradition, some secret hidden book or knowledge, some brother who supposedly has a new revelation, or any of that deviation from the Bible! Stick with the Scripture! 2 Timothy 3:16 says this:

"The Scripture was written by men moved by the Holy Spirit, which is profitable for teaching, reproof, correction, and training in righteousness."

In 2 Peter 1:20, the Bible says this:

"But know this first of all, no prophecy of Scripture is a matter of one's own interpretation, for no prophecy was ever made by an act of human will, but men moved along by the Holy Spirit spoke from God."

So, what we learn is that all Scripture is inspired by God and profitable for relaxing reading at the beach, increasing your self-esteem, building up how well you feel emotionally, and teaching you how to be financially successful. Oh wait, I'm sorry. Where did I get that? I must have been reading the Apocrypha. Actually, all Scripture is profitable for what? Teaching is one thing Scripture is profitable for. Yay!! Then there is reproof, which is not as easy to say yes to. There is also, correction that deals with our sin just as reproof. And then there is training in righteousness. Well, that one is positive. Okay, so half the time we should be squirming when the Bible is being taught; that is, the real Bible. Why? Is it because God wanted to ruin our happy thoughts and He's just being mean? No! It is so the man of God may be adequately equipped for every good work.

In the next chapter as we continue our examination of the five areas that define a group as a cult, we're going to take a look at another source of authority for Catholicism, which is the popes.

Chapter Eight

A Works Based Salvation

What we saw in the last chapter with the source of authority issue is how Catholicism came up with a lot of their false beliefs. The first place is their Bible because their Bible contains the Apocrypha. Again, "Apocrypha" means "secret or hidden things." However, the only secret to uncover about the Apocrypha is that it is where a lot of Catholicism's false teachings come from. That's why it was rejected for inclusion in the Protestant Bible.

Now if that's not bad enough, number two, Catholicism also gets their authority from man's decrees. Conversely, Christians say, "Sola Scriptura", which means, "The Bible Alone" or "By Scripture Alone." We believe all authority is derived from the Christian Bible as the lone source of our truth. Christians agree on that. Well, Catholicism also has a Bible but again, their Bible isn't the same so that's their first mistake.

Secondly, down through the years they've also gotten their authority from simple church council decrees. If that's not bad enough, they actually give those declarations equal weight with the Bible. Catholicism has had twenty-one different council meetings that produced doctrine they say is on par with the Bible. Hey, leadership meetings can be cool, but I can't even begin to understand how they could make decisions from those groups of guys absolute like Scripture.

Catholicism even takes it to another level, so it gets worse, if that's possible. We'll get into that in this chapter with the writings of the popes. The popes were all just individual fallen men but still they tell us that decisions from these random guys over the centuries, who at the time were asked to be group leaders for these priest and cardinals, is on par with the Bible?

Another source of authority Catholicism holds as supposedly on par with the Scripture is their Code of Canon Law. It's an unwieldy group of 1,752 laws they came up with. And if that's not enough, they believe that church liturgy is also on par with the Bible. So that means they think all their stand up, sit down, do this, go there, perform your Penance, confess this, work at that, say your Hail Mary's, and all that is supposedly on par with Scripture. Again, I want to reminder you that this stuff is really what they teach.

Another source of authority for Catholics is their Catechism. With their catechism we excerpted exact verbiage from their own official workbook, which is basically what catechism means. Their catechism defines their belief system. Still more of their source of authority that they put on par with the Bible is their famous theologian named Thomas Aquinas.

Of course, in the last chapter, we saw that another big source of authority with them that is put on par with Scripture is their tradition. Those who are traditionalists might say something like this: "Well that's the way they've always done it so therefore it has to be right." And supposedly it must be on par with Scripture too, they say. Wow! So how many different sources of authority, outside the Christian scripture, was that? They've got their 'Apocryphied' Bible, the council meetings, the popes, 1,752 Code of Canon laws, church liturgy, their catechism, Thomas Aquinas, and Catholic Church tradition. I count eight. We Christians believe the Bible, period! They say the Bible is one of their sources, but their Bible is not even the same one as the Christian Bible and then they say our source of authority should also include this and that and that and this and on and on. It's no wonder they espouse so many false teachings. Anytime you get outside the Scripture, you're in a heap of trouble. Eventually it's going to start to crumble.

So, let's now examine why we should reject the popes, with each succeeding generation of new ones they come out with, as authoritative. Besides tradition, Catholicism really believes that when this guy called the Pope speaks, it's as good as the Bible. But let's analyze that and see if it should be rejected. Here's a spoiler though— yes! Here is some analysis of the Catholic doctrine:

"Concerning the Pope, the Catholic Church believes that its hierarchy, culminating with the Bishop of Rome [the Pope], derives his authority from three beliefs."

So of course, Christians would say, *"Are you kidding me?! The Pope is supposedly speaking new Scripture as he goes along as Catholic leader?!"* Where do they get that? Apparently, there are three places they cite in that regard.

Number one, they say Christ made Peter the head of the Apostles and the Universal Church.

What's interesting at the end of that sentence is that the word, 'Catholic', as in the Roman Catholic Church, started shortly after Constantine with the Roman Empire, and it means "Universal." So, it's literally the "Roman Universal Church." So, they're still working on achieving that worldwide universal religion status to this day. The Pope supposedly has all this authority like the Bible because this religion of Catholicism, or "Universalism", claims the following:

"Christ made Peter the head of the Apostles of the Universal Church, and secondly, they say the Apostles appointed bishops as their successors, and number three, they say the pope is Peter's successor."

Of course, the problem is that each of these beliefs is in error! Later we'll look at that in much more detail, but in this chapter, I'm trying to finish the papal [Pope] area of information and then we'll start smacking them right down the list on each of their different false teachings. First though, let's examine this belief system as far as why they say the Pope's opinions parallel the authority of the Bible, which includes whatever he says and rules. Here are the reasons we should reject their three false arguments for the Pope's authority:

"Number one, Peter was not the head of the Apostles and the universal church."

So, there is the first lie. Matthew 16 is the verse Catholicism twists. Let's examine that and the key word to remember with this is, "context." That's because anyone can remove verbiage from the full text and cause readers to get your wrong idea instead of the truth. In Matthew 16, was Jesus making Peter the first pope? No. In fact they missed it on several different levels. Let's take a look at Matthew 16:

"Now when Jesus came into the district of Caesarea Philippi, He asked His disciples, 'Who do men say that I, the Son of Man, am?'"

Right in the context what is this paragraph about? It's very simple. Jesus asked His disciples who men say He, Jesus is. He's not asking whom Peter, the popes, or the Roman Catholic Church is. None of that stuff is involved. The whole context from the beginning is about Jesus asking who men say Jesus is. The disciples respond in this way:

"Some say [you, Jesus, are] John the Baptist, some Elijah, and still others say Jeremiah or one of the prophets."

Jesus then adds a second question: *"But who do you say I am?"*

So, we're still in the middle of Jesus and His disciples talking about who Jesus is in men's eyes? Now Simon Peter replies to Jesus' question of who the disciples say Jesus is:

Simon Peter: *"You are the Christ, the son of the living God."*

So, what is Simon Peter saying? In this context, Simon Peter is just filling in the blank to the question of who Jesus is. It's still about Jesus, right? Now Jesus responds to Simon Peter with this:

"Blessed are you Simon Bar-Jonah,"

As a side note, "Bar" means "son of." So, Bar-Jonah is "Son of Jonah", in this case. Barnabas, for example is from "Bar-Nabas", which means "Son of Nabas." So, when someone says Jesus' last name was Christ, they are confusing it with his title. His title from the Greek is "Christos", or Moshiach, in the Hebrew. Moshiach means Messiah, or "Anointed One." So, Jesus' last name in those times would be what? It would have been "Bar-Joseph." His full name would have been Yeshua bar Joseph. If that helps you some day on Jeopardy or a crossword puzzle, you can take me out to lunch. Now we'll get back to Matthew 16:

"Blessed are you Simon Bar-Jonah, because flesh and blood did not reveal this to you but My Father who is in heaven. And I also say to you that you are Peter, and upon this rock I will build My Church, and the gates of Hades or the grave will not overpower it. I will give you the keys to the kingdom of heaven, and whatever you bind on earth shall have been bound in heaven, and whatever you loose on earth shall have been loosed in heaven."

Now I've got to stop here because there is another issue, even in the interpretation of Scripture we just read. I've talked about this in other studies. Besides the Roman Catholic Church abusing this text to say it's where the papacy [popes] came from. What we just read about binding and loosing, is also an abuse of the Scripture. How many times have you heard religious people, when talking about something evil, say something like, "I bind you and loose you"? But that's not even what the text is about! It's talking about Church authority. It means when the Church is in accordance with the Word of God and Jesus Christ, those words carry God's authority. So, when the Church gives a ruling on something like maybe a discipline issue, the Church can say, "According to God's word, you are disciplined." And then, guess what; that sets the discipline in place to be the way it was laid out. God gives us that authority.

At my church, like any other Church, we have had to discipline. All churches need to at some point. Where do we get our discipline practices? Is it from us? No! It's of course from the authority of God's word. That's all the Matthew 16 binding and loosing is about. In fact, the binding and loosing, in the Greek means, "forbidding and permitting." That's all those words pertain to. Where is the word, "demon", mentioned in that? How about spiritual warfare? No. None of that is in there. It's a church authority issue. Also, what I've always thought was interesting, and kind of weird, is that even if you want to say Matthew 16 is about getting rid of demonic issues, why would you ever bind them only to turn around and let them go (loose them)? Hello?! Keep them down. Anyway, let's move on with Matthew 16:20:

"Then Jesus warned the disciples that they should tell no one that He is the Christ."

So right there at the very end he wraps up the issue. He says to tell nobody that He, Jesus is the Messiah. Peter just happened to get the right answer, but it really didn't even come from Peter. Who gave the answer to Peter? It was from God. And what is the whole context about? It is only about Jesus and who He is.

Now let's analyze the same passage as far as how Catholicism claims it has to do with the papacy. The Roman Catholic Church says the passage shows that Peter is the rock upon which Christ will build His Church. However, first of all, we just saw how the context certainly doesn't support that contention and secondly, the Greek meaning definitely doesn't support that interpretation. Peter is "Petros", the masculine noun, which means "boulder." But "rock" is feminine! If it were meant to be the same thing, it would be the same. It would be masculine with masculine. It's impossible in the Greek to mean that Peter is linked with the rock because Peter is masculine, and the rock is feminine. And the noun, Petra, means "massive rock."

So, the verse is actually equivalent to Jesus saying, "you are Peter", and then the separate issue is the massive rock, upon which Jesus will build His Church. So, the question is, "What's the massive rock?" What is the bedrock, upon which Christ will build His Church? It's Jesus and who He is, right? It has nothing to do with Peter. It certainly isn't saying that now we should have a string of popes from today forward and by the way, whatever they say is as perfect as the Bible. Where do they get that from?! You talk about twisting the Scripture! The context in this passage is about Christ and who Christ is. It's about the Christ, who is the Son of the living God. The foundation of the Church is Christ. It is not Peter! It's Jesus! He is the foundation of the Church. In fact, that's what 1 Corinthians 3:11 says:

"For no man can lay a foundation other than the one which is already laid."

So that must be talking about Peter and how, from him forward you'll need to install a whole bunch of popes. Oh, I'm sorry, that's the wrong translation. That must be the Popocrypha or whatever false book they're calling infallible now. Hello?! It's Jesus Christ! An interesting tidbit here is that, while it's true Peter is usually first in the list of the Apostles, it does not mean he was the head of the Apostles and it certainly doesn't mean its time to break out a line of popes, who can do and say no wrong.

How about we tell everyone that these pope guys will be putting down new Scripture the whole time they serve? That's not crazy, is it? Just because you're at the front of a list, how does that equate to being the leader? For example, we just had our annual Church Chili Cook-Off Contest. It's a Potluck. What I've noticed is that it seems like every single year; Bobby is always in the front of the line. That's every single time. So, I guess it's obvious that Bobby is the pastor of our Church and from now on we can only hire pastors that come from the lineage of Bobby. I mean that's a logical conclusion, right? What?! No. That's crazy. It does not matter if you're at the top of the list. What does that have to do with anything and especially with being an authority figure to be inherited down through future generations? That's nutty and a complete rip off of the context.

Secondly, the Apostles did not appoint bishops as their successors. That's another lie! Let's take a look at this claim by the Catholic Church because the Scripture Catholicism uses to justify that is 2 Timothy 2:2. But the passage only talks about disciplining men who will go on to disciple other men. It's the reason why we have an internship program at our church. If you apply Biblical teaching correctly, you will want to do what we're doing. When you find other men who are capable of trusting God's truth, what do you do? You train them to go out and do the same. It has nothing to do with bishops and certainly not the idea that you need a bunch of doctrine producing popes to put out ideas that should be revered and followed just like the Bible. Let's take a look at 2 Timothy 2:2 but we'll start with verse 1:

"You then, my son, be strong in the grace that is in Christ Jesus and the things that you've heard me say..."

In this passage we can see that Paul is investing his life and time into whom? It's into Timothy and Titus. That's why the three books of 1 Timothy, 2 Timothy, and Titus are called the Pastorals. With these young men who are becoming pastors, Paul is investing in them so they can pastor. Then Timothy and Titus in turn will infuse Biblical principles into other young men in the congregation. They aspired to replicate Biblical teaching like we're doing here to create more pastors for replicating God's truth. So that's what Paul was talking about here in Timothy 2:2:

"...and the things that you've heard me say in the presence of many witnesses, entrust to reliable men, who will also be qualified to teach others."

Well there you have it! That's why we've got popes! When you actually examine what they point to, it's actually funny! They're using that simple discipleship verse to justify having popes. They say its biblical proof but what in the world are they talking about?! All this Scripture is simply advocating is for men to teach/disciple other men to be pastors and share the gospel so there's another rip off. It's crazy! Nowhere does Scripture call these men out as popes. Paul simply calls them partner and fellow worker. Catholicism put their justification of these offices into the text because it is certainly not there.

Number three: The pope is not Peter's successor. There's no evidence of that. They don't say what they rely on for their contention except that maybe it's that word they use and put on par with the Scripture, which is, "tradition." While I have no doubt it is their tradition, it doesn't make it true. Here is commentary from the research:

"There is no scriptural evidence to support this claim by the Catholic Church."

The Pope, the office of the Pope, and certainly the supposed lineage of popes going back to Peter, is all completely out of context. It might be their tradition but it's not Biblical. And their traditions certainly don't have the same authority as Scripture! Those traditions are of man just like any other man.

"Clearly we must join with the reformers and declare that it is Scripture alone. The Bible is the authority for the believer. The Scriptures are authoritative and constitute the believers only source of faith and practice. Only Scripture is perfectly adequate for all matters of faith and conduct, for salvation, and sanctification."

"Scripture is all sufficient in regards to the soul of man in a relationship with God and our relationship with other people."

So, in other words, basically that's what our Protestant reformers, or if you will, our Protestant forefathers of the faith, relied on. That's why they were murdered, drowned, and burned alive and then even after they were dead, the Catholic Church was so mad at the reformers, that Roman Catholicism dug up their bones, burned the bones, and then chucked them in a river. Again, why did Catholicism do these heinous acts? It was because reformers would not go along with Catholicism's doctrines that came from Catholic men. The reformers said they would only follow God's word that is in the Bible. They said that neither the popes, nor any Catholic council would be their authority. They said, we're not going along with this apocrypha thing and we don't care about your 1,752 laws, your church liturgy, or your catechism. They also didn't care about the words of some theologian named Thomas Aquinas back in the 13th century. They *only* cared what the Bible said and for that they were exterminated like flies. And folks, if you think the Vatican has changed, they have not!

So that's where Roman Catholicism gets their authority and it's the reason their doctrine is all messed up. Christians point to the Bible and Catholicism says they revere the Bible but even their Bible isn't like ours and then they also add in bunch of other authority sources to hang their miters on.

The second reason Catholicism is a cult, is that it's how they view the **Nature of God, including the Trinity**. Again, we're dealing with the five signs of a cult. Number one pertains to where a group gets their **authority**. If they point to anything other than the Bible, it's a cult. And that's certainly what we saw with Roman Catholicism. Number two is the Nature of God and here's what makes Catholicism appear Christian so it's able to suck people in:

"The Roman Catholic Church agrees with historical Biblical Christianity on the nature of God and the doctrine of the Trinity."

Okay, there it is then. Since Catholicism got that right, it must be a true faith, right? They believe in God the Father, God the Son, and God the Holy Spirit. They'll even say so. But even though they have that aspect correct, that doesn't mean the rest of the religion is Biblical. We just saw how their authority is all messed up. Then they do get the nature of God correct. There's also a little bit of similarity to Christianity in the next aspect we'll look at, which is their idea of the "person" of Jesus Christ. HOWEVER, they get the "work" of Jesus Christ completely wrong. Then looking at the fourth and fifth ways to spot a cult, we'll see that with those last two aspects, Catholicism greatly perverts them just like the first issue of authority.

If Catholicism wants to assimilate with Christianity, they have to agree completely, not partly. It's no different than Mormons, who say, "Yeah, we believe in Jesus." But they corrupt Scripture because their Jesus is different. And it's like Mormons when they also twist the Scriptures to teach that there is not just one God. They believe that they themselves can become gods, so they believe in multiple gods. The overall point is, it's not acceptable to get just some of it or even most of it correct. It must all be Biblical. God doesn't speak with a forked tongue. He didn't have multiple Gospels. He doesn't have multiple sources of truth. There's only one.

The third way to spot a cult is by looking at the group's view on the **personal "work" of Jesus Christ**. The Roman Catholic Church agrees with historical Biblical Christianity on the "person" of Jesus Christ as far as Him being the second person of the Trinity, His deity, His humanity, the Virgin Birth, Him living a sinless life, dying on a Roman cross, resurrecting from the dead, His return to Heaven, and that He is seated at the right hand of the father, so they might get those aspects right, but they're wrong on the "work" of Jesus Christ. Concerning Christ's death on the cross, Catholicism doesn't believe in the sufficiency of the cross of Christ to take away our sins. We'll get to that in a minute. But again, because it's important, let me emphasis this:

ROMAN CATHOLICISM MIGHT GET THE PERSON OF JESUS RIGHT BUT THEY ARE NOT CORRECT ON THE WORK OF CHRIST!

The number four gauge of a cult is how they view the "Nature of Man." They get this one completely wrong. Let's take a look at that:

"The Roman Catholic Church teaches that human beings are created in God's image. Every person is a unique precious being of dignity and worth."

Whoa! There's some self-esteem building but what's the problem with that? They didn't read their Bible before making up that statement. You only need to read Romans 3, which we mentioned in our study; *The Holiness of God,* which is also in our book, *The Character of God*. It's one of those verses you might want to read when you're feeling awesome about yourself but maybe getting a bit too high and mighty. This verse will put you back in your place. Paul is talking about how no one is righteous; not even one. Then it gets to verse 12, which I specifically point out because in the above verse, Catholicism talks about us humans as beings of dignity and worth. Here's God's take on it in Romans 3:

"All have turned away. They have together become 'worthless.'"

Or at least we were all worthless before getting saved. Our value comes in Christ. It's not in the self-esteem, self-love, self-respect, self-inflated self, or self-statements of self-love. What makes us so valuable and precious is the blood of Jesus Christ. We've been adopted into God's forever family. It's Jesus Christ who makes us worthy and special. Do you see what I'm saying? I really think this self-love, self, self-stuff is not only false teaching, but people are getting ripped off and I really think it's adding to life's problems and people experience. It's because we're told the panacea for being down, blue, and depressed is to just puff yourself up. You need to love yourself more.

Excuse me?! That's pouring gas on the flame! Why do we sin? It's because at that moment in time, who are we choosing above God? We are choosing our self so you're making things worse. Again, you're going to run into a conundrum. As you sit there looking in the mirror saying to yourself how incredible you are and how much you just love yourself, you are on your way to blowing it. You're going to sin. And how do you feel when you sin? You feel bad about yourself! But then they'll say you just need to put on more self-love, and you will feel great. That's not true!

Folks, there are times when we Christians do things that are very wretched, and I am including myself. But do you know why you're still able to fall asleep at night? Is it because you feel great about your self-esteem? No! It's because the blood of Jesus Christ forgives us of all our sins. The whole world can be against me and I could make a million mistakes but unlike Catholicism teaches, I'm completely washed clean by the sacrifice on the cross of Jesus. God loves me. Through Jesus I have peace with God! I'm going to Heaven! Isn't that exponentially better than knowing you did something rotten, yet you still gaze into a mirror and tell yourself how much you love yourself? That's why I say people are getting ripped off from these false teachings. The real value is in Christ. That was just a little detour so let's continue with the statement from Catholicism on the nature of man:

"By their freewill, human beings have chosen <u>to sin</u> against God, rejecting his nature, and pursuing a course of life that is opposed to his essential character and revealed law."

The following is an analysis of the problem with Catholicism's corrupted view on the nature of man as far as his sin:

"The Roman Catholic Church distinguishes between two types of sin; Mortal and Venial."

We dealt with this near the beginning of this book but let's take a quick look at it again. Here's where Catholicism gets the nature of man wrong. When man blows it, what do we do with his sin? Here again is Catholicism's explanation of their two categories of sin:

"Mortal sin, the Roman Catholic Church teaches, destroys the sanctifying grace of God within the individual and necessitates the forgiveness through..."

Hey, do you think they're going to says it's through Jesus' work on the cross alone?! No, they are not! It continues:

"...the forgiveness through a sacrament of reconciliation..."

Their sacrament of reconciliation involves works that Catholicism prescribes to be performed by you. And again, this is from their catechism.

"...the forgiveness through a sacrament of reconciliation, which reconciles one with God and obtains forgiveness of sins committed after Baptism."

So basically, Roman Catholicism teaches the great importance of getting your kid sprinkled (baptized) quickly in the Catholic Church because they say that's how you get the child kick started. When the Catholic Church baptizes you, you're supposedly kick started into grace but now the rest of it from then on is up to you. And when you start committing sins after your Baptism and especially the mortal ones, man, you're in a heap of trouble. You're going to have to work! For the rest of your Catholic life, you'll need to be doing the works prescribed to you by the Catholic Church, or else! If you neglect your assigned works, you're really in a mess, according to Catholicism. You'll probably still end up in Purgatory where you must burn for some undetermined amount of time to purge off your sins anyway.

Wow! This is really what Roman Catholicism teaches. It is not at all Christianity! It's not even close! Here is more from Catholic teaching:

"Sin causes exclusion from heaven and results in eternal death and hell. Catholics classify a sin as mortal when it meets the following conditions..."

Again, who made Catholicism the arbitrator of being able to categorize sin? What does God say about <u>every</u> sin no matter whether great or small? All have sinned and fall short of the Glory of God and the wages of any and every sin, period, ends in death. Every sin, no matter how horrible or insignificant in a human's conception, causes us to deserve to die and go to Hell. But knowing that from the Bible, Catholicism still decides they're going to put sins in categories with subcategories and then hand out a works-based prescription program. That's exactly what they're doing and by doing so they show themselves to not trust in the loving merciful act that Christ did for us on the cross. Let's take a look at more of this Catholic doctrine from their catechism on pages 1857 to 1859:

"Catholics classify sin as mortal when it meets the following conditions: The sin is a serious or 'grave' (murder, adultery, stealing, and bearing false witness, etc.), when it is committed with full knowledge and complete consent."

What is bearing false witness? If you've lied, you've done it. So according to the Catholic Church, you just committed a mortal sin. You're going to Hell. Isn't that wonderful and encouraging? No, it is not, so according to Roman Catholicism, those under that burden better find out quick what the prescription is to fix that mess and get busy performing those tasks or paying the cash required. That's their work-based system! It's really what they believe. And we're just getting started.

Now the other supposed lower category of sin is venial sin. But does God play games with sin where He labels one greater than another? No, the Bible says all sin is serious and an offense to a holy God. But listen to what Catholicism does with this one:

"A venial sin is a sin that either is not serious or grave, or does not involve full knowledge or complete consent."

Again, the Bible says all sin is serious. But Catholicism says, Oh, no, these venial sins are not as bad. The catechism continues on page 1863:

"Unlike mortal sin, venial sin does not destroy the saving grace of God in the individual. Venial sin does not deprive the sinner of sanctifying grace, friendship with God, charity, and consequently eternal happiness."

So apparently there are some sins you can get away with. Isn't that really what they're saying? And again, you can check this out for yourself. Now what's the Biblical response? This is what the Bible tells us:

"By man, man chose to sin against God and is therefore under the condemnation of the physical and spiritual death, i.e. eternal separation from God."

In other words, we deserve to die and go straight to Hell.

"The corruption of sin extends to every aspect of our being including our intellect and our conscience. The heart is deceitfully wicked."

So, we are not just wicked. We are deceitfully wicked. How then are we supposed to know how wicked we are? Only God knows, right?

"All people are therefore unable to enter into a personal relationship with God on their own initiative."

Here's your Crone translation of that: We're messed up! In John, Chapter 6, Jesus said that nobody can come to the Father unless the Father draws him. Here is more on what the Bible teaches:

"For the believer, the Bible does not distinguish between big sins and little sins."

Now listen, this is talking about after a person gets saved. What would Catholicism characterize as the period after being saved? Well, if we look at their version of being saved, we can see what supposedly comes after. Their idea of getting saved is vastly different than the Christian view. Theirs is that you must get baptized. But as a Christian, do you have to be baptized to be saved? What's a perfect example in Scripture that disproves this Catholic doctrinal lie? It's the thief on the cross next to Jesus. How much time did that thief have to be baptized? None, yet Jesus said the thief would be in Paradise with Him. Hey wait! I know what probably happened. Remember how it was dark there for three hours? I'll bet Jesus got down from His cross and then took the thief off his cross and they got that baptism done! Right? No, He didn't. The thief didn't have time to be baptized. And how many good works were performed by that thief? He didn't have time for any works and yet, what did Jesus tell him? Jesus said, today you will be with Me, Jesus, in Paradise.

With that said, is Baptism something important to do? Yes! We do it in remembrance. It's symbolic of salvation, which takes place by faith in the cross of Jesus Christ. The same applies to communion, which Catholicism unfortunately also gets wrong. They call their communion the Eucharist and believe it's the actual body and blood of Christ. However, we only do communion in remembrance. It's symbolic of the body and blood of Jesus Christ.

We're not saved by Baptism. But Catholicism says you start out being saved by getting baptized and typically the Catholic Church wants you there ASAP, as a baby. The important question is, how can a baby make a choice about Christ? A baby doesn't know anything. All they usually do is sit there and scream during the Baptism ceremony. Even with that distress for the baby and annoyance for many present, those in attendance often say it was so special. But the kid was screaming his head off. I would be too if a strange guy was saying stuff and waiving a hand over me. Personally, I'd be freaking out too. Again, how does that child know what to decide? He didn't know about Jesus, the cross, and sin. How can he make a choice?

Baptism doesn't save you. If all that's involved in salvation is to sprinkle water on people while reciting some words, then let's get outside with a fire hose and as everybody drives by, we can hit them with salvation! Do you know how many people we could save that way?

What?! It's crazy but that's how Catholicism believes you are saved. You just get baptized and it's preferably as a kid. So, there's a double no, no. A child doesn't even know what's going on and Baptism certainly does not save you. But what Catholicism says is this: After you get saved, supposedly through Baptism, from that day forward, keeping your salvation is all up to you. As you commit what they say are the more serious sins, including lying, you repeatedly become doomed again and again. Is that what the Bible teaches? No! The Bible says Christians are going to blow it, but does it tell us we are then doomed and headed straight to Hell because we sinned after getting saved through Jesus? No! If that was the case, none of us would get there, right? So, all sin is serious, and it still happens after we're saved but you don't lose your salvation! Salvation is complete for you in Christ. There are however effects from sinning for Christians and that's what this tells us:

"The Bible doesn't distinguish between big and little sins. However, as a result of sin, if you do sin as a Christian [a true Christian], there is sometimes a loss of fellowship."

What's he talking about there with loss of fellowship? Well, do Christians do things they refuse to acknowledge and repent of so as a result, they are kicked out of their church? Of course, even at my church, this issue has become personal to us. Unfortunately, there are people who are not welcome here until they take the Christian road and do what Scripture demands for reconciling by owning up to what they did. We're all about reconciliation! Come on back, man! We're the family God and that would be such a great victory for Jesus. But until such time, the Scripture says for them to stay at bay until they come and reconcile so it's a loss of fellowship. They are absolutely still saved but they lose out on some fellowship. Scripture talks about it.

A second effect of sin on a Christian concerns church discipline. Again, here we've had to do that. Being saved and then sinning still has consequences. Though the difference in what the Catholic Church claims is that the sin of a saved person dooms them straight to Hell and the only way out is by performing works that are prescribed to attempt working your way back from damnation. For Catholicism, it's not just a Biblical falling away from fellowship with other Christians, Catholics teach that you have to try getting your salvation back, or at least their version of salvation.

So, for Christians, discipline happens, including the Lord's discipline. And sometimes people run from their church's discipline. Maybe a certain Christian who has lost fellowship is not even interested in coming back to apologize. In that case, what do you suppose God will do if they are truly born-again? What does the Bible's book of Hebrews say about this issue? God disciplines those whom he loves so you're not going to escape. If we blow it as Christians, including myself, can we avoid the consequences? No. What does God do? He spanks us right back on track. You can try all you want to escape but He's still going to love you enough to chase you down.

So that's the Lord's discipline and sometimes it even includes physical death. What am I talking about with that? Well hey, for example, God may forbid you, Christian, from giving into the sin of drunkenness. Is He just trying to ruin your Super Bowl party? Is your party going to be lame now without the alcohol? No! Guess what, all of God's commands are for our own benefit. If you get drunk and drive around, what has a better chance of happening? It's more likely you'll crash and die! And you could kill someone else. So sometimes physical death takes place because God is saying, 'No, I won't let you do that!' Sometimes the consequence of sin by a Christian can take their life.

Sin hurts, harms, and destroys even after you get saved. God takes it very seriously and the Church should too. The Catholic Church though, categorizes them, apparently for your convenience, so if you commit a sin in the big category, you're doomed. So that is a monumental difference with eternal consequences. It's not at all like Christian teaching.

When sin occurs in a Christian's life, the fallout does not involve all of the Catholic mumbo jumbo works-based Penance with Hail Mary's and all their other prescriptions created by men like crawling up the steps and getting your knees bloody to prove how sorry you are. The remedy for a believer's sin is repentance and confession to God. It is <u>not</u> repentance and confession to a priest so they completely desecrate Biblical discipline.

In dealing with signs of a cult, that was a look at our fourth sign with Catholicism's idea of the nature of man**.** Now here is the fifth sign with more on how they get the **means of salvation** wrong too. Here is some analysis of Catholicism's view on that:

"According to Catholicism, justification is the process in which God's grace is poured into the sinners heart making that person progressively more righteous."

Is that what the Bible says? No! When you get saved, right at the moment of salvation, all your rottenness is accredited as righteousness. It's an accounting term. All of our rottenness is placed on the cross of Christ and his righteousness is put on our ledger. At that point it's 100% done. Bang! That happens instantly and completely at the moment you get saved. Praise God! There is no progressive aspect to it. It's all fully done. But again, Catholicism says that's not true. They say it's progressive.

"During this process, Catholicism says it's the sinner's responsibility to <u>preserve</u>, [which means retain], and increase that Grace by <u>various good works</u>."

It's a work-based salvation! Catholicism is not Christianity at all. And again, with that in mind, remember that our media gets on the television putting a Christian stamp of approval on Catholicism by saying, *"And now for the Christian perspective."* Who do they roll out? It's a Catholic priest. Well, they may as well put a Mormon or Jehovah's Witness up there because none of them are Christianity.

"The means by which justification is initially obtained is not faith but the sacrament of Baptism."

That's how Catholicism, if you will, kick starts you.

"Furthermore, justification is forfeited when the believer commits a mortal sin such as hatred or adultery."

And as we saw earlier, that list even includes lying.

"In the teaching of the Roman Catholic Church then, works are necessary, both to begin and continue the process of justification."

Continue?! Wait a minute. Who completes the work that He began in us? It's Jesus Christ and the Bible is very clear about that. It's not up to you, Praise God! I've said it so many times because it's so true; if our salvation is based on our works being counted as even 0.00001% of the equation, how many of us would ever get to Heaven? It would be none! We'd all go straight to Hell and burn. That's because we can't possibly do it! We're not capable. We still have to deal with that old sin nature we've been dragging along with us since birth.

Plus, what is the crucial question that puts this into perspective about what's really being taught by Catholicism here? The logical question is about why Jesus died on the cross! If all that sprinkling of water on my head as a baby was to get me started, and the rest was up to me, why did Jesus die?! You are denying the actual cross and atonement of Jesus Christ! How is that at all like Christianity? It's not even close! Catholicism is a works-base salvation! It's crazy to think you can equate Christianity and Catholicism at all.

And yet when we talk about this stuff, I start to get flak online. They say, "You mean to tell me that Roman Catholics aren't Christians?" Yes, that's exactly what I mean! You can look at it yourself so it's not me saying so, it's the Scripture. My authority is not in myself. My authority is in my appeal to the word of God in the Scriptures. If it's not said in the Bible, then yes, what you are teaching is wrong. You can take it out on me, but your problem is not with me. It's with the Bible that came from God and guess what? You'll never win because God's word never changes. Oppose the Scripture to your own detriment. I wouldn't recommend attempting that.

"In the teaching of the Catholic Church, works are necessary, both to begin and to continue the process of justification. The entire system of sacraments is a genuine rejection of the true grace of God and salvation by Grace. Salvation in Roman Catholic theology is not by Grace through faith but a complex..."

Yes, remember that we looked at how complex their doctrine is? Their system is as convoluted as saying something must happen on a Thursday but only if it's raining and a cat is running by. Their prescriptions for ridding yourself of sin are things like performing a bead rubbing fifty times while turning right and then left as you get water splashed on your head and then you're good to go. You wonder how their followers even keep up with all that, right? How would you know what to do at any point? But see, that's what keeps them going back to their spiritual elite leadership for the Catholic Church. The people have to go to the priests regularly to figure out what to do. It's like a religious Christian slavery that is leading people to Hell.

"It's a complex adherence to sacraments and rituals as legislated by the church hierarchy."

It's a fake false demonic pseudo-Christian cult.

"The Roman Catholic Church teaches that grace is granted through the sacrament of Baptism. This so-called sanctifying grace is a gift, they say, of the Holy Spirit, but can be lost."

Can you lose your salvation? No! What sin do you know of that Jesus can't forgive? There isn't any He doesn't forgive! He forgives them all. But then people say, "Well, what about the blasphemy of the Holy Spirit? Jesus said that's one sin that can't be forgiven." But what that is not mentioning is how we can't commit that sin today. If you look at the context, the blasphemy of the Holy Spirit statement happened when Jesus was physically present on the Earth. He was performing miracles and the people physically walked up to him and accused him of achieving those miracles through the power of Satan.

So, first of all, would any born-again Christian approach Jesus and say that? No, so that supposedly unforgivable blasphemy of the Holy Spirit argument is what's called a straw man argument. Secondly, is Jesus physically right now in front of us performing miracles so that we can even possibly make that statement, which we wouldn't do in the first place? No. So in other words, you can't possibly commit that sin. Now I will give you this: Maybe during the Millennial Kingdom period, which is fast approaching, when Jesus is back on the planet ruling and reigning, that could come into play. But it certainly won't today and certainly not by a born-again Christian. And even with us Christians who as the Church get to be a part of the Millennial Kingdom, are we going to have a sin nature in the Millennial Kingdom to be able to even do anything like that? No. So we'll never ever do that.

I'll say it again: Christ forgives all sins! But Catholicism teaches that salvation can be lost through serious conscious and deliberate sin. They say it can then be regained through what? Of course, it's through your works of religious Penance the Catholic Church prescribes that you must do.

Catholicism also says there is "actual grace", which is temporary supernatural assistance to perform these good works that are necessary for salvation. Catholic sacraments are Baptism, Penance, the Eucharist, which is their version of communion, Confirmation, Matrimony, Holy Orders, and the Anointing of the Sick. Catholicism believes those sacraments are:

"...the primary means, by which God provides sanctifying and actual grace. This enables the Catholic to do good works, which are rewarded with heaven after final purification in Purgatory."

Wow, they are saying you can work your tail off and you still don't get to Heaven! You will supposedly end up in this mythical place they call Purgatory, which is an idea that is not at all supported by the Bible. This Purgatory is said by Catholicism to be a kind of holding place where you are to purge away your own sins in this horrifying burning rotten place. So, Catholicism teaches that by your own pain and torment, you atone for your sins. Of course, that is only after you do all the other religious stuff throughout your life that they prescribe for you. No one knows how long a person who has died is going to be in Purgatory, but luckily, after your friend, father, mother, or other relative dies, you'd probably feel guilty if you didn't take a large portion of that inheritance money and hand over those big bucks to the Catholic Church to show your loved one that you "love them enough" to pay that cash so Catholicism will supposedly shave off some of their time in that Purgatory place.

What a racket!! I'm just telling you what they believe. I'm only stringing it all together here and when you do so, it is kind of comical if not for the tragic consequence of eternal damnation in Hell. But when reading their doctrine, you just have to keep asking; Are you serious?! And let me go back again to a pet peeve of mine here after I've set the stage more for you to better understand the literal outrage I feel when our media decides to give us the "Christian perspective." They plop down a priest to pontificate his supposed Christian view. But instead he is delivering his opinion from the perspective he's gained as the follower of a pseudo-Christian false, fake, demonic cult called Catholicism. It's not Christian. It is the Catholic cult perspective. When you see that, don't you wish you had one of those big theater stage hooks that you could use to pull them out of the picture? Then you could put a real Christian out there to give God's word on the subjects. It's so crazy!

Now you may think, oh come on, Catholicism doesn't really believe this kooky stuff, do they? Well, let's break it down for you with quotes from their own catechism, which again is what the Roman Catholic Church supplies as their official workbook of their belief system. Catholicism believes the following:

"Infants receive Grace through the sacrament of Baptism and adult converts also receive grace through the sacrament of Baptism after proper preparation."

Here's are quotes from the Catholic Catechism 977 and 2020:

"Baptism is the first and chief sacrament of <u>forgiveness of sins</u>..."

That is a direct quote. This is not make-believe. It's what they teach. Let's continue in their catechism:

"...because it unites with Christ who died for our sins and rose for our justification so that we too might walk in newness of life."

Well, that's correct but they say the way you get there is by being baptized and preferably as a child. Here is more from their catechism:

"Justification has been merited for us by the passion of Christ but it is granted to us through <u>Baptism</u>."

They are actually saying Baptism is where you are granted salvation. What?! No, it is not! Catholicism reemphasizes that point with this:

"Spiritual rebirth and the lifelong process of sanctification, which begins at the point of the sacrament of Baptism."

So basically, they believe the sacrament of Baptism, again preferably as a child even though the child has no idea what he's doing and is probably freaking out anyway, temporarily saves you and then the rest is up to you to do works for the rest of your life to retain it. When you blow it, according to Catholicism's long list, luckily, they have a lot of works to prescribe for you. Oh, and by the way, even after performing those works throughout your entire life, you are probably still not going to make it anyway or at least not until you go burn in Purgatory while hopefully your loved ones will be throwing some cash at the Catholic Church to shave off some of your burning time. This is coming from their own stuff!! Here is a second point to discuss from their catechism about how good works has been added to the sacraments:

"Good works increase Grace."

What?! So according to Catholicism, the way to receive God's grace is by doing Catholic sacraments like Baptism, Penance, the Eucharist, Confirmation, Matrimony, Holy Orders, the Anointing of the Sick, and your own good works. How does that compare to the Biblical definition of Grace? The Bible tells us that Grace means, "unmerited favor." So basically, what Roman Catholicism teaches is that we have to work for God's unmerited favor, or, said plainly; work for God's unworked-for favor. Yes, it's an oxymoron. Grace means the very opposite of what Catholicism says Grace means. You cannot work for it! It's unmerited! You cannot earn God's Grace because Grace is a gift. Yet Catholicism claims we need to work for Grace. That's the complete opposite of what the word itself even means. Let's continue with what Catholicism teaches:

"Good works increase Grace and the cooperation with the Grace preserves Grace in the soul."

And here is the proof text of that from page 1821 of the Catholic catechism:

"We can therefore hope in the glory of Heaven promised by God to those who love him and who do his will. In every circumstance each one of us should hope with the grace of God to persevere to the end and to obtain the joy of Heaven, as God's eternal reward for the good works accomplished with the grace of Christ."

So how do you get to Heaven according the Catholic catechism? It's by your own good works.

"Moved by the Holy Spirit and by charity, we can merit ourselves and for others the graces needed for our sanctification."

But Grace means "unmerited favor." So, you can't work for it! Yet they say and teach as doctrine, the exact opposite, which is that you need to work for what you can't possibly work for. Yes, that is very messed up! Now here is a third point about Catholicism's doctrines:

"They say Grace is lost through a mortal sin and can be regained through the sacrament of Penance..."

Which is the work that Catholicism prescribes for you. This is from their catechism:

"Christ instituted the sacrament of Penance for all sinful members of the church: above all for those who, since Baptism, have fallen into grave sin, and thus lost their Baptismal grace and wounded ecclesial communion. It is to them that the sacrament of Penance offers a new possibility to convert and recover the grace of justification."

So, if you blow it, according to Catholicism, you lose your salvation, which the Bible says is not possible in the first place because our sin is all covered by Christ— praise God! But Catholicism teaches that you then have to do what they say to do to get your salvation back. This is no different from what you'll find sometimes even in so-called Protestant circles with Protestants who say you can lose your salvation. Those people wouldn't claim to be Catholics but they're basically saying the same thing. Those Protestants may not use the word, "Penance" as the Catholic Church does but they have their list of no-nos and it goes something like this:

'You went bowling?! You're doomed to Hell! You better come to the Church and stack these chairs for the next 50 years. If you do that, I think God will let you slide on the bowling, brother. You better get here to the altar and repent!'

Hey folks, I'm telling you there are churches like that. It's bizarre. One time I had some fellow elders who served a pastor with me and these guys had come out of what was called "Freewill Baptists", which was a doctrine where basically you could lose your salvation. One guy said it was a horrible existence growing up like that. He said you never knew if you were saved, even for one whole day. They had to go up to the altar every day. He said it could be a great feeling after the altar session because we would cry, repent, and do all the things they taught us that we were supposed to do. He said then I would feel clean and content because I did my thing and got my salvation back. However, by that afternoon I knew I blew again but I had to wait until the next Sunday to get back to the altar. He said it was a horrible dreadful existence. And they dealt with it year after year until, praise God, they finally came to the knowledge of grace in Christ and Christ alone. After that experience, these guys could smell works-based religions from a mile away.

Along those lines, one of the greatest problems happening today in Mormonism and Jehovah's Witnesses is suicides. I really think part of the reason why its suicide is because, like Catholicism, there is no assurance of salvation. You can't know you're saved. You're so busy doing good works and maybe you calculate that you'll accomplish 100,000 good works, but what if you get to the judgment seat you are expecting, and it actually takes 100,001 good works to get in? So, you never have any assurance of salvation. How do you know what's enough?

Well first, there is no number that is enough! To get into Heaven you must be Holy, which means being completely without sin. None of us can do that. You could try to clean things up after you acknowledge your sin, but you're still doomed because you'll never be perfect. That's why the Scriptures say that when you come to Christ, you have peace with God. It's all done and taken care of. But when you follow these works-based doctrines, it's a torment! Catholicism is a pseudo-Christian torment system that is also leading people to Hell. It's a hellish existence that the followers have to live before they even get to Hell because they have no assurance and therefore, no peace. They're always wondering how it will end for them. Will it be salvation or burning in Hell?

Now again, are we called to do good things? Yes. But with those helpful acts, Catholicism is not advocating you do them with the same motive Christianity has. Why do we Christians do what we do? Is it because Pastor Billy said so? No, for my congregation I hope that's not what it is. It's because of this: Who wouldn't want to serve Jesus after we've received a complete, clear, and full salvation that gives us peace with God? We're fully justified and fully forgiven once and for all! He loves me and that's where my worth and value come from. And it can never be taken away. Nobody can snatch me from my Lord's hand. Doesn't it make you want to wash Jesus' car or shine His sandals? Paul says Christ's love compels us.

But you don't have that with these Catholic type works-based systems. Instead, you're worried to death and then you're even told in this Catholic system that you're most likely not going to make it anyway. Before you can supposedly get to Heaven, you are still going to have to suffer in this mythical place they named Purgatory. And don't forget to give the Vatican more cash to throw on top of their, arguably, largest pile of treasure stored up anywhere by any group on earth. What a shallow tedious horrible existence that must be.

So why would Christians ever link hands with Catholicism who is promoting this stuff? You may say, 'Oh, you're being intolerant.' I'd say I'm rescuing people from something that's leading them to Hell and it's a system that keeps them apart from Christ, even before they would supposedly get to a fictitious Purgatory, as they have a rotten existence here on earth. Hopefully they do get saved somewhere along the way, but this system is not the way they'll do it.

The good news is that through Christian's testimonies, Catholics can get to the freedom that we already have in Christ. We need to love them enough to speak up, tell them the truth, explain the better way, tell them how there is only one way, and help them understand how that one way is awesome! And that path is Jesus!

Let's continue on with what this person explains about Catholic beliefs beyond what we already mentioned about losing and recovering salvation:

"The fathers of the church present the sacrament, they say, as the second plank of salvation after the shipwreck is loss of grace."

Again, Catholicism says you can lose it, but you can gain it back through Catholicism's works-based system. Here is the excerpt from the Catholic catechism (Para 1493):

"One who desires to obtain reconciliation with God and with the church, must confess to a priest all the unconfessed grave sins he remembers after having carefully examining his conscience."

How many of you remember what happened at 7:53 this morning? I don't. As cool as that moment probably was, I have no clue. And that's just one day. Catholicism says you need to give them all the unconfessed grave sins you can remember. And apparently, according to them, it's crucially important because this is how you get back into reconciliation with God and the church. You not only have to go confess all your sinning ways to this guy, but you have the added pressure of remembering all the sins you committed. It's impossible! There's no way! And hey, my heart is so wicked that even if it did know all I did, my heart probably wouldn't tell me, so I'm doomed! Nobody can remember them all!

Aren't you glad Christ forgives them all? And I say this all the time: He even forgives the ones I don't know about. We know logically that sin is going to happen, and no one is condoning it. People may say, "Hey, you're just giving people a license to sin!" Excuse me?! Before I got saved, I didn't need a license. Nobody needs a license to sin. You don't take a class on it to pass a test so you can sin, and you don't get a sinning tag at the Department of Motor Vehicles. We just sin because of the sin nature in all humans so it's a misnomer that just because Christ forgives us of everything, we will go on a malicious sinning spree.

If we're honest with ourselves, it seems like people who believe Christians can lose their salvation are usually referring to someone other than themselves. They are always about "that person." They're always looking down on that other person but it's never them. What they have is called "spiritual pride." Of course, that pride can't happen with the bishops, right? And spiritual pride certainly doesn't affect the Pope because under Catholic doctrine, the Pope never gets anything wrong. The spiritual pride problem only lies with you little people down below who are low on the pecking order so you must do everything we high-minded clergy say you must. And you need to do it in the right order (as they snicker behind your back at how gullible you are). They'll also have you give them some cash while you're at it. But last time I checked, spiritual pride is a sin too.

So, the whole system is a horrible existence. Praise God Christ forgives all our sins because you'll never remember them all. Here's more analysis of what Catholicism teaches:

"By Christ will they say, the church possesses the power to forgive the sins."

Do we as the Church have the power to forgive sins? Do I, the deacons of our church, or anyone have the power to forgive sin? Who forgives sin? It's Jesus and Him alone!! But the Catholic Church says they have the power to:

"...forgive sins of the baptized and this authority is exercised by the members of her clergy..."

So, the Catholic Church delegates that sin-forgiving authority to the bishops and priests, normally in the sacrament of Penance, which again is whatever a priest feels you need to do like, maybe fifty Hail Mary's, or stacking chairs for a few years. Here's more analysis of another precept of Catholicism:

"Eternal life is obtained by dying in a state of Grace."

Well that's true because when you're truly born-again, you're "placed in Christ." It's a wonderful phrase in the Scripture. You should do a study on this one. You are placed in Christ, so if I'm placed in Christ who is holy and perfect forever and has never committed sin, how can I not be in a state of Grace, especially when Jesus said nobody can take you out of the Father's hand. That includes me, by the way. So, I'm in a state of Grace.

But that's not what Catholicism means by the above statement, which continues here:

"Eternal life is obtained by dying in a state of Grace. If one has not attained the state of holiness required to enter directly into heaven..."

Well, wait a second! You can't attain a state of holiness on your own. It's only through Christ! But they say if "you" don't do it "yourself" then you go to:

"Purgatory to make atonement for sins that was not made on Earth."

In other words, you blew it according to our system. You didn't do enough Penance on Earth so now you're going to have to finish the job yourself by making your atonement in this place we call Purgatory. Now the following analogy may sound kind of graphic, but I've used it in some instances to try shaking people into understanding:

"Let me tell you what this works-based stuff is basically saying. It's saying you might as well just crawl up the cross, slap Jesus in the face, and say, 'You know what? You didn't finish the job. I had to finish it for you.'"

That hurts to even give that as an analogy but isn't that what you're saying? What he did was not good enough. You had to finish it for Him, and you can't even complete that work on Earth. You have to finish it in some mythical place. What?! And yet, people will say Catholicism is Christian like us and we need to all work together. Here is more analysis of the Catholic view:

"All who die in God's grace and friendship, but still imperfectly purified..."

Whoa! Who purifies us completely? It's Christ.

"...are indeed assured of their eternal salvation; but after death they undergo the purification, so as to achieve the holiness necessary to enter the joy of salvation."

Now what we're going to see in the next chapter is that in contrast to Roman Catholic doctrine with their salvation of works, the Bible teaches clearly that salvation is by Grace, which means unmerited favor so it's by faith alone. Salvation is the work of God completely whereby he saves an individual from the penalty, the power, and one day the very presence of sin. It is completely by God and not on the basis of merit or works. I don't want to cover that information from the next chapter yet, but just to give you a little tidbit, let's take a look at how many times Catholicism gets it wrong. Let's take a look at Scripture and you tell me if works play a part in any of it, if the cross of Christ is not sufficient by itself, and if your salvation is not absolutely completely 100% secure in Jesus.

In John 5:24 Jesus said this: *"I tell you the truth. Whoever hears my word and believes Him who sent me, has eternal life and will not be condemned. He's crossed over from death to life."*

In John 6:37 Jesus says this: *"All that the Father gives me will come to me and whoever comes to me I will never drive away."*

Jesus, in John 10:28, says this: *"I give them eternal life and they shall never perish. No one shall snatch them out of my hand."*

Romans Chapter 8:35 and 38-39: *"Who shall separate us from the love of Christ? Shall trouble or hardship or persecution or famine or nakedness or dangerous sword? I am convinced that neither death nor life, neither angels nor demons, neither the present nor the future, nor any powers, neither height nor depth, nor anything else in all creation will be able to separate us from the love of God that is in Christ Jesus our Lord."*

1 Corinthians 1:8 says this: *"He God will keep you strong to the end so that you will be blameless on the day of our Lord Jesus Christ."*
2 Corinthians 1:21-22: *"Now it is God who makes both us and you stand firm in Christ. He anointed us. He set his seal of ownership on us. He put his seal in our hearts as a deposit <u>guaranteeing</u> what is to come."*

Ephesians 1:14: *"The Spirit is God's guarantee that he will give us everything he promised and that he has purchased us to be his own people. This is just one more reason to praise our glorious God."*

Philippians 1:6: *"Being confident of this, He God who began a good work in you, will carry it out to completion until the day of Christ Jesus."*

2 Timothy 14: *"The Lord will rescue me from every evil attack and will bring me safely into his heavenly kingdom."*

Hebrew 7:25: *"Therefore He, Jesus is able to save completely, those who come to God through Him because He always lives to intercede for them."*

Hebrews 9:12: *"He, Jesus did not enter by means of the blood of bulls and goats and calves, but He entered the most holy place once for all by His own blood having obtained eternal redemption."*

Hebrews 9:15: *"For this reason Christ is the mediator of a new covenant, that those who are called may receive the promised <u>eternal inheritance</u>."*

1 Peter 1:3-4: *"He has given us new birth into a living hope, into an inheritance that can never perish, never spoil, never fade. It's kept in heaven for you."*

John says this in John 5:13: *"I write these things to you who believe in the name of the Son of God that you may know..."*

He says you will KNOW! It's not for you, Christian, to wonder, doubt, or even work your tail off in this life or some mythical place, that you may know you are saved. If you've become a Christian, you can know right now that you have eternal life. That's what the Bible says for the Christian. When you get saved, praise God, it's all then on the shoulders of Jesus Christ just as Hebrews says about how you enter into God's rest because it's not up to yourself anymore.

According to Ephesians 2:8-9, *"It's by grace through faith that you are saved"*, so once that happens, God not only seals you with His Spirit, guaranteeing you get to Heaven and that you belong to him now forever and ever so you're going to get there, but He also gives you the Holy Spirit because He wants you to do certain things in His name to lead souls to Him. Not because we're trying to earn it, that's all been taken care of by Christ.

In fact, Paul explains this when he asks why we do what we do as Christians? He also asks why we do not do what we do as Christians? And he asks why do we take a stand on issues as Christians? Because I'm personally so thankful that I'm not going to Hell! It's because I know I deserve to go straight to Hell and burn forever, not just for the sins I committed before I got saved but even for the sins I've done since. I'm so thankful that my salvation is absolutely complete, and God considers me, as He says in His word, spotless, blameless, pure, and holy, with the latter word meaning "saint." According to the Bible, a "saint" is a "holy one" and my salvation is guaranteed so that no one, nothing, and not even myself, can take it away from me. That's why the Gospel is called the "Good News"!

No one has a brighter future than a Christian! Nobody has a more secure future than the Christian! No one has better news to share with people in a rotten world full of manmade religious religion, than us, and that's what God wants us to do but he wants us to do it in full knowledge that He's not asking you to do so to earn something. Instead, He's giving you something that He labeled as a gift and you can't earn a gift. Take the gift and understand it as such. It's complete and full. Then, after you have received the assurance of salvation by accepting what he did on the cross for you, He wants to use you to do works so that other people can be saved also. Here's an often, overlooked concept: God wants other people in Heaven besides us!! As Paul says, *"How beautiful are the feet of those who bring the Good News."* But how are they going to know unless someone tells them!

A works-based salvation gets the cart before the horse. Yes, we're called to do good works, but they take those good works passages out of context and put them in a primary position. They have it exactly backwards. Yes, we're called to do good works but it's not because we're trying to earn or keep salvation for a loved one or ourselves. It's also not to attempt to keep from losing it. All that is complete! So as a Christian, I do good works for the reason that I love Jesus and I am so thankful to Him. That's the freedom we have in Christ. You don't get that with this cult called Roman Catholicism.

Chapter Nine

Salvation and Mariology

We have discovered by looking at the facts about Catholicism and what the Bible says, that Catholicism's means of salvation is not Biblical Christianity. The Bible says it is by grace through faith that we are saved so it's only through the work of Jesus Christ. But clearly, what Roman Catholicism prescribes to people is a system of works. They have their whole list, which requires good Catholics to do this and that, say this and that, recite some Hail Mary's and a few Our Fathers, stand up, sit down, kneel, and do all these other works. But that's not the Gospel! Their means of salvation is works-based and that's a classic sign of a cult. Catholicism solidly lines up as a cult.

You might say, okay, that's what they believe as their false system of works but what does the Bible specifically say. Here is the Bible's approach:

"In contrast to Roman Catholicism's salvation of works, the Bible teaches clearly that salvation is by grace; unmerited favor through faith alone. Salvation is the work of God whereby He, God saves individuals from the penalty, the power, and one day from the presence, of sin."

Are you looking forward to that? When we get to Heaven there will be no more sin nature! In fact, go ahead and encourage a member of your family by telling them that they too won't have a sin nature so you might finally get along with each other, right? It's going to be awesome! The analysis of the Bible's approach continues:

"And that's the gospel. It is <u>completely by God</u>. It is completely by God and is not on the basis of merit or works."

Is that just what I believe? No, that's also what the Bible teaches, so in contrast to Catholicism's salvation by works, with their false gospel, amongst the other signs of a cult, let's talk about what the Bible specifically says concerning salvation. This is number one on the list of how Roman Catholicism gets salvation wrong:

"The Bible says it is by grace, not by any good works of Catholicism."

So, it sounds like salvation is achieved through good works, good deeds, and trying to at least do 51% good versus 49%, bad, right? <u>No!</u>

Ephesians 2:8-10: *"For by grace you have been saved through faith. That not of yourselves; It is a gift from God, not as a result of works, so that no one may boast. For we are God's workmanship, created in Christ Jesus for good works, which God prepared beforehand so we should walk in them."*

And here is more analysis: *"But if it is by grace, then it's no longer on the basis of works. Otherwise <u>grace is no longer grace</u>."*

So, wait a second. Catholics, and even many Protestants, sit there and say Catholic doctrine is the same as Christianity. But the Bible says we're saved by grace. Catholicism says we have to finish the job because what Jesus did wasn't enough. But then it's no longer grace, is it? And this is not some nifty profound saying from me. That's from Romans 11:6. Here is more:

Galatians 2:21: *"I do not nullify the grace of God,"*

You say, well, yeah, who would dare do that? So, let's flip it around. How do you nullify the grace of God?

"...for if righteousness comes through the law [good works], then <u>Christ died needlessly</u>."

Did Christ die for nothing? No, of course not. So how do you nullify the whole message of the Gospel? You do so by saying the opposite, which is saying we can attain salvation by our own works, and then with that, what are you basically saying? You're saying that what Christ did on the cross was needless because I can do it myself. Hey, that's pretty profound of me to come up with that, right? No! I'm just quoting the Bible. Saying we can be saved by our works is completely wrong.

Titus 3:4: *"But when the kindness of God our Savior, and his love for mankind appeared, He saved us, not on the basis of deeds which we have done..."*

That includes all this stuff from Roman Catholicism or any other false works-based salvation teachings, which are false gospels. Works-based doctrines are those from the Mormons, Jehovah's Witnesses, Catholicism, or pick whichever you'd like.

Titus 3:4 continued: *"...not on the basis of deeds we have done in righteousness, but according to his mercy, by the washing of regeneration and renewing by the Holy Spirit whom he poured out on us richly through Jesus Christ our Savior. So being justified by his grace, we will be made heirs according to the hope of eternal life."*

That tells us clearly that salvation is by grace, period! It is unmerited favor! Regardless of your works, it's something that is a gracious act of God. We can't measure it because He just blesses us with it, if only we would receive His gift. That's what the Bible says so the first way Catholicism gets salvation wrong is their **denial of salvation through grace**. The second way is that the Bible tells us **salvation is through faith.**

John 5:24: *"Truly, truly, I say to you,"*

He who burns in purgatory and suffers endlessly all alone...
Oh, I'm sorry, that's the wrong translation. John 5:24 continues with this:

"Truly, truly, I say to you, he who believes has eternal life."

So then, can you just believe Jesus existed, as in historically? No! People get themselves into big trouble with that one. What it means to believe on the Lord Jesus Christ is to believe on what the He did for you and I. It's a phrase meaning Jesus died on the cross, God is holy, and we are not, Jesus is our savior, it's His work and righteousness that takes the place of my unrighteousness, and the only way I can be forgiven is through Him. That's what it means to believe in Jesus Christ or believe on Him.

Romans 3:28: *"For we maintain that a man is justified by faith apart from works of the law."*

Romans 4:5: *"However, to the one who does not work, but believes in Jesus, who justifies the ungodly, his..."*

...prescribed Catholic penance is to crawl up steps at the shrine of Fatima on his bare bloody knees and elbows and that is going to save him. Oh, I'm sorry, that again, was the wrong translation. Here is the rest from the Bible:

"...his faith is credited as righteousness."

Romans 5:1: *"Therefore having been justified through..."*

...saying fifty Hail Mary's and twenty Our Fathers!
Oops, again, that was a wrong translation too. Here's how the Bible finishes that one:

"...justified through faith, we have peace with God through our Lord Jesus Christ."

Galatians 2:16 *"...nevertheless, we know that a man is not justified by..."*

...anything Roman Catholicism says you have to do in order to be saved!! Of course, that was my words but it's accurate to what's being said here in Galatians:

"...we know that a man is not justified by the works of the law but through faith in Christ Jesus. Even we have believed in Christ Jesus so that we may be justified by faith in Christ and not by works of the law, since by works of the law no flesh shall be justified."

After all those verses, what would you say the Bible is telling us about everyone who is trying to get to Heaven by their own works and deeds? The Bible clearly says that no one will benefit from their own works or anyone else's beside what Jesus did for them! It says no flesh, which means, no one! So, if your own works are the way you've chosen and the path you're on, you are going to Hell. Salvation is <u>only</u> by <u>*grace*</u> through <u>*faith*</u> in Christ.

Galatians 3:24: *"Therefore the <u>law</u> has become <u>our tutor to lead us</u> <u>to Christ</u>, so that we may be <u>justified by faith</u>."*

The whole point of the law is to show us that it's not possible for us to even do those ten things. It leads you to the knowledge that God is holy, we are not, we're in a heap of trouble, and therefore we need a savior. So that's what Paul is telling us in the book of Galatians. The law leads us to Christ. It points us to the conclusion that we can't get there on our own. No matter how many things you prescribe for me, how many Our Fathers I say, or all the other religious deeds I can possibly do, I still can't get there. I need a savior!

Now besides **salvation by grace** and **salvation through faith**, a third way Catholicism gets it wrong is the aspect of how, once we have been saved, **we keep our salvation forever**. Do you appreciate the fact that once you get to Heaven, you're not going to get kicked back down to Earth? Romans 8 says <u>nothing</u> can separate the believer from Christ. All true believers, once saved, are kept by God's power and they are always saved from that point on and forever. We went through all those verses at the end of the last chapter. I ripped through a bunch of them for you. Here are a couple such verses:

In John 6:37, Jesus says, *"All those the Father gives Me <u>will</u> come to me, and whoever comes to Me, I will <u>never</u> drive away."*

In John 10:29, Jesus says, *"I give them eternal life, and they will never perish. No one [not even yourself] can snatch them out of My hand. My Father, who has given them to Me, is greater than all. No one can snatch them out of My Father's hand."*

Man, that is such a comforting truth and it's just two of many such Bible verses. When you're saved, praise God, it's complete and God has saved you forever more. In fact, God uses specific terms to drill home the point. Of all things to describe our salvation, He uses the term: "born again." There is a reason why He's using the words, born again. It's because of the procedure involved. He's talking about what happens to Christians at the point of their salvation. We literally became born again.

Now logically, if we took a survey of those reading this book, what percentage of us were actually born of our mother at some point in the past? And no, I'm not including those who have been scientifically cloned, so assuming all readers are not clones, we were all born at one time. Here's the question: Can you reverse that procedure? No. You can't reverse your birth and end up being unborn. It's too late. It's an irreversible procedure by nature. God uses the same thing for our salvation. If you are "born again" through Christ Jesus, how can you possibly get "unborn" from that? Is there a state of being "unborn again?" No, you can't do that. It's an irreversible procedure.

Now besides born again, the other term God uses is when He says He not only gives us life, but He actually gives us "Eternal Life." Now here's a perplexing question for you: How long is eternal? Yes, that's right. It's forever. Eternal life lasts forever, which is what God gives us. We are born again, it can't be reversed, and it's also forever. Well, wait a second. If it is, by nature, forever and eternal, how does something eternal then become <u>uneternal</u>? It doesn't, yet <u>eternal</u> life is the exact term Jesus uses to describe our salvation.

Earlier we saw that Jesus talked about **salvation by grace**. On top of that, He uses another term in the Bible, which is "gift." Jesus lets us know that salvation is a <u>gift</u>, so let's make an analogy for clarity. Say I offered you a free piece of gum as a gift, but before I hand it to you, I just ask that if you take the gum, you would then come by my house tomorrow, and wash my car. What?! No? You don't want to do that? But I've given you a piece of gum, as a free gift. You say, that doesn't sound like a gift! You're right, because it's not a real gift! By what I've outlined for you, apparently you have to earn it. There are strings attached so it's not a gift. But what term does Jesus use for our salvation? Jesus says it's a <u>gift</u>. There is nothing you can do to earn it. Salvation, according to Jesus, is purely a gift of mercy from God. That's exactly what Jesus says in the Bible. For the Christian who accepts it, salvation is complete and yours to keep forever. From that point where you get saved, nothing can separate you from God.

Now how about when a person <u>professes</u> to be a follower of Christ and then turns away from their faith in Christ? People bring up that <u>supposed</u> example as some sort of proof that you can lose your salvation. They'll usually say something like this: "Oh yeah, well I know a guy who said he was a Christian, did all the Christian things, prayed all the time, was very active in the church, but then he went through a hard time and just walked away from being a

Christian and he became a Mormon." Or they'll say he became a Catholic, an atheist, something else, or whatever. We've probably all heard these stories about guys or ladies like that who supposedly "lose" their salvation. They say something like, "Don't tell me people can't lose their salvation. I've seen it happen." But that's not true! What does the Bible tell us? In 1 John 2:19, Jesus basically says that a person who professes to be a follower of Christ and then turns away, just shows that true salvation for that person never took place. Here's that verse:

"They went out from us because they never belonged to us. If they had belonged to us [because God keeps his own], they would have remained with us. But their going made it clear that none of them belonged to us."

So, if anyone professes to know Christ and then walks away from Christ, they never belonged to Christ. They were not Christian so you can't lose your salvation. And the idea of those among us not being truly saved in their own hearts is kind of a creepy thing, right? How many people are coming to church services thinking they're heading to Heaven, but they're not truly saved? They can fool some of us in the Church or maybe even all of us, but they can't fool God. He knows who His children are who trust only in His one and only Gospel, which is by grace through faith in Jesus Christ. It's only the work of Christ. If you're trusting in yourself, even a tiny bit, you're in a heap of trouble. So again, salvation is kept forever, and Christ's work is a fully sufficient sacrifice.

Hebrews 10:10: "We have been sanctified through the offering of the body of Jesus <u>one time for all</u>."

Here's an excellent comparison of what Hebrews says there and Catholicism's practices: *"And every priest stands daily ministering, offering time after time the same sacrifices, which can <u>never ever take away sin</u>."*

He's saying that Catholic priests can stand there every day doing the Eucharist, saying their religious sounding liturgy, having the followers stick out their tongues for the wafers, having them stand up, sit down, kneel, and say their Hail Mary's, but none of it can ever take away even a single sin. That's what the Scripture says. But Jesus offered one sacrifice, for all sins, for <u>all time</u>. That means it's done! For all time, means you are good to go for the rest of eternity. We are forgiven for all sins; past, present, and future. It is even true for the sins we haven't committed yet or those we don't know about or remember. Woo

Hoo!! Those sins are gone for all time! Why? As Jesus said on the cross, "It is finished." Then He sat down at the right hand of God to wait from that time forward until his enemies are made a footstool for Him. By one offering, He, Jesus, has perfected for all time, those who are sanctified by faith in Jesus Christ as their savior.

Once a person knows they have been saved from Hell by what Jesus did for them and that they will be with God for eternity even though they are a corrupted sinner deserving of Hell, then at that point, the acceptance of free salvation through Christ results in good works. And that's where, in many places, the Bible does talk about doing good works. But you can't get the cart before the horse. As we read earlier in Ephesians 2:8-10, we're saved by grace through faith. Verse 10 goes on to say that as a born-again Christian, we're in Christ Jesus, and as a new born-again creation in Jesus, we are created for this time to do good works. Now that you've become a born-again Christian, God wants to use you to do good works by letting other people know about Him, by you serving Him, and for you to be a good example of a Christian for others to see.

However, all that does not mean those good works have anything to do with your salvation. Again, that's because you can't earn salvation or lose it. Doing good works for our Father is the after effect of your gratitude for His act that allowed you to have salvation.

The whole argument is a common-sense thing. If someone saves you from falling over Niagara Falls, they didn't have to do so, right? They just did it out of their kindness and mercy. And what's the natural response to a person who just saved your life from plummeting over the falls? You of course thank them profusely. But you also think about what you might do for them in return. You naturally think, "How can I return the favor?" You probably feel like, "Hey, can I mow your yard?" You'd want to wash their car or do something for them. And that's the same thing as what Christ did to save our eternal life. How much more is that worth? So, the understandable result is our desire to do good work for Christ.

As Paul says, *"It's Christ's love that compels us."*

You naturally want to serve him, right? As a side note and now speaking of those in the Christian Church, it's kind of scary when you see people in the Church who say things like, "Oh, I love Jesus. He's the greatest thing in my life and I'm so thankful for Him." But then when someone working in the Church asks that person for help, to maybe stack a few chairs or something, what is sometimes certain peoples repeated response? Some in the Church often reply with things like, "Oh, sorry, I've got to run." Yet they'll say, "Jesus Christ is so important to me, He means everything, and I'm so grateful to Him for what He's done!" But again, when someone from the Church tries another time to get some help from that same person, maybe this time for the youth group, the response is more of the same: "Oh, I'm sorry. I've got a cold coming on."

That person may never serve Christ and it makes you wonder why? Again, our works do NOT save us. That's what Catholicism teaches and it's a false gospel. But for someone to sit in the Christian Church and profess their indebtedness and thankfulness for what God has done for them, yet they never do anything in return to help the Church, there's something wrong there. This isn't meant to be a guilt trip. It just logically doesn't make sense. I don't care if it's just stacking chairs. If you are doing it for Jesus, then praise God! But do something, because that shows how maybe something really did happen to you that changed you. Maybe there was a spiritual exchange where something changed in your heart when you realized what Jesus did for you. Nobody should have to pull your teeth to get you to serve Christ.

I used to have what I called the 50/50 rule. To me, this seemed to apply across the American Christian Church. Now just for background, let me say that I don't know everyone's heart and certainly only God does but if you go with the odds in the Church today, it is so infected with non-Christians because the Word of God is not being preached and the Gospel is not being given. Any particular congregation might be a large bunch of people coming in the doors, but that doesn't mean they're Christians. So now back to the 50/50 rule. No matter where I was teaching or preaching, I'd apply that rule, which says about 50% of the people I'm talking to are probably not saved. If there were two hundred in the audience, I'd figure about a hundred of them listening to me were not saved.

Along those lines, I remember reading the biography of D. James Kennedy. His number was 80%. He figured 80% of the people were not saved. Only 20% were. What he based that on was his experience with the 80/20 rule as it applies in the Church. In the Christian Church, 20% of the people in the Church do 100% of the work, while 80% of the people do nothing. Why is that? What Kennedy would say is this: How in the world can you sit there and say you understand what Christ did for you on the cross and say that you're so thankful, but week after week after week, you do nothing to help? You never serve Christ or maybe even talk about Him. You just punch the time clock every Sunday and then go on your way. Something isn't right there.

We are saved FOR good works. We are not saved BY our works.

Hebrews 12:28-29: *"Therefore since we receive a kingdom, which cannot be shaken, let us show gratitude, by which we may offer to God acceptable service with reverence and awe. For our God is a consuming fire."*

So that's what the Bible says about the **means of salvation** and we're just quoting Bible verse after Bible verse after Bible verse. Again, we've been looking at the five areas, to examine if you want to know whether someone is in a cult. And this last one we've talked about has been, the **means of salvation**. The Bible says when it comes this last aspect, salvation is by grace, it is through faith, it's kept forever so you can't lose it, salvation is a complete sacrifice, it's all from Jesus' actions and none of it is by our own doing. That's it! That's what the Bible teaches, so that's the true Gospel.

Now with all that said, do you know that Roman Catholicism not only gets it wrong with their doctrine and teaching of a system of works, but then they have the audacity to tell us Christians that if we believe what we just studied right there from the Bible about salvation, we are under their curse? They profess to curse all, including Christians, who believe salvation is not through works. Let's take a look at that proof:

"The Council of Trent, from 1545 to 1563 declared the following canons, and they maintain these today: Canon 9: 'If anyone says that the sinner is justified by faith alone, meaning that nothing else is required to cooperate in order to obtain the grace of justification and that it is not in any way necessary that he be prepared and disposed by the action of his own will, let him be anathema."

Let him be anathema means, "Let him be accursed." Catholicism says you are cursed! They're saying, we in the Catholic leadership and those followers we teach to do so, curse you if you believe a sinner is saved by grace alone. In Canon 19, Roman Catholicism says this:

"If anyone says that nothing besides faith is commanded the gospel, that other things are indifferent, neither commanded nor forbidding but free, or that the Ten Commandments in no way pertains to Christians, let him be anathema [cursed]."

Catholicism says they curse you if you believe that. What?!

Canon 24: *"If anyone says that the justice received is not preserved and is also not increased before God through good works; but that the said works are merely the fruits and signs of Justification obtained, but not a cause of the increase thereof; let him be anathema [cursed]."*

So, Catholicism says that if anybody tells you that you shouldn't have to work for your salvation and that works are merely the fruits and signs of a person already saved and not the cause of increase, let him be cursed. If you dare say that salvation is not by your own works and you instead believe or teach Biblical principles about how Jesus alone secured our salvation, the Catholic Church curses you. Catholicism is not content with disagreeing with you. They say, "We curse you!" That's what anathema means. Let's continue on:

Canon 27: *"If anyone says that there is no mortal sin except that of unbelief, or that grace once received is not lost through any other sin however grievous and enormous except by that of unbelief, let him be anathema."*

Catholicism is telling you that if you don't believe you can lose your salvation, Roman Catholicism curses you. They are saying, how dare you teach that salvation can't be lost after it's been obtained. We curse you! If you don't believe that you can lose your salvation through any sin, no matter how grievous or enormous, except by unbelief, we curse you! But again, I'm not teaching that. The Bible does and Catholicism curses us for teaching the Bible. Wow!

Canon 30: *"If anyone says that after the reception of the grace of justification the guilt is so remitted [removed] and the debt of eternal punishment so blotted out to every repentant sinner, that you are not going to hell and that no debt of temporal punishment remains to be discharged either in this world or in purgatory before the gates of heaven can be opened, let him be anathema."*

If you dare have the audacity to say you can know for sure today through Jesus Christ that you're going to Heaven and you will not go to Hell, we in the Roman Catholic Church curse you. Now I have one more canon to mention but again, what is a tragic misnomer out there in our media? Once more I'll mention that they love to say, *"and now for the Christian perspective*", as they roll out a Catholic Priest. And yet the barebones of what we believe with the Gospel of Jesus is something the Catholic Church curses Christians for believing. But we're supposed to get the Christian perspective from those who curse Christians?! And then, on top of that abomination, we actually see Christians all over the world saying Catholics are the same as Christians. What?! No!! They are cursing Christians! The whole thing is just wild.

Canon 33: *"If anyone says that the Catholic doctrine of justification as set forth by the holy council..."*

Notice that the authority they point to is not the Bible. Instead it's the leaders of the Catholic Church.

"...as set forth by the holy council in the present decree, derogates [detracts] in some respect from the glory of God or the merits of our Lord Jesus Christ, and does not rather illustrate the truth of our faith and no less the glory of God and of Christ Jesus, let him be anathema."

In other words, if you disagree with their version of justification, which is by works, we, Catholicism, curse you. So apparently the point is not to be discussed. If we Christians even think differently from Catholic doctrine on these important issues the Catholic Church is going to curse us. The Bible curses you for that doctrine of yours! I didn't say that. Paul did. And where did Catholicism even get the word, anathema? It's from Paul in Galatians. Paul curses anyone who would dare say you could achieve salvation in any other way but by faith and trust in the work of Jesus alone. Let's take a look at Galatians 1:6. You have to see this with your own eyes. Literally every central tenet of the Bible that Christians believe in like grace through faith, it's all Jesus, it's complete, and I'm not going to Hell. Yet, if we just agree with what the Bible says on these issues, Catholicism condemns us with language like this:

"I curse you. I curse you. I curse you. How dare you say that? How dare you disagree with Catholic doctrine? You have no right to disagree with Catholicism and no; I'm not leaving it at a disagreement. I curse you. I curse you. I curse you."

Really? Well, as defenders of the Christian faith, let's take a look at what the Bible says to that from Paul in Galatians 1:6-8:

"I am astonished that you are so quickly deserting the one who called you to live in the grace of Christ and are turning to a differing gospel, which is really no gospel at all. Evidently some people have thrown you into confusion..."

What's the background of the Galatians? People were professing that yes, it is Jesus, "but" it's also this and that. Remember, anytime someone tells you the true gospel is "Jesus or", "Jesus and", or "Jesus but", that's not the Gospel! Yet that's exactly what's going on here with Catholicism in their canons. They are saying it's Jesus, but you need to worship Mary, you've got to do penance, and you've got to keep the rest of the sacraments. Paul says that's no gospel at all and he adds this:

"Evidently some people are throwing you into confusion or trying to pervert the gospel of Christ. But even if we or an angel from heaven should preach a gospel other than the one we preach to you, [that salvation is only through Jesus alone], let him be eternally condemned."

Anathema means, "eternally condemned", which is, "cursed." It's the same word Catholicism uses against Christians and against the Bible. If you do that, as Catholicism has done, Paul says, "Excuse me? You're the one that's condemned. God curses you." For emphasis, in Galatians 8, Paul reiterates:

"As I've already said, so now I'm going to say it again: If anyone is preaching to you a gospel other than what you accepted, let him be eternally condemned."

Paul is pronouncing anathema on them. They are the ones that are cursed by their own doing. And it's also because, apparently, Christians can't even discuss this with most Catholics and even less so with the Catholic leadership. What does the Bible say about that? It tells us that these people, with their false teachers, have seared consciences. When you have a seared conscience, it means you are so set on lies that it's like nothing is going to change your mind. Your heart is so hard and your conscience is so seared that I can't even talk to you. All you do is sit there and say, "I curse you. I curse you. I curse you." But you know what? You yourself are cursed straight into Hell because we can't even have a discussion on this. Again, Paul says, you're the one who deserves eternal condemnation. That's what the Bible says. Here is more analysis of Catholic doctrine:

"Roman Catholicism places an undue stress on human works. Catholic doctrine denies that God justifies the ungodly without first making them godly."

Before getting saved, many future Christians have a conception of Christianity that tells them they need to clean up their act before they can get saved. That's what Catholicism teaches. But that's not what the Bible tells us. Aren't you glad the Bible says God accepts you where you are, no matter what you've done? However, the good news is that he loves you, so he doesn't keep you there. By his spirit he begins to clean you up. But don't get the "cart" of wanting to do good things for Jesus because of what Jesus did for you, ahead of the "horse", which is that salvation gift he gave us. Here is more analysis:

"Good works therefore become the grounds of justification, according to Catholicism and as thousands of former Catholics will testify, Roman Catholic doctrine and liturgy obscure the essential truth that the believer is saved by grace through faith; not of his own works. In a simple sense, Catholics genuinely believe that they are saved by doing good works, confessing sin, and observing ceremonies."

That's a perverted gospel! Galatians, Chapter 1 says this about anyone who teaches that: "Let him be eternally condemned." That false teaching is leading people to Hell. It's profoundly serious stuff. When you realize all this about Catholicism, you really understand what I'm going to point out again for emphasis: "*And now for the Christian perspective*." Again, that's what is said as another Catholic priest is presented as a Christian to the unsuspecting audience. It blows me away!

Here is more analysis and it addresses the idea of some who think of, or advocate for, Catholicism being just another denomination, or sect of Christianity, which of course it is not:

"The Roman Catholic system is not a group of wayward [Christian] brothers. It's an apostate form of Christianity. It's a false religion. It's another religion."

It's not Christianity at all! Catholicism is no more Christian than Mormonism, Jehovah's Witnesses, or any other works-based cult. And yet the media and the Vatican have done a masterful job of brainwashing people into thinking Catholicism is the same thing as Christianity, or at worst, just a little different, maybe because they wear robes. But, no! It's not!

Now all that has been leading us to what we're going to cover over the next couple of chapters. What else is there to look at and point out with Catholicism? The Catholic doctrine and its false teachings that we already examined was bad enough. They get it wrong on a lot! But as you'll see, they're messed up on a whole bunch more and that's what we're going to cover now. In this chapter, we will only get started on it.

An important aspect of Catholicism that we have to address is "Mariology." The Catholic Church will often say they don't do this, but they certainly do. Mariology is basically the worship of Mary. We'll find that Catholicism literally worships Mary of the Bible. So, there you see another false doctrine! Excuse me?! That's an idol. Let's go down that route:

"Roman Catholicism and Christianity are not the same thing. Christianity is properly defined by certain doctrines, i.e., revealed in the Gospel."

And what are those basic core beliefs of the Biblical Gospel that make up Biblical Christianity?

"There is only one God, you are to serve no other gods, Jesus is both God and man, Jesus rose from the dead physically, salvation is by grace through faith; the Gospel is the death, burial, and resurrection of Jesus according to the Scriptures, God is the Trinity, and Jesus was born of the Virgin Mary."

So, here's the point: when someone is a true Christian, they will believe these things and not violate them. That's just the bare bones, right?

"Roman Catholicism violates many of them; first of all, by its practice of promoting Mary."

In a later chapter, we'll get into the saints as well, because it's all part of the Catholic practice of praying to dead people like Mary and the saints. Besides Mary, they pray to a whole bunch of other dead people and they even attribute to these dead people, including Mary and the saints, God-like powers. They have the saint of this, a saint of that, a saint to stop the rain, one to fix your flat tire, a saint for finances, and one for most anything else you need. But those appeals in prayer are all for stuff only God can do! And last time I checked, all the Saint So-and-So's are dead. Would you agree that a dead person does nothing? And maybe don't test that concept. Just acknowledge it because that could get weird. But let's continue:

"In Roman Catholicism they say that Mary is the mediatrix, she made atonement for the sins of man, and she is the subject of preaching and worship."

But let's go even further in exploring this. In fact, I'm just going to rip through Catholicism's view of Mary. I'll be quoting the Catholic catechism and the different popes, which is all their source of authority equivalent to the Bible. You tell me if this is a Biblical view of the Biblical person, Mary. Here's what it says:

"According to Roman Catholicism, Mary is the all holy ever-virgin mother God - (catechism 721), she is the queen over all things (catechism 966), she's our advocate, helper, benefactress, and mediatrix [the latter means we go through her to get to God] (969), who is full of grace (722), she's the mother of God and our mother (2677), the new Eve (726), the seat of wisdom (721), she had no original sin (508), never committed sin (493), she sits on the right hand of the majesty on high (Pope Pius X), no man can go to Christ but by his mother (Pope Leo XIII), Mary crushed the poisonous head of the most cruel serpent and brought salvation to the world (Pope Pius IX), delivers souls from death (catechism 966), continues to bring us gifts of eternal salvation (969), Mary made atonement for the sins of man (the fundamentals of the Catholic dogma, page 213), we could entrust all our cares and petitions to her (catechism 2677), give ourselves over to her now (catechism 2677), we need to pray to her (2679), have devotion to her (971), she was taken up body and soul into the glory of heaven (catechism 974), we need to be looking to Mary (972), in her, the church is holy (867), and in paradise the Church gathers around Jesus and Mary (catechism 1053)."

Here's the $64,000 dollar question: *"Has the Roman Catholic Church exceeded the scope with its teaching about Mary?"*

After reading all those quotes, I'm sure you agree the answer is, "absolutely"! But again, whenever a Christian starts to bring this stuff out, Catholicism will obfuscate the truth by saying something like, "Oh no, you misunderstand. That's not really what we're doing. We don't worship Mary." Really? Well you might want to take that up with some of your leaders whose title rhymes with "popes." That's right, the popes have been worshiping Mary. Let's take a look at Pope John Paul II. This has been going on a long, long time, but let me just give you some more modern-day proof.

"Pope John Paul II had a massive devotion to Mary."

And it was not just devotion. It was worship. By the way, what I'm quoting is secular information. This is not some anti-Catholic literature. This is just information in the news. The media doesn't think anything is wrong with it, so they print the truth about it. Listen to this:

"Pope John Paul II was well known for having a deep and abiding love for the Blessed Virgin Mary. His devotion to her was evident in all he did; his teaching, his prayer life, and even his papal motto and coat of arms were dedicated to the blessed mother. When he was nearly fatally shot during his papacy, he credited the intercession of the Virgin Mary and specifically Our Lady of Fatima."

What is Our Lady of Fatima? It's one of many such visions that appeared on the scene, out of the blue, and said it was the Virgin Mary. Of course, we know it was actually a familiar spirit, or in today's language, a demon. We'll get to all the Marian visions in the next chapter, but John Paul II said Mary, as Our Lady of Fatima, saved his life. He didn't say it was God or Jesus. He claimed it was Mary who saved his life. Here is more analysis of his devotion to Mary:

"How did he develop this lifelong devotion to Mary? In his book, Gift and Mystery, Pope John Paul II credited his home parish, the nearby Carmelites [An order of Marion brothers at Mount Carmel, founded in the 12th century], and also his father, who regularly took him out on pilgrimages to local Marian shrines."

Now let's stop there for a second. It says, "Marian Shrines." This is their terminology used for these shrines, which the Catholic Church has built all over the world. Yet Catholicism then says, "We don't worship Mary." Really? Well, someone paid a whole bunch of cash to build these Marion shrines. No! The Catholic Church built Marion shrines all over the Earth. Hey, what do you do at a shrine? You worship! So, Catholicism says they don't worship Mary, yet they build edifices, which are shrines, around the globe. By the nature of their terminology, they are building shrines to worship Mary. It's crazy that they actually do so but even more wild that they then try to deny that worship is worship. But let's continue:

"John Paul II was also influenced by another guy; Louis de Mountford who says, 'yes, Mary does bring us closer to Christ. She does lead us to him, providing that we live her mystery in Christ.' When John Paul II was elected pope, he chose his papal motto with words written by Louis de Mountford [to Mary]: 'I am all yours and all that I have is yours.'"

And this next one is really crazy. Listen to a direct quote from Louis de Mountford:

"There is no better way to advance quickly in holiness, no better way to please God, and no better way to guarantee one's present sanctity and eternal salvation, than with true devotion to Mary."

Whoa! Who is your God? Who are you worshiping there? In a nutshell, this is all just flat-out run-of-the-mill idolatry. That's all it is.

Well hey, I don't know about you but I'm certainly relieved that fortunately for the Catholic Church, it was only that one Pope who did this sort of thing. Oh wait, no, I'm wrong. Let's take a look at the current guy; Pope Francis. Of course, he's doing the same stuff, because it's a core thing in Catholicism. They worship Mary and that's called Mariology. Again, here is information from a recent secular article. Go check it out for yourself.

"Pope Francis heads across Rome to put the traditional crown on the statue of the Virgin Mary in the Piazza di Spagna for the Feast of the Immaculate Conception,"

What's the Immaculate Conception? Is that just the Virgin birth? No! It's the Catholic false teaching that Mary was immaculately conceived, which means she was supposedly conceived as a person without sin and continued sinless for her entire life. The Virgin Birth and the Immaculate Conception are not the same thing. Catholicism teaches a sinless Mary but what does Scripture tell us about that in Romans, Chapter 3? It says this:

"All have sinned and fall short of the glory of God."

So even Mary needed a savior and she says so herself. In the Bible, in what is called her "Magnificat", meaning her "statement", Mary says, *"My spirit rejoices in God my Savior!"* There it is. Even Mary, in her own words, admitted she needed a savior. Only those free of sin do not need a savior. She admitted she does and it's because of her sin. So that's what Pope Francis was doing when he placed a crown on that false teaching of Catholicism's represented by the statue of a supposedly sinless Mary. Now continuing on with Pope Francis:

"...in the Piazza di Spragna for the Feast of the immaculate Conception, as a reminder not only of his personal devotion to Mary, but a broad papal love affair across this century. Maintaining a tradition that began in 1953 where the column [Mary statue] of the Immaculate Conception, stands tall, Pope Francis, surrounded by thousands of locals and curious bystanders, will bless a crown of flowers that will be hung around the right arm of the image of the Virgin and a second flower arrangement, with the S.P.Q.R., that will be placed at the bottom of the statue."

Now from history, you may know that SPQR are the initials of the Latin expression; "Senatus Populus que Romanus", which dates back to the time of the Roman Empire. The English translation is, "the Roman Senate and the people." So, remember how we took the time to explore the history and found out where all this Roman Catholic stuff came from? It's not just from "Catholic", which is Latin for "universal", it's not only the "Catholic Church", or "Universal Church." What is their full name? It's the "Roman Catholic Church." Why? It's because the papacy with its false teachings and the entity that wants to have this universal church with all the world's religions coming together under them, started with Constantine who was a Roman Emperor. The Roman Catholic Church kicked off shortly after him. But it was his edict meant to bring all religions together as one under Rome's leadership. Shortly after that, Roman Catholicism grabbed control of the government.

So even sowed into their own words used to this day, you get hidden clues to what they're really all about, which is what Revelation 17 addresses with the prophesies of events to come. It's not just a Woman with a One World Religion. It's a Woman who rides the Beast. That beast is the One World Government. These guys want what they had but then lost at the Reformation. They want control of all religions and all governments on the planet and the Bible talks about how the last days will bring a revived Roman Empire that arrives back on the scene. Catholicism still wants what they had because they were birthed out of that Roman Empire. It's remains their focused motivation and is constantly promoted by Catholicism to this day. Here is more on Pope Francis and Mary:

"Francis' love affair with our lady is well documented from his yearly attendance to Argentina's massive pilgrimage to the Shrine of Our Lady of Lujan, patroness of the pope's country, when he is in Buenos Aires, to his regular visits to Rome's Basilica of St. Mary Major to venerate the famous icon of Our Lady..."

Notice that these places are all over the world. Pope Francis goes to all these places and worships there because these are worship shrines.

"Earlier this year he also made a politically charged trip to Mexico...delivering a strong appeal in favor of immigrants,"

Do you remember that one? Pope Francis chastised the United States for talking about building a wall on our southern border, yet anyone can quickly do an Internet search for "Vatican wall" and see that the Vatican has a massive wall surrounding them even while the Pope is making that statement about how the United States should have no walls. Do you know what they call that in the south? They would say he's a, "Hypo-Crite", or more carefully pronounced: a hypocrite. Let's move on:

"...delivering a strong appeal in favor of immigrants, he said, time and time again, he had to make the trip to visit Our Lady of Guadalupe,"

Our Lady of Guadalupe is another of their Marian shrines that happens to be in Mexico. Pope Francis talked about this particular shrine:

"'How could I not come?', Francis said...'Could the Successor of Peter, called from the far south of Latin America, deprive himself of seeing [the Virgin]?'"

"In 2013, soon after his election, he changed the already planned trip to Brazil, to participate in World Youth Day in Rio de Janeiro, to include a day-trip to the...Shrine of Our Lady of Aparecida."

"Francis has spoken about how his devotion to Mary has helped him through his election to the papacy, about praying the rosary three times a day, and he always

makes a point of stopping and even presenting flowers at the feet of Our Lady when he's in St. Peter's Square or whenever he celebrates Mass during his trips abroad."

So, wherever he goes, he puts in the effort to visit Marian shrines so he can worship Mary in them. But oh, no, Catholics don't worship Mary. Really? Again, Catholics might want to tell that to their leaders.

"During Pope Francis' papal visit to Poland last July, he tripped and almost fell while celebrating the Mass at the Jasna Gora monastery, in Czestochowa. Speaking to journalists on the flight back, he said he was simply 'looking at the Madonna, and I forgot about the step.'"

Yeah, this stuff is hazardous to your health! Now remember, this is a secular article and I couldn't believe this part of it:

"Pope Francis even gave up TV in 1990 because of a promise he made to the Virgin of Carmel."

So, if he made her a promise, does that mean he talks to her/it? Yes, he does!

"The pope's devotion to the Mother of God wasn't always as strong as it is now,"

This level of admiration makes you wonder how Francis began on his path to Mary worship. Here's a quote from Pope Francis:

"If I remember well, it was 1985. One evening I went to recite the holy Rosary that was being led by the Holy Father [Pope John Paul II]. He was in front of everybody, on his knees...I got lost in prayer."

Can I translate that for you? Pope Francis was listening to Pope John Paul II recite the rosary while Francis was humming, moaning along, and flipping through those rosary beads. In Hinduism, when Hindus go into those prolonged mindless chanting sessions, they often get into an altered state of consciousness. So, Francis did most likely get "lost" during his prayer. Let's continue with that altered-state experience that Pope Francis recounts:

"I got lost in prayer...I felt that [Pope John Paul II], chosen to lead the [Catholic] Church, was following a path back to his mother in the sky... From that moment, I recite the fifteen mysteries of the Rosary, every day."

Wow, what was probably his state of mind there?! I mean, there can be serious demonically influenced consequences when you get yourself into an altered state of consciousness. That's just bizarre! But what is monumentally worse is that he claims to practice this mindless bead rubbing, reciting, moaning, and groaning, every day!! That's crazy! But remember, to Catholics, that stuff is all part of their Catholic penance that is performed to supposedly work off their sins. Again, we know from earlier in this study and from other parts of our larger study, like *New Age*, that this sort of mindless recitation is the recipe to enter into an altered state of consciousness in order to communicate with familiar spirits, which are demons. So, Pope Francis is not only trusting in that dangerous practice, but listen to what he said through an interpreter about the cross of Christ, which we know is the only way to get to Heaven:

"I'm going to tell you something private. In my pocket, I always carry two things: The rosary to pray and something, which seems odd. This here, this item is the history of God's failure. It's the way of the Cross."

God's what?! His failure? Pope Francis goes on to say that those things in his pocket are where he places his hope. So, his blessed hope is flipping through his beads and dwelling on the failures of Christ. He always carries them in his pocket to remind him of the rosary.

At this point, I just have to say it one more time: "And now for the Christian perspective!" And we still have a few chapters left but by now, as Christians, I hope that when we hear our fellow brothers and sisters in Christ say something about how Catholics and Christians are similar and all part of the same Christian community, that we would take hold of that ill-informed Christian and in a Biblically profound way, "lay hands on them." Not literally of course, and the correction should not be out of fleshly anger. Catholicism is so diametrically opposed to everything we Christians live in our faith. Even their top leader today, Pope Francis, says that the cross is God's greatest failure. I'm not saying this. They are! You too can find this information right there in the news. It's unbelievable!

Now the interesting question this brings up is this: Where do they get the whole Mary-worship thing? Catholicism is bad enough with all this other stuff from their sources of authority that are outside the Christian Bible, but where does this Mary worship come from? Well, they get it from two things. One is from that same authority issue, which, as we've seen, comes by following the teachings of man.

Secondly, as we'll get into in the next chapter, and this might sound harsh, but believe it or not, it's from demons. You saw in the article about how they mention Our Lady of Fatima. That is one of their demonic visions. Nowadays they actually derive a lot of their false teachings from this other alarming area of the authority for Catholicism. Remember, their authority comes from the popes and what they say, the church councils, their version of the Bible, which is not the same Bible as our Christian one, from all their church rulings, and from their supposed theologians, tradition, and many other things. But even after that whole long list, you can't leave out this one more extremely bizarre source of authority that they look to at the same level as Scripture. They literally get their source of authority from these demonic visions appearing around the world that Catholics say is the Virgin Mary. So, with the next chapter, we'll get into that aspect. Why do they worship Mary? Where did all this come from? How did it get started? Again, it was from the false teachings of man but also, believe it or not, from this demonic issue.

Chapter Ten

The Truth about Mary Worship

In the last chapter we started to explore Catholicism's Mary worship. They worship Mary from the Bible. Now Mary was a great godly woman and praise God, what an awesome privilege it was that she was tasked to give birth to the Messiah. But frankly, the Catholics have turned her into an idol.

In this chapter, we're going to dive deeper into that. We'll see that the popes have been in on this stuff just like so much we've already seen. Throughout this study, we've been quoting from Catholic teachings like the writings of the popes and the Catholic catechism. So, let me give you more of the smattering of claims and statements that Catholicism makes about the Biblical Mary. Again, frankly, these doctrines that have been laid down by Catholic leaders for their Catholic followers, literally turned the Biblical Mary into a very unbiblical idol. Then they proceeded to worship that idol. Here's a recap of the analysis we saw in the last chapter and it's important to repeat because of the severity of deviation from Scripture:

"The Catholic Church says that Mary is, 'the all holy ever Virgin Mother of God. She is our advocate, helper, benefactress, and mediatrix. She is the one who is full of grace. She's mother of God and our mother, the new Eve, and the seat of wisdom. She had no original sin. She never committed sin. She sits at the right hand of the Majesty on high. No man goes to Christ but by his mother, i.e., Mary. Mary is the one who crushed the head of the serpent. She is the one who delivers our souls from death, continues to bring us the gifts of eternal salvation, and she

is the one who made atonement for the sins of man. We can entrust all of our cares and petitions to her. We need to give ourselves over to her now, pray to her, and have devotion to her. Her body and soul were taken up into glory [heaven]. Looking to Mary is how the church is made holy and in paradise, the church gathers around Jesus and Mary."

Again, that was just an assortment of quotes and I didn't quote the sources since we listed those in the last chapter. This is not make-believe. This is what they have done to Jesus' mother from the Bible, Mary. The Catholic persona of Mary has become their centerpiece and we saw that includes more than just a small faction of Catholicism. Their leadership does it now and previous leadership has as well, for a long time into the past. Unfortunately, that is very true and we're going to see more of it in this chapter.

Catholicism promotes our devotion, not to Jesus, but to Mary. Let me give you a couple more quotes on that. This first one is from the Catholic catechism, 971:

"The liturgical feasts dedicated to the Mother of God and Marian prayer, such as the rosary, <u>is the epitome of the whole gospel</u>."

What?! So, the best representation of the whole Gospel is flipping through a string of Rosary beads while ripping off your prayers to Mary so that you can supposedly work off your own punishment for your sins? They are actually claiming that as the epitome of Christ's Gospel. And I'm just quoting right from their doctrine. Here is more analysis of Catholic doctrine:

"Catholicism says we need to entrust ourselves to Mary, we need to ask Mary to pray for us, and we need to pray specifically to Mary: 'Mary is the perfect prayer, a figure of the church. When we pray to her, we are gathering with her, adhering with her to the plan of the Father (catechism 2679).'"

What?! Never once does the Bible say to pray to Mary, let alone any other person who is dead! In fact, it says *<u>not</u>* to. In the next chapter we'll get into that dead issue more with the discussion of their saints. It's not just Mary that they pray to. Again, Mary is prayed to and deified, as this goes into:

"Mary, they say, is to be worshiped. Vatican Council II, page 420 says this: 'When she, Mary, is the subject of preaching and worship, she prompts the faithful to come to her son.'"

What was that teaching? What are good Catholics supposed to do? Make Mary the subject of preaching and worship. That is a direct quote. So, they can claim whatever they want, but in their own words, worship is what's going on there.

Catholicism give titles to Mary and a lot of them are titles that make it sound like she has the same qualities as God and Jesus. In fact, they have a very interesting title we're going to explore. They call her, "The Queen Over All Things", and literally call her a name directly from ancient history; "The Queen of Heaven." Of all the verbiage to use for Mary, Roman Catholicism chose "The Queen of Heaven", which was already in existence long before they latched onto it and most likely was already very well known to those Catholics who chose it. Unfortunately, most people don't recognize that term because they're not studying their Bible enough and certainly not the Old Testament. The Queen of Heaven is the same false female deity that Israel worshiped in the Old Testament and that caused God to let Israel know they were in big trouble because of it. Let's look at that in Jeremiah 7:16, and also answer the question of whether this passage even mentions Jesus' mother, Mary of the Bible. In this verse, God is speaking to Jeremiah and you tell me if God is not happy with their affinity to this Queen of Heaven entity:

"Do not pray for this people nor offer any plea or petition for them. Do not plead with me, for I will not listen to you."

Would you say that whomever God is talking about, they really messed up? Yes, and remember, he's talking about Israel. But why can't people even pray for these particular Israelis? God continues with this:

"Do you not see what they are doing in the towns of Judah and in the streets of Jerusalem? The children gather wood, the fathers light the fire, and the women knead the dough and make cakes of bread for the Queen of Heaven;"

That is the exact same title the Catholic Church has ascribed to Mary. Isn't that interesting?

"...for the Queen of Heaven; they pour out drink offerings to other gods to provoke me to anger. But am I the one they are provoking? declares the Lord. Are they not rather harming themselves, to their own shame? Therefore, this is what the Sovereign Lord says: My anger and my wrath will be poured out on this place, on man and beast, on the trees of the field, and on the fruit of the ground and it will burn and not be quenched."

Wow! What in the world is going on there? God tells them to not even intercede for these people because it's over. They pushed things over the edge so it's over and that's it. They are getting my wrath because I've had it with this behavior. What behavior? Well, it's their behavior toward their idol, this Queen of Heaven. What is the Queen of Heaven? As it occurs here in Jeremiah, it is referring to the Assyrian Babylonian goddess known as "Ishtar." Ishtar is actually where we got the word, "Easter."

"Ishtar, also called Ashtoreth or Astarte [depending on the translation], was thought to be the wife of the false god, Baal..."

You may know of Baal from Scripture. He was the god that the Israelites got seduced by.

"...Baal, also known as Moloch."

Who was Moloch? Moloch, or Baal, was basically a big ole huge statue that was hollow on the inside because they put flammable materials inside to start a fire and heat up the statue so much that the outstretched arms of Moloch would get flaming red hot. Then they would throw their live children into the arms of Moloch. It was a fertility rite. These pagans did so because they thought these child sacrifices were going to give them prosperity. That's what was going to ensure their pleasure, good living, and things of that nature. Can you believe that?! Can you imagine a society that would literally murder children for the sake of personal convenience? Of course, we can because it's happening today in abortion centers across our country and around the world. The Old Testament is coming alive, isn't it? And you wonder why God says, 'That's it! If you are going to worship these entities, I'm through with you!' And the Queen of Heaven is one of these entities they worshiped. God says, they are going to get His wrath for worshiping the Queen of Heaven. Let's continue:

"The motivation of women to worship Ashtoreth stemmed from her reputation as a fertility goddess, and as the bearing of children was greatly desired among women of that era, worship of this 'queen of heaven' was rampant among pagan civilizations."

Unfortunately, the Israelites got seduced into it as well. Here is another analysis of a reference to the Queen of Heaven, from the Bible:

"Jeremiah warns them that greater punishments await if they don't repent. They reply that they have no intentions of giving up their worship of idols, promising to continue pouring out these drink offerings to the queen of heaven, Ashtoreth, and even going so far as to credit her with the peace and prosperity they once enjoyed because of God's grace and mercy."

So, in other words, the pagan Queen of Heaven worshipers said, "No, we're not going to repent. We're going to keep on worshiping this thing even though you're trying to warn us. We won't stop." And that's why God said he was done with them. Let's continue with the analysis:

Now first of all, there is no queen of heaven. Did you know that? There's no queen of heaven, there's never been a queen of heaven, but there is a King of Heaven. There is the King of Kings and Lord of Lords. That's Jesus. He alone rules in Heaven. He does not share His rule, His throne, or His authority with anyone. The idea that Mary, the mother of Jesus, is this queen of heaven has no scriptural basis whatsoever. Instead, the idea of Mary as the queen of heaven stems from the proclamations of priests and popes of the Roman Catholic Church. Mary obviously was a godly young woman. She was blessed to be chosen to give birth to the Savior of the world, Jesus but she was not in any way divine. She was not sinless nor is she to be worshiped, revered, venerated, or prayed to.

In fact, if you look at the Scripture, when people are approached to receive worship, they decline. That's what you see in the Scripture with Peter and the Apostles. They refused to be worshiped. Paul and Barnabas had people say to them that they must be gods and those people even tried to make sacrifices to them. But Paul and Barnabas said, 'No, no, no! We're just men like you. What are you doing?' Even angels in the Scriptures refused to be worshiped. What's the typical phrase in the Scripture that angels and men replied with when other men tried to worship either one of them? It was, 'Don't worship me. Worship

God.' So why is the Catholic Church telling us to worship Mary? That's completely unbiblical. Worship is to be reserved for God alone.

Now basically what has happened is that the Biblical Mary, who I'm sure was a wonderful godly woman and is now in heaven, has frankly been turned into one giant idol by the Catholic Church. So, let's take a look at what constitutes an idol and whether the Catholic Church is, in fact, guilty of turning Jesus' mother from the Bible into an idol and worshiping her as an idol.

First of all, the first two commandments say that you shall have no other gods, you shall worship only God, and you are told not to worship idols. In Exodus 20, the actual word there for, "worship" is the Hebrew word "shachah." It simply means to bow down, or prostrate oneself, before one who is your superior. You're basically bowing down before somebody who is superior to you. In fact, in Hinduism, it's their prevalent greeting, which is even popular in our culture these days. That is, "Namaste" [nuhm'-uh-stey]. Namaste means, "I bow before the god in you." What?! That greeting violates both of God's first two commandments. When you bow and say, Namaste, you are treating the other person as a god and making an idol out of them.

Again, worship, in Hebrew means that you bow down to a superior; prostrating yourself and giving them homage. Now let's take a look at that and see if it is what the Catholics have done, and are doing, to the Biblical Mary. First of all, the Bible not only prohibits us from worshiping idols, it gets specific by breaking it down to an itemized list about the subject. In 2 Chronicles 33, the Bible specifically says you shall have no altars dedicated to idols. And verse 15 says this:

"He also removed the foreign gods and the idol from the house of the Lord, as well as the altars, which he had built on the mountain of the House of the Lord and in Jerusalem and he threw them outside the city."

So, it wasn't just the idol itself. It was the altar built for and dedicated to the idol, along with the housing for it, the platform it stood upon, the flowers, and everything else connected to the idol. The Bible tells us to get rid of it all. It's not just idols. God doesn't even allow the altar for the idol. Well, what do we see with the Catholics when you go into their buildings and other structures? And again, they may say, "We don't worship Mary", but then why do they have these things all over the world that they have bought and paid for, called Marian

Shrines? They are shrines, so they have entire temples built all over the world to worship her.

And with those idols, what do you see when you go into a Catholic "Church" sanctuary? I hesitate to say the word, "church" because that's a Christian word, but when you go into their edifices, what do you see? You see statues of Mary and they are usually where in their "churches"? As a rule, they place their Mary idols in a prominent position and normally put them on a pedestal. They are right there in front of you so you can't miss them. It's an altar! And that's clearly a violation of Scripture.

Leviticus 26:1 says we are not to bow down to images:

"You shall not make for yourselves an idol or set up for yourselves an image or sacred pillar or place a sculpted stone in your land to bow down to it, for I am the Lord your God."

So, when you see a statue of Mary, it's probably best to turn and go the other way.

With Catholicism, you take a look all across the world and images of Mary are being elevated during feasts. Later we're going to look at the transcript of a video involving this Mary worship but oftentimes with these Mary statues, what are the Catholics doing toward these shrines and statues in their churches? They are bowing down to those sculpted stones that are in the likeness of Mary, which is a violation of Scripture. And regardless of a statue or shrine, you are not even to have an idol in your heart. Because again, that's worship, and worship is to be only for God.

Ezekiel 14:3: *"Son of man, these men have set up their idols in their hearts and put, right before their faces, the stumbling block of their iniquity."*

Again, what do you see with Mary? Are the statues present but Catholics aren't really into them? No, unfortunately they are all over the idols! These people are crying alligator tears while venerating the statues and shrines of Mary from their hearts. They really believe the idol they have made Mary into, is going to do what they ask it to do like getting them into Heaven. She (the idol) is going to intercede to Jesus, putting in a good word for them. The idol is going to be responsible for getting them the blessings they need. And they are deadly serious! They're doing it from the heart. But the Bible says we are NOT to venerate an idol from the heart. You're also not supposed to kiss an idol.

Hosea 13:2: *"Now they sin more and more and make for themselves molten images, idols skillfully made from their silver, all of them the work of craftsmen. People say to them, 'Let the men who offer human sacrifice, kiss the calves!'"*

Why does the Bible specifically say not to kiss the calves? It's because golden calves were unfortunately one of the idols they had made. So, with that Biblical directive in mind about not kissing idols, what do you see all over the Catholic world? Catholics not only bow down to the statues of Mary, they're not only weeping, wailing, and worshiping the idols from the heart, but also ceremonially, they kiss the statue, or idol's feet.

"There is no record found from the Vatican denouncing such a practice."

And the Bible says, 'Don't you dare do that!' Again, it's because that's an attitude of worship and homage being paid to an idol. The Bible also forbids the making of graven images. But of course, where can a cult make huge cash? They do it by selling idols. And again, as we're going to see in the next chapter, it's not just Mary. The Catholic Church makes all kinds of figurines. They do Jesus, Joseph, and many others. Then when you throw in their multitude of saints, it's a big ole list! They have a saint for everything. Catholicism seems to have a saint for anything you're dealing with or desire. They have a saint for corns on your feet. You think I'm joking but wait until you see the list! And it's all just a bunch of dead people. The Catholic Church wants me to buy their figurines and pray to dead people to fix things? Wow! It's crazy, folks.

But apparently a massive number of Catholic followers believe they can pray to so-and-so saint and that particular dead guy is going to bring you good luck, this other dead guy is going to cause it not to rain, or if you contact this other dead saint, he'll give you some money and that's important because you need to buy a bunch of those little graven images, sculpted stones, or sculpted plastic from the Catholic Church! But all that is happening there is the purchase of expensive trinkets to line the pockets of the Catholic Church and then in an attempt to talk to dead people. You can call it a figurine, says it's a fig tree, or label them Moe and Schmoe, but whatever you choose, it's still just an idol. If you pray to that thing, it's an idol. If you think that thing is going to give you good luck, it's an idol. Again, we'll get into the Catholic saints more in the next chapter but that's a quick idea of what the Catholic Church has set up for their followers with this massive money-making idol manufacturing operation.

With all that said, it starts to make sense about why they manipulated the Ten Commandments to create their revised version of it. What Catholicism did was actually <u>remove the second commandment</u>, and of course that was because they didn't like what that commandment talked about. What do you suppose it is about in the Christian Bible? It says, you shall have no idols! God knew this would be a pervasive issue throughout the ages so he made very clear that it was not to be done. But if Catholicism took out the second commandment, that would leave only nine, right? Does Catholicism's altered Bible have "The Nine Commandments?" Of course, they could not get away with that, so how did they get the number back to ten?

What they did was take the tenth commandment on coveting and turned that one into two separate commandments. So that way, they could still show a total of ten commandments. Now that's not only trickery, it's twisting the Scripture. But now you see why they had to do it. It's because they couldn't have the second commandment against worshiping idols, if everything they do is based on idol worship, including how they present Mary. The whole thing starts to fall apart. The Bible also warns against making male and female images in Deuteronomy 4:15-16:

"...be careful that you do not act corruptly and make an idol for yourselves of any form or shape, whether in the likeness of a male or female..."

Isaiah 44:17 talks about praying to idols: *"From the rest of it he makes a god, his graven image. He bows down before it and worships; he prays to it and says, 'Deliver me, for you are my God.'"*

Even with all these warnings from the Bible, what is Catholicism teaching? What are they telling you and I that we need to do? The Catholic Church not only wants you to pray to Mary, but to pray to her to get us to Heaven, forgive us of our sins, get us to the Father, and even outright delivers us. That's a direct violation of Scripture. At this point, you might be saying, "Come on! You can't be serious that Catholicism is pushing this kind of crazy doctrine. Maybe it's just a fringe group or maybe it's only factions of Catholicism in certain backwoods areas." Unfortunately, that is not the case. This stuff is mainstream in Catholicism today. If we're being honest about it, this false teaching is commonplace with the Roman Catholic leadership.

So, we're going to take a look at a bunch of different anti-biblical Catholic practices, even here in America and over in Israel. The video transcript to follow is of Catholics turning Mary into an idol. They are venerating, kissing, worshiping, and praying to her. This is an everyday Catholic practice today. It's not a fringe issue. Let's take a look at that from the transcript from a video and it starts with a reporter's introduction:

"Some people believe this is just a carving in a tree. Others believe that it's a miracle. It's a small carving in a tree, measuring about six inches in length, but now hundreds of people are coming by just to take a glimpse of the carving; a carving they believe is of the Virgin Mary."

Reporter interviews a local: *"Why do you believe?"*

Interpreter for Elba who is being interviewed by the reporter: *"She say that she feel it in her heart. She feels it inside that it is the Virgin of Guadalupe [Mary]."*

Reporter: *"Elba was the first to spot the carving Tuesday afternoon on her way to the store here on busy Bergenline Avenue in West New York, New Jersey. By nightfall, word began to spread and the faithful began to gather; so much so that police had to put up barricades and station several officers here. The site has become a sort of tourist attraction with pictures of the carving now being sold here."*

Reporter asks a young man named Gianni about his experience: *"The spiritual energy in that one carving of her, it's amazing."*

Reporter: *"Gianni and his mother Lillian are among the many also praying here. People here believe this carving resembles the Roman Catholic icon known as Our Lady of Guadalupe. Many in the crowd tell FOX 5 that they believe the carving also holds mystical powers."*

Another woman tells the reporter about her experience: *"Right now I'm having a lot of sensation or feelings and a lot of energies flowing through my body and when I touched her, it's like my fingers felt numb."*

Switching to a second news report: *"Believers are flocking to this Baton Rouge neighborhood to see a statue of Mother Mary with their own eyes."*

One man who came to see the Mary statue: *"The faith of all the people who are coming here is at stake."*

Reporter: *"You see everyone here believes the statue is bleeding. Hai Nguyen is the owner. His daughter translated for us and says he was doing lawn work when the unexpected happened."*

Hai's daughter: *"He looked up and he saw blood flowing down."*

Reporter: *"Blood [was] dripping from the side of Mary's face and the word spread quickly."*

Hai's daughter: *"He don't know how to explain it. He say he just known that maybe the God send a message through Mary."*

Reporter: *"One faithful says he has seen these manifestations before."*
Switching to a third news report: *"A possible miracle right in their living room; a family in northern Israel bought a statue of the Virgin Mary last year. Now they say the statue appears to be crying. Osama Corri, his wife, and children are Greek Orthodox. Some Muslim neighbors have seen the tears, as well. It started when Amir Corri recently noticed the statue was seemingly covered with oil. She says it even spoke to her telling her not to be afraid. Word of this has quickly spread. Some 2000 people of all faiths have come to see the statue in just the last week."*

So not just Catholics, but 2000 people from all faiths came to see that last one in just one week. And did you catch when they said that even the Muslim neighbors came to see it? Wow! Sounds like these Mary "appearances" are an idol. This is a woman figure that is custom made for all religions to gather around. What does that sound like? It's a foreshadow of Revolution 17 with the Woman that rides the Beast. And this extreme adoration and worship of Mary is going on today, and believe or not, that includes inside Israel.

I also want to point out that the second report supposedly shows bleeding from near the top of the Mary statue's head. But if you see the video, you can tell it's most likely not bleeding. It's called pigeon droppings. Give me a break; that wasn't blood. I'm sorry. It's just crazy. Again, notice what they were doing. People discover these supposed Mary-related appearances often from obscure images that loosely resemble Mary on things like tree bark, stains on the sidewalk, frost build up on a window, or whatever, and then the people leave flowers, money, or other adornment, and they burn candles. What did Jeremiah say the people were doing for the Queen of Heaven idol? They were presenting bread and cakes, pouring out drink offerings, and lighting the fire. It's the same stuff being repeated today, and the warnings are all there to see in the Scriptures.

Now I'll just give you one more and it's a direct quote from their Handbook called, *Today's Catholic*, and it's on page 31. According to Catholicism, Mary is preparing a home for you. But again, that claim is a direct violation of John 14. Here's the Catholic quote:

"This mother [Mary] is waiting and preparing your home for you."

Wow! So, the question is: Where in the world are they getting this Mary stuff? There are a couple different areas and again, this is a look at how to know if you're getting involved in a cult. Of course, you know it's a cult when a group's source of authority starts coming from places and people outside the Bible. And with Catholicism, even if you stick with their Bible, we saw that it's not even the same Bible as our Christian one. Their Ten Commandments aren't the same as the Christian commandments God gave Moses because Catholicism had to twist the Scripture to cover their idol worship.

For their source of authority, they put their trust in their version of the Bible, the teachings of the popes, and the rulings of their church councils, among other things. It boils down to the fact that they put their faith in the lap of man instead of the Word of God alone. Those are sure signs of a cult. So, the first reason why Catholicism is perpetrating this Mary centered idol worship, is because they are listening to the teachings of man. It stems from their doctrine built on the teachings of man. And in the next couple of chapters, we're going to see a whole bunch of other false teachings they follow because of their teachings from Catholic men.

And they don't just worship Mary. They have other examples of twisting Scripture concerning Mary like the false teaching they call the Immaculate Conception. As we saw before, that is not the same thing as the Virgin Birth. The

Immaculate Conception is their belief and teaching that Mary was without sin. Is that what the Bible says? No! Romans 3 says this:

"All have sinned and fall short of the glory of God."

That includes Mary. And in Luke 1:47, right after Elizabeth says Mary is blessed among women, Mary replies with this:

"My spirit rejoices in God my Savior."

If someone professes to need a savior, they need to be saved from sin so Mary herself even admitted that she was a sinner just like everybody else and she was in need of saving. That is just as Paul said in Romans 3:10 about there being no one righteous and for emphasis, not even one. Mary was someone, so that includes her. In fact, if Mary was sinless, then why was it, in Luke Chapter two, that after the birth of Jesus, they needed to go and offer a sacrifice for sin with the turtle doves, or pigeons? You can't get around it!

But again, why do we shake our heads and make that puzzled look when we hear this kooky stuff? It's because as Christians, we think everybody follows the Bible. We know if a doctrine is not Biblical, you don't put your faith in it. But of course, not all people believe in the Christian Bible like we do. And again, their bible is not even the same as the Christian Bible. That's problem number one. Number two; they follow the teachings of man. It's the same thing that happens when you try to witness to the Mormons who always say they believe in the Bible but when a Christian points out directly from the Bible about where they get it wrong, what do they do? They shift over to the sayings of the Book of Mormon, Joseph Smith, or the prophets. Those false teachings disagree with the Christian Bible. And it's the same thing that happens with Roman Catholics.

Catholicism has another false teaching called the "Perpetual Virginity of Mary." They claim she was not only sinless, which is heresy, but they also say she was a perpetual virgin which means she was supposedly a virgin for her whole life. Now I will agree that Matthew 1:25 tells us Joseph did not have sexual relations with Mary until after Jesus was born; hence the virgin birth. That is important to believe in but it's not what Catholicism teaches as far as their doctrine of the perpetual virginity of Mary. They say Mary was a virgin her whole life. Of course, the Bible says different. In Matthew 13:53-55, Jesus is preaching in His hometown so as you'd expect, local folks recognize Him. They know who He is and in fact, they know who His family is. Let's take a look at what they say about Jesus' family. Was He an only child? Of course not, as you'll see here starting with verse 53:

"When Jesus had finished these parables, He moved on from there and coming to his hometown, He began teaching the people in the synagogue and they were amazed. 'Where did this man get such wisdom and miraculous powers?' they asked. 'Is this not the carpenter's son [Joseph]? Isn't his mother's name, Mary, and aren't His brothers James, Joseph, Simon, and Judas?'"

What? I think we all realize you can't be a virgin if you have kids! It mentions four brothers while verse 56 adds even more siblings:

"Aren't all His sisters with us as well?"

Wow! "Sisters" is plural too. So, God obviously gave Joseph and Mary, after the virgin birth of Jesus, a whole slug of kids which is a blessing, according to God. Psalm 127:5 says, "How blessed is the man whose quiver is full of them." So, excuse me?! How in the world could you say that she was a perpetual virgin when it's clear from the Scripture that she had a whole bunch of other kids? It's absolute nonsense. How could you even go there? Again, when we Christians quote Scripture, they have to get around it by firing back with what pope so-and-so said or the words decreed by some Catholic council. But who cares what those guys said?! There's the central problem with cults. They don't stick with Scripture and that's why, today, we have so many different world religions, cults, and the occult. It's a source-of-authority issue.

Now I don't want to go into this next one too deeply, but Catholicism has what's called the Four Marian Dogmas. Those are their four important teachings about Mary. We just talked about the first two, which are the Perpetual Virginity and the Immaculate Conception. They also say Mary is the Mother of God. Now if you just stop and think about that, it's a logical absurdity. God by definition is Supreme. He's the Supreme Being. And what makes Him Supreme? It's the fact that He's all-powerful, everywhere present, all-knowing, and self-existent. Even a secular philosopher would have to admit that if there is a God, a Supreme Being, he has to fit those aspects. So, He has to be all-powerful because if somebody were more powerful than Him, He wouldn't be supreme so, by definition, He couldn't be God. He has to know everything because if He didn't, there would be a deficiency so then how could He be supreme, which means the one most high Lord of Lords.

And He's got to be everywhere. He can't be limited because if He's limited, someone would have something over on him, so to speak, so he couldn't be God. And He has to be self-existent. What does that mean? It means He's not dependent on anyone for his existence. That's why God is eternal. He always is. He's the same yesterday and the same forever. He's the alpha and the omega, which is the beginning and the end. He just is. When we get to Heaven, we'll find that it is in a state of eternity so there is no time. God is above and beyond time. He's self-existent.

Knowing all that then, in order for God to be born from someone as His mother, so that He even could be born, that would mean God would have a beginning point. But God can't have a beginning point, by definition. So how could Mary be the mother of God? It's ridiculous, right? Plus, if she's the mother of God, then that would make God dependent upon her for His existence so she would have to be God. She would then have to be eternal and all the rest that describes the one God. But again, it makes no sense to Christians, and it certainly isn't Biblical, but that's because Roman Catholicism isn't listening to the Scripture in this area just like so many other teachings of the Christian Bible.

Catholicism also claims that there was a "Bodily Assumption of Mary." That became official Catholic doctrine in 1950. Basically, they say that she did not die but instead was bodily taken into Heaven. Again, and by now this probably won't be a shocker for you, there's no Biblical evidence of it.

We've now, at length, discussed the question we asked: how in the world did they get this Mary worship? And by the way, can you imagine the real Mary in Heaven knowing what's going on and how Catholicism has twisted her story with this idol worship? But as we saw, the first way Catholicism developed Mary worship was from the **Teachings of Man**. The second reason it's developed in Catholicism is from, believe it or not, the **Visions of Demons**. Whoa!! That sounds pretty creepy, right? But unfortunately, these demonic visions are another big reason why Catholicism prescribes the worship of Mary. It's these so-called **Apparitions of Mary [Visions of Demons]**, that have been appearing all over the planet and they've been happening for quite some time.

Again, it's not just some fringe group in the Catholic Church or a non-authoritative minority, and it's not like Catholicism doesn't promote this stuff. Yes, they do! I'm going to quote from their information on the official apparitions that have been sanctioned by the Catholic Church. So, the Vatican has approved of and promoted these. What the Catholic visions of demons are, is when people have said that they see a vision of an actual apparition of Mary and this apparition speaks to them. What do you suppose these apparitions normally advocate for? It, of course, wants people to worship it and claims to be the provider of salvation for humans. Let me give a couple of examples:

In 1531 at Guadalupe, Mexico, there was an appearance to a guy named Juan Diego. This is what the apparition said to him:

"Know, know for sure my dearest, littlest, and youngest son, that I am the perfect and ever Virgin Holy Mary...I am truly your merciful mother, yours and all the people...my lovers, who love me, those who seek me, those who trust in me. Here I will hear their weeping, their complaints and heal all their sorrows, hardships, and suffering...Am I not here, I, who am your Mother? Are you not under my shadow of protection? Am I not the source of your joy? Are you not in the hollow of my mantle, in the crossing of my arms? Do you need anything more?"

This entity thing claims that it, "Mary", takes care of us! What?! That isn't Mary! But this is from the Catholic Church's officially sanctioned [accepted, approved, confirmed] apparitions.

Another of the more prominent apparitions was in 1858 at Lourdes, France. A young girl named Bernadette Soubirous claimed to have seen Mary several times in a <u>cave</u>. Folks, there it is again! It was in a cave. Turn to someone and say, "Don't go into caves!!" We have seen this so many times with corrupted and false doctrines, including Islam. That's the same place it started for the Muslims. Muhammad went into a cave and had an encounter with an entity there. So, stay out of caves and out of dark places. Now back to the young girl. Several times she supposedly went into a cave and saw Mary. The apparition told her this:

"Kiss the ground as a penance for sinners", and "I am the Immaculate Conception."

In 1917 there was another prominent apparition and it is arguably the most famous one. But again, it's not the only one because there are tons of them. This was the Fátima apparition of "Mary" that happened in Portugal Spain. Fatima was a hundred years ago last year so of course Pope Francis did some interesting ritual stuff on the hundredth anniversary and we'll get to that, but first, here's the story about what happened back then:

"In 1917, three children, Jacinta Marto, Lucia Santos, and Francisco Marto said that an apparition of Mary appeared to them that was brighter than the sun. And here's what the apparition said, amongst other things: 'Are you willing to offer yourselves to God to bear all the sufferings he wants to send you as an act of reparation for the sins, by which he's offended?'"

What?! So, you suffer to pay off your sins? No! The Fatima apparition continues:

"Establish the devotion to my Immaculate Heart throughout the world [Remember, this is supposed to be Mary]. I promise salvation to whoever embraces it. These souls will be dear to God like flowers put by me to adorn his throne."

But you may think this stuff was just happening way back then and Catholics don't do it today. Well, listen to this one from March of 2008 and it's an actual article out of India so I'm not making this up.

The headline: *"Fifty people go blind after staring at the sun trying to see the Virgin Mary."*

The report: *"At least fifty people in the Kottayam district have reportedly lost their vision after gazing at the sun looking for an image of the Virgin Mary. Though alarmed health authorities have installed a signboard to counter the rumor that a solar image of the Virgin Mary appeared to the believers, curious onlookers, including foreign travelers, have been thronging to the venue of the miracle."*

So, in our world today, if word gets out that some tomato sauce stain or a piece of split wood looks like Mary, people will get to it as they did to this sun apparition. The description of that event continues:

"St. Joseph's ENT and Eye Hospital in Kanjirappally alone has recorded 48 cases of vision loss due to the photochemical burns on the retina...The damages to the macula, the most sensitive part of the retina. They have developed burns after continually gazing at the sun...When the doctors found a pattern in the case sheets, they reported it to the district medical officer."

In other words, people kept coming in with fried eyes and they started to wonder what was going on.

"The health department has now put up a signboard at the hotelier house near Erumeli, where the divine image is said to have appeared, warning people about exposing their eyes to the sunlight...The hotelier, who has since moved to another house, had claimed that statues of Mother Mary in his house have been crying honey and bleeding oil and perfumes."

Now, I guess there's a certain element of bravery in that. For me personally, if some of the artwork in my house started bleeding, I'm going to scream and run. Or I would probably try to stomp on it and then attempt to burn it. You've got to be kidding me!

"Though people have been flocking to the blessed land—hastily christened Rosa Mystica Mountain—the mad rush for the image in the sky, began a week ago. There are quite a few people still seeking the miracle, despite the experiences of their unfortunate predecessors and strict health warnings against gazing at the sun with the naked eye...They are mostly girls in the 12 to 26 age group. The youngest, of course is 12 and the oldest is 60. Most of them were looking at the sun between 2 and 4 p.m., when the UV rays are at their worst."

This is still happening in our time. There are people all over the Earth who are getting all worked up over this silly stuff. Why would they do something like that? It's because they're worshiping Mary, which is really an entity. And they're not worshiping Jesus. It's a seduction by false teaching from Catholicism in conjunction with this the so-called Queen of Heaven and followers are worked up even to the point of frying their eyeballs. How sad that is! How tragic is it that people are being led astray, and I'm going to bring this up again because it can't be said enough: How appalling is it that our television media are repeatedly saying, "And now for the Christian perspective", as they bring up a Catholic priest to talk about Christianity. Talk about fried eyeballs; it fries your eyeballs when you see that on TV, or at least it does mine. Here are some other apparitions the Catholic Church puts their stamp of approval on to testify that these events really happened and that it was from the Biblical Mary:

"Guadalupe, Mexico; Poland, 1578; Lithuania, 1608; France, 1664; France, 1830; Italy, 1842; France, 1846; France, 1858; Wisconsin, here in the United States in 1859; Czech Republic, 1866; France, 1871; Poland, 1877; Ireland, 1879; Portugal, in 1917, was Fatima; Belgium, 1932; Belgium, 1933; and even Rwanda, in 1981, where this so-called vision of Mary appeared to several children reminding them of the efficacy of fasting and of prayer, especially the reciting of the rosary."

So, the apparition was promoting the rosary. These events are still going on and notice that's it's happening in multiple countries around the world. The apparitions are a global event. Well then, what is this apparition, or entity, because we know it's not Mary? The answer rhymes with, "demon." Yes, it's a demon, or demons. That's exactly what it is. Now how did I come up with that idea? People would argue: "You Christians blame everything you disagree with on the devil or demons." But no, it's not Christians saying it. It's what the Bible says.

First of all, in Luke 16, Jesus tells us that when a person dies, there is a great chasm fixed. He specifically states that people can't cross over, or go back and forth, so when you die as a Christian, you go to Heaven and if you're not a Christian, you go to Hell, and you do not come back. I'm sure that Mary was a godly woman and a Christian so when she died, where did she most likely go? In 2 Corinthians 5:8, the Bible says, "To be absent from the body is to be present with the Lord." Contrary to the false teachings of Catholicism, there is no place called, "Purgatory." We saw many times that purgatory is a lie. Christians go straight to be with Jesus and aren't you glad that when you get to Heaven, you don't come back? You can't get kicked out. Praise God! That's a blessing, right? Then where has Mary been for approximately 2000 years on our time scale? She's in Heaven and she's not coming back.

Then what are these apparitions? I'm not discounting that people are seeing and hearing something, or even that these apparitions are speaking to people. But what's the Bible say? In 2 Corinthians 11:14, the Bible says that Satan can masquerade as an angel of light. In the Old Testament, Scripture actually has a name for this type of masquerading entity, they are called, "Familiar Spirits." And that's what God says in Deuteronomy 18:9:

"When you enter the land that the Lord your God has given you, do not learn to imitate the detestable ways of the nations there. Let no one be found among you who sacrifices a son or daughter in the fire..."

What is that in reference to? It's the pagan god we described earlier in this chapter; Moloch. God says, 'How dare you murder your own children for the sake of your personal well-being!' Here is the rest of that from Deuteronomy:

"...who Sacrifices a son or daughter in the fire, practices divination or sorcery, interprets omens, engages in witchcraft, casts spells, or who is a medium or spiritess."

For that last word, some translations say, "familiar spirit", instead of "spiritess." The word, "familiar", in Latin is "familiaris." It means a "household servant", and that's the basis of the occult's whole belief. These people believe they are conjuring up sorcerers and witches. You may have heard my testimony about a girl at a party where I was who drew a pentagram to conjure up demons. This really happened to me, so I know it's not make-believe; of course, besides the fact that the Bible mentions it, these things really do come out. But what occultists believe is that when you use certain techniques, what comes out of it is contact with familiar spirits. In other words; they are a sort of household servant supposedly there to serve you. The idea is that you conjure them up and bind them by your words and rituals. Occultists have many different practices used to do that, but the familiar spirits are supposedly bound to do what you want them to do. They're your household servants, or familiar spirits. They're there to do what you say whether it is to give you information, to go put a curse on someone for you, or do whatever else you say.

Well, that's a lie! There's one and only one who controls the demons and of course that's Jesus Christ. Now, praise God we have the strongest weapon possible if you ever have a demon show up in your house or you're experiencing demonic warfare. And yes folks, demonic warfare still happens today. For example, what are witches doing on a worldwide basis right now? They are using demonic warfare as they pray against President Trump. This is real stuff happening in our day.

So, if you do encounter this issue, what do you do? The privilege of being a Christian is that you can command, in the name and authority of Jesus Christ [because it's not from us], for a familiar spirit, or demon, to leave. With that, they must cower, obey, and flee. There is something about the name of Jesus Christ and praise God, that's a privilege we Christians have. But these occult people think demons are familiar spirits, or household servants that exist to serve them. However, God says not to mess with that because this contact with you from demons is a way that you are going to be duped. God says that anyone who practices this stuff, and unfortunately Israel was even doing this to the point of appealing to Moloch with the sacrificial burning of their own children, is detestable to the Lord. God told the Israelites that they must not do these things in the promised land that He gave them.

Here's another interesting aspect of these visions of demons:

"Some other avenues, through which demons, or familiar spirits, can gain entrance into a person's life, is through divination [Again, that's where you do the rituals to conjure up a demon.], transcendental meditation [where you get yourself into an altered state of consciousness], visualization [which is another way to get into an altered state of consciousness], necromancy [communication with the dead], witchcraft, drugs, and alcohol."

Why are drugs and alcohol included? It's because those are mind-altering substances that get you more easily into an altered state of consciousness.

"These are all activities that believers are exhorted to avoid; when you look at the Scripture."

Let me add another to this list: the apparitions of the supposed Virgin Mary will also get you connected with a familiar spirit [which is a demon]. These Marian apparitions that the Catholic Church endorses, are not the Virgin Mary. It's a familiar spirit that is appearing, acting like Mary, and giving the impression of Mary but the demon is only masquerading as her. It is a demon that is leading people astray. Now why would these familiar spirits appear all of a sudden while you're in a cave? Well, when they were by themselves, what were these people often doing in a cave or other isolated place? What's a practice in the Roman Catholic Church? It is to rub beads and mindlessly chant. It's the same thing we found with the mantras in Hinduism and Buddhism. The Hindus and Buddhists perform repetitive movements and repetitive speech to the point where it becomes mindless so that they are susceptible to shifting into an altered state of consciousness. It's a form of self-hypnosis.

So even in the very practices of Catholicism and similar to aspects of Eastern religions, people are going to these sacred places and even caves, flipping through beads, and reciting the same words over and over. And the next thing you know, an entity appears. It's a setup. That's what is going on there. Again, it is <u>not</u> Mary. Oh, and by the way, the Bible's book of Job is replete with testimony about the finality of those leaving the body at the point of death. He calls it the "place of no return." Over and over again, Job tells us that when you die, you go to the place of no return. You do not come back from there!

Catholics really believe all these demon apparitions are Mary from the Bible, and of course, demons, or familiar spirits, are more than happy to go right along with the deception because it leads to the worship they are seeking anyway. A demon is thinking, "Yes, that's right! You need to worship me; 'Mary', because I'm the one who's going to get you to Heaven. Now build me a shrine, kiss my feet, and bring me some incense and flowers." And yes, the apparitions are actually decreeing that Catholics need to build these Marian shrines all over the world in worship of the apparitions.

So, it's not just the false teachings of man. Catholics are listening to the visions and teachings literally coming from demons. And do you remember 1 Timothy 4:1? As it talks about, and what's interesting with this stuff, is that Paul tells us about the last days and how people are not only going to turn aside from the truth, they are also going to listen to the doctrines of demons. It specifically uses that word, demon. Could you say that's true of what's going on with these apparitions? Absolutely! But again, is this all just a fringe group of Catholics? No, it isn't. The popes really line up directly behind these demonic apparitions.

In fact, Pope Francis remembered the apparition of Fatima. It started when the apparition happened in 1917 and of course in 2017 completed 100 years since. Here was a recent article:

"Pope Francis, on Wednesday, recalled that this year marks the Centuri of the Apparitions of Fátima. Speaking to German pilgrims during his general audience, the Holy Father said, 'Let us entrust ourselves to Mary.'"

What?! Is that what the Christian Bible says to do? This is a direct quote and just happened in 2017. Francis continues:

"Let us entrust ourselves to Mary, Mother of Hope, who invites us to turn our gaze toward salvation, towards a new world and a new humanity."

Yeah, that new world is called the Antichrist kingdom with a Woman riding the Beast. But you certainly don't want to trust in or be any part of it. It's better known as the Seven Year Tribulation. From it, you need to run!! That's exactly what Pope Francis is talking about and the article goes on with this:

"Last December, the Vatican confirmed that Pope Francis will go on a pilgrimage to the Sanctuary of Our Lady of Fatima on the 12th and 13th May of [2017]."

In 2017, Pope Francis went to visit that Fatima shrine in Portugal just as we saw in the last chapter about how he has been visiting many of these apparition shrines. He's been rolling through Mary's shrines, big time. And in fact, Pope Francis didn't just say, 'Let us entrust ourselves to Mary', he performed a ritual in front of a crowd of over 100,000 people, outside the Vatican where he entrusted the world to this image of Fatima, which is a demonic apparition. I have video from this time with Pope Francis leading the ritual. You can find it on the Internet and after you watch, you tell me if Catholicism doesn't really worship idols and Mary, even from the top of their leadership and right on down. The video is from the Catholic News Service and opens with a crowd waving at the statue of Mary as it is carried through the huge gathering. Then Pope Francis is seen doing his incense spreading and toe-kissing stuff around the large statue of Mary. The closed caption on the video reads,

"Pope Francis presided over a prayer vigil for a special Marian day organized for the year of faith, Saturday, October 12th. On Sunday, the Pope formally entrusted the world to Our Lady of Fatima, before a crowd of over 100,000."

That's on their own Catholic news channel. But, no, they don't worship Mary, right? You can hear it now: 'What are you Protestants? Are you a bunch of whackos? You Protestants don't know anything.' And the statue of Mary in this video wasn't just an idol mounted somewhere around the Vatican. They were carrying this idol of Mary through the crowd on their shoulders and when they put it down at the front of the crowd, it was on an altar. Then Francis paid homage to the idol, which was surrounded by flowers and other things. Then Pope Francis got out the bug-smoke censer thing and whirled it in the air to get rid of the mosquitoes, or whatever he was doing. I guess he got tired of swatting at them. No, actually that's a container for burning incense. But why is Francis really using incense? It's for worship! So, there it is again! I'm not making this up like some conspiracy theory. Remember last chapter when we learned about what he carries with him in his pockets everywhere he goes? He's always got that rosary thing he rubs his fingers on while humming out that repetitive wording. How many times a day did he say he does that? And if he keeps getting into a mindless state...I don't know but it starts to add up.

But again, I may have sounded harsh to you the first time I mentioned how it bothers me so much when I see our media introducing a priest or bishop by saying, "And now for the Christian view..." You know, you hope it's righteous indignation and not the flesh but I hope you're starting to understand, not just how the media is duping people into thinking that Catholicism is Christianity, which of course, it is not at all, but when you hear other so-called Christians argue with us about that, it just blows me away! And that's because we Christians are supposed to be the ones who know the truth and lead people, including Catholics, away from the false teachings. This is serious stuff and that's why we're doing this study. Among other things in the next chapter, we're going to get into another unfortunate false teaching from Catholicism and that is what's called, Saint Worship.

Chapter Eleven

Catholicism & Saints

It's not just Mary they worship, pray to, and expect the blessings from. They also expect to get that from the dead people they call saints. The idea is that these dead people are deemed to have been super-amazing religious people during their time on Earth. After their death and over time, at a Catholic leadership meeting, the Catholics decide this super-amazing Catholic person, who is long dead, will now be designated as a saint. And because they are now a saint, you can start praying to this newly added super-amazing dead guy and he will get you all kinds of cool stuff. And at about that time, the Catholic Church normally manufactured a huge number of new trinket figurine things that look just like their new saint and it's can be yours for just $19.95!

Now I know you think I'm joking, but, in a nutshell, that's really what is going on there. Unfortunately, it's another moneymaking venture for the Catholic Church that is already extremely wealthy. To be honest with you, I really think it's the wealthiest institution on the planet. We saw that in a previous chapter, so I won't go there again.

We'll get more into why we certainly shouldn't pray to dead people but before that, it's important to understand that Catholicism's whole premise, with their version of saints, is completely wrong. In four different ways, the Bible actually does use the term "saint." However, that is <u>not</u> a dead person being called a saint by the Catholic Church because they died and is later deemed to have been a super duper Catholic.

In Scripture, saints are the "people of God." There are four different kinds of saints but with all of them, the Bible is talking about the people of God. Whoever belongs to God, is a saint. Let me give a couple of examples. Psalm 106:16 is about Old Testament saints:

"They envied Moses also in the camp, and Aaron the saint of the Lord."

Aaron is an Old Testament saint. You and I as Christians are New Testament saints. Everyone who is born again, is a saint. Philippians 4:21 is just one example:

"Solute every saint in Christ Jesus" Paul says, "the brethren which are with me greet you also."

Who is Paul talking about? It's a Christians whom he calls New Testament saints. There's also what is called a "tribulation saint." Revelation 13:7 says this:

"He [the Antichrist] was given power to make war against the saints."

Who is John talking about? It's not the Church. The tribulation saints are the people who get saved during the Seven Year Tribulation. Then the fourth example is the millennial saints who are those that will still be in their natural bodies during the thousand-year Millennial Kingdom of Christ. It's not the Church because the Church is taken up at the Rapture, which is prior to the Seven Year Tribulation. Christians in the Church, at that time, will get resurrected bodies. Revelation 20:4 goes on to talk about the tribulation saints who were murdered after the Rapture:

"They [the tribulation saints] come to life and reign with Christ for a thousand years."

These tribulation saints get to be a part of the Millennial Kingdom along with the people that somehow survived the Seven Year Tribulation with their natural bodies. Also going into the Millennial Kingdom, will be the Jewish elect.

So, the Bible talks about four different kinds of saints. They are Old Testament saints, New Testament saints, tribulation saints, and millennial saints. As a side note, this information is important to know when people want to say that the Church is going to go through the Seven Year Tribulation just because the word "saint" is used for those who will be in the Tribulation. But that doesn't mean it's those saints who make up the Church. In fact, contextually, it's not the Church.

Now with all that background on saints, are saints what the Catholic Church portrays? Are we supposed to wait for the Vatican to decide that someone deserves that label? No! Anyone who belongs to the people of God is a saint. In fact, saint is the Hebrew "kadosh", which simply means "a sacred holy one, or saint." And it's the same in Greek where the name is "hagios", which is "a most holy one, or saint."

So, whether it is in the Old Testament or New Testament, in Hebrew or Greek, a saint simply refers to the people of God. That leads us to the conclusion that the whole saint aspect of Catholicism is bogus so right there we can just dismiss the Catholic version of saints. It's not even Biblical! Their whole portrayal of saints is wrong! But beyond how they wrongly define a saint, let's go ahead and play their little game to see if what they do with their version of a saint is even right. And the spoiler, as you expected, is "no." Even what they do with their version of a saint is wrong! Here's some analysis of that:

"Is prayer to saints [dead people] and Mary [she also died] Biblical? No. It is the official position of the Roman Catholic Church that Catholics do not pray to saints or Mary, but rather that Catholics can ask saints or Mary to pray for them."

All that is just double-talk, which is also apparent in the very next statement:

"The official position of the Roman Catholic Church is that asking Saints for their prayers is no different than asking someone here on Earth to pray for us."

Well, wait a second. On the one hand you say you don't pray "to" saints and Mary but in the next sentence you say your official position is that you're asking the saints and Mary to intercede for you. The last time I checked, that's praying "to" them. So, Catholicism's obfuscation of the truth here is just double-speak. Yes, they do pray to the saints and Mary! We're going to see that is abundantly clear. It's the same as we saw in the last chapter where they say, "Oh, we don't worship Mary." We learned how ridiculous that lie is and now it's the same thing with this statement: "Oh, we don't worship saints. We only talk to them." Come on! Besides Mary, you worship the saints too and we're going to take a look at that.

"The point is [praying to Mary or the saints] has no Biblical basis whatsoever. The Bible nowhere instructs us as Christians to pray to anyone other than God. The Bible nowhere encourages or even mentions believers asking individuals in Heaven for their prayers, yet, the Catholics view Mary and the saints as intercessors before God. They believe that a saint has more direct access to God than we do. Therefore, a saint delivers a prayer to God and it's more effective than us praying to God directly."

What?! What are you talking about? It is the same thing they do here on Earth. Catholicism tells you that you can't go all by yourself and just ask God for forgiveness. According to them, what do we need to do? You have to go to this super-duper spiritual person, the priest. Then you must confess to the priest and only the priest can make it right. No! That's not what the Bible says. Hebrews 4:16 tells us that we believers here on earth can "approach the throne of grace with confidence." Praise God, we individually, through Jesus Christ, can go directly to God! We are to communicate directly to God. We have direct access to God, so we don't need any man on earth and especially not a dead man, or woman. Besides all that, these dead people, if they weren't trusting in Christ alone for their salvation, are in Hell. You don't want to pray to a dead person and you certainly don't want to pray to a dead guy in Hell. That just seems like common sense. Wow!

First Timothy 2:5 says there is one God and <u>one mediator</u> between God and man and that is...Mary. Oh, I'm sorry. I meant to say it's all these saints. No! It's Jesus Christ! What is Catholicism even talking about with this stuff! Why would we go to anyone else? But that's what they claim. Catholics use these supposed saints and supposedly Mary to supposedly intercede on their behalf. What do you call that? By definition it's a mediator! But according to the Bible, the only mediator is Jesus. How could they sit there, do that, and promote that? Now if you want to talk about intercession, what do the Scriptures say? Here is some analysis of what real Biblical intercession is:

"Jesus is the only mediator, which indicates Mary and the Saints cannot be mediators."

They cannot mediate our prayer requests to God. Further, the Bible tells us that Jesus is interceding for us before the father. Here is Hebrews 7:25:

"Therefore, Jesus is able to save completely those who come to God through Him [Why?] because he always lives to intercede for them."

So, who is it that is interceding for us? It's Jesus and I like how this author puts it about what the Scriptures tell us on this subject:

"With Jesus himself interceding for us, why would we need Mary or the saints to intercede for us and whom would God listen to more closely than his own son?"

But see, that's Catholicism's problem because that's how much they have elevated Mary and the saints, but especially Mary, as we saw before. Roman Catholicism is now calling Mary the "Co-Redemtrix." With that profoundly false doctrine, they teach that we must go through Mary to be saved by her putting a good word in with Jesus. And if that's not blasphemous enough, Catholicism says it is only because Jesus loves Mary, that Jesus will relent and allow us into Heaven. That's their false teaching!

Not only that but listen to this: Romans 8:26-27 describes the Holy Spirit interceding for us. So now you have the second and third members of the Trinity interceding for us before the Father, which is the first person of the Trinity in Heaven. Why would you need dead people to intercede for you, as if they even could? Why would you even go there? It makes zero sense! Yet Catholics argue that praying to Mary and the saints is no different than asking somebody here on Earth to pray for them. So, let's examine that. Number one: The Apostle Paul asked other Christians to pray for him in Ephesians Chapter 6.

So, the Bible does talk about interceding but it's about living Christians, who do the interceding for other living Christians, which makes perfect sense.

Many Scriptures also describe believers praying for one another, like 2 Corinthians 1, Ephesians 1, Philippians 1, and 2 Timothy 1. The Bible nowhere mentions anyone asking someone in Heaven [that of course assumes these Catholic saints are even in Heaven] to pray for them. The Bible nowhere describes anyone in Heaven praying for anyone on Earth.

That said, here's what Catholicism does: They bring up Revelation 5:8. So be prepared for that and let me quote it for you:

"And when he had taken the book, the four living creatures and the twenty-four elders fell down before the Lamb. Each having a harp and golden bowls full of incense, which are the prayers of the saints."

So that it! That's all they have. Does it sound to you like absolute proof we need to pray to dead people so they, in turn, can pray to God with some supposed supercharged prayer? See, according to Catholicism, if you can connect with the appropriate saint for your condition or whatever you're going through [We'll get to the massive assortment of saints in a minute] it's like turbo-charging your prayer. Apparently, that's what this process created by the Catholic Church does. According to them, the church-designated saints can send turbocharged prayers that really get through to God! And Revelation 5:8 is supposedly their big proof for that false doctrine so let's read it one more time:

"And when he had taken the book, the four living creatures in the twenty-four elders fell down before the lamb. Each having a harp and golden bowls full of incense, which are the prayers of the saints."

Again, that is their justification for teaching how it's perfectly fine to attempt contact with dead people by praying to them and asking them to pray for you so they can kick in the turbo by putting in a positive word for you. But that's not what the verse says. Let's more closely examine Revelation 5:8.

I'll grant that I believe the 24 elders mentioned there is the Church that is in Heaven after the Rapture. However, all it says is that they have bowls full of incense, which are the prayers of the saints back on Earth. That's it. That's all it says. Now, what it did ***not*** say is that the 24 elders [the Church] then turned around, dug into those bowls, rifled through all the prayers, and then communicated those prayers back to God. Did it say that? No, it didn't say any of that. It didn't say anything they may have done with the prayers. All it said was that the elders were holding these bowls containing the prayers of the saints that were back on Earth. It also didn't say the saints on Earth prayed those prayers to the 24 elders [the Church]. It just said the elders were sitting there holding bowls full of incense, which is symbolic of the saint's prayers. Again, that's it! The saints, who are Christians living on Earth, did not pray to the 24 elders, who are the Church-age Christians that are now in Heaven. Neither did the elders look through those prayers or then pray them to God. It said none of that stuff. All it said was that they had bowls of incense, symbolic of the people's prayers. That's it.

But according to the Roman Catholic Church, that verse is their justification for why we need to pray directly to these dead people who Catholicism has designated to be saints even though they may or may not have been Christians. Then these dead people can supposedly pray directly to God instead of you doing so.

So that Revelation verse is Catholicism's supposed best evidence for praying to saints and Mary? It's crazy! Let me give you an analogy: If I were holding the keys to your brand-new car in my hand, does that mean, by virtue of me holding those keys, that I own your car? Please say, yes! Unfortunately, as a truthful Christian, you're probably saying, no. Of course, it doesn't mean the car is mine, it only means that I'm holding the keys. Let's take it a little farther. Likewise, because I'm holding your keys, does that mean you have to pray to me in order to use your car? No! You don't have to do that. Well, let's keep following this logic: you pray to me so you can use your car because I hold the keys but I can't give you an answer yet about whether you can use it because I have to, in turn, take that prayer request and go to the car dealer to get his permission. It's goofy!

In a nutshell, that's what they've done to this verse. All it says is that they're sitting there holding the prayers of the Christians. There's no communication going anywhere. And yet that's Catholicism's supposed huge proof text as to why their doctrine is Biblical. But the Bible clearly says not to do that! Don't pray to dead people! And there is only one mediator, that is Jesus! We pray only to God, period! Over and over again, the Scripture tells us this. First Timothy 2:5 says there is one mediator and that's Jesus Christ. Hebrews 7:25 says Jesus lives to make intercession for us. John 14:13-14 is Jesus saying,

"Whatever you shall ask in my name, I will do."

It's not Mary's name or any saint so-and-so. Jesus says if it's in His name, He will do it. The Scripture never tells us to pray to dead people and you certainly don't ask dead people to pray for you. Hey, even without the Scripture, not praying to dead people should be common sense. In fact, here's a deep question and I have faith in you already just because you picked up this book so I think you'll give the correct answer: Would you say that dead people don't pray? Of course, they don't. Again, it's common sense, right? This stuff is nonsense! The Scripture never says to pray to a dead person or to ask them to pray for you. In Matthew 6:9, Jesus said to "pray like this", so it's our model of prayer, which is the Lord's Prayer. What does he tell us to do when praying? He says to pray like this:

"Our Father..." He didn't say our mother in heaven. He didn't say, "Depending on your problem or ailment, you should take your pick of dead guys to pray to." He didn't say to "go down the list of saints to get the right one in order for your prayer to be effective." Instead, He said: "Our Father in heaven, hallowed be your name."

Philippians 4:6 says this: *"Be careful for nothing, but in everything by prayer and supplication with thanksgiving let your requests be made known unto God."*

Lamentations 3:40-41: *"Let us test and examine our ways. Return to the Lord. Let us lift our hearts and hands to God in heaven."*

There is no biblical basis whatsoever for prayer to, or asking for, intercession from Mary or the saints.

Now continuing to put it to the test, here is the second way Catholicism twists what a saint does, regardless of how wrong they already are about what a saint is:

Contrary to what Catholic doctrine teaches, "Mary and the saints are not omniscient."

What does that mean? God is the only one who is omniscient, which is all-knowing and everywhere present at the same time. It's because they are not God. Only God has those attributes. And that's the problem, isn't it? We saw that Catholicism certainly gives those attributes to Mary and in this chapter, we'll see with their own sample prayers, that they also attribute those abilities to saints.

Because Mary and the saints are not omniscient and don't have God's powers and abilities, the point is this: they are still finite beings so how could they possibly hear the prayers of millions of people? Many millions of the billion plus Catholics all over the world are praying to those Catholic saints right now as you read this. They're praying to dead men and Mary too, who is also dead. Besides the fact that they are not alive anymore, how could these normal finite humans even handle more than a couple prayers at a time? How do these normal finite human Catholic guys handle the omniscient job that Catholicism says they are doing for huge populations of people all at one time? Of course, that is on top of the fact that now they have to do it while dead. And as far as them even being saints in Heaven, they probably aren't because they followed the Catholic Church so they're probably in Hell. At least we know Mary is in Heaven, but she too is just a finite being like the rest of us. How could she handle millions of prayers every moment of the day?! It would be utter chaos and impossible! The idea is crazy! Only God can do that.

Now when the Bible does mention the practice of praying and/or speaking with the dead, it is always in the context of sorcery, witchcraft, necromancy, and divination, which the Bible obviously condemns. Leviticus 20:27 says this:

"Men and women among you who act as mediums and who consult the spirits of the dead..."

Isn't that exactly what we've just learned that Catholicism is teaching and practicing? Catholics are taught to consult with what? It's the spirits of the dead! Mary is dead and I believe she is in Heaven but these Catholic so-called saints, if they were following the Catholic way to supposedly get to Heaven, *are not there*. They are in Hell. But either way, they're still dead people. Again, what does the Scripture say?

"Men and women among you who act as mediums and who consult the spirits of the dead must be put to death."

So, it's an abomination to God! In Deuteronomy 18:9, Moses tells the people:

"When you go into the land that the Lord your God has given you, don't imitate the ways of the nations there...There shall not be found among you who makes his son or daughter pass to the fire,"

Remember how they worshiped Moloch by throwing their babies on the red-hot arms of the giant hollow metal idol in order to gain prosperity? We talked about how it's similar to abortion happening today to keep from inconveniencing lifestyles.

Moses continues: *"or who uses divination, or an observer of times, or an enchanter, or a witch, or a charmer, or a consulter with familiar spirits, or wizard, or a necromancer."*

A necromancer is someone who communicates with the dead! Hello, Vatican?!

Moses continues: *"For all that do these things are an abomination To God."*

Why? It's because God wants us to know the truth, this is demonic and you're going to be deceived. But the other thing too is, prayer is no small thing. When you pray to God, what is that? Prayer is a form of worship. Only God is worthy of our prayers because He alone is the only one worthy of worship. But with this Mary and saints prayer you're giving worship to dead people when you do that. That's a major, major problem. And we see in the Bible about how people tried two different times to worship people and angels but were asked not to and turned away. Let me give you those and the first is Revelation 19:10, which says this:

"Then I bowed down at the angel's feet to worship him, but he said to me, 'do not worship me.'"

So, a true angel from God is going to tell you not to worship him.

The angel said this: *"I'm a servant like you and your brothers and sisters who have the message of Jesus. Worship God."*

So again, if it's a true angel from God, what's he going to tell you to do even if you were close to messing up? He's going to tell you to worship God! Here's another one. Listen to this from Peter in Acts 10:

"When Peter entered, Cornelius met him, fell at his feet, and worshiped him."

What did Peter say? Did Peter gloat a bit and say, "Hey bud, if you think I'm cool now, just wait until I've been dead for a while because the Catholic guys are going to consider me for bigger things. Hopefully though it won't take too long because I want that free ticket out of Purgatory just as soon as they canonize me into being a saint?" No!

By the way, that is something the Catholic Church teaches. One of the perks of being a Catholic "saint" is that the new saint apparently gets to skip Purgatory and go straight into Heaven. Of course, there is no such place as Purgatory in the first place. It's an abomination. Still, they say you supposedly go there to purge (work off or suffer for), your sins before going onto Heaven. But again, the idea of Purgatory is an abomination. The only way your sins are going to ever be forgiven is through Jesus Christ, when you're alive, so Purgatory is not even a real place but that's what they say happens for their saints. The saints get a short cut and do not pass through Purgatory.

In fact, I got to thinking about that. Did you know that they finally turned Mother Teresa into a saint just a couple of years ago? It was in 2016 but she died in 1997. So, for those of you hooked on math, that's nineteen years that they left Mother Teresa supposedly floating around somewhere in limbo. Do you think she was knocking on the door at the Vatican saying, "Hey, I want to go now! Can you make a decision?! Am I going to Purgatory or not?" Here's the question: there were nineteen years, so did she go to Purgatory and then get out? How does that work? That's what Catholicism teaches. When they canonize a saint, that saint does not have to spend time in Purgatory. But there is usually a delay until sometime after the death so how does that work? Anyway, whatever. Let's move on.

When Cornelius met Peter and tried to worship him, what did Peter say? Peter helped him up and said,

"Stand up; I too am just a man."

Now, you're thinking, "Oh, come on. They don't really do this stuff." When confronted with Catholicism's Mary issue, Catholics are conditioned to say, "We don't worship Mary." But then you have only to look at their practice, behavior, and the official Catholic teaching, even from their own catechism. If you just look at all that, you can safely reply: "Yes, you do." It's the same thing with the Catholic saints. They say they don't pray to saints. They only ask the saints for things. But what does that sound like? It is praying to them. Hello?! Just like with Mary, Catholics say they don't worship the saints. But yes, they do.

What I'm going to show you is from Catholic Online, which is on the Internet at Catholic.org. Again, this is their website and their words, and not mine. Here are their sample prayers in case Catholics don't know how to come up with prayers by themselves. The Roman Catholic Church is always available to help you get kick started in your prayer life by buying these figurines to remind you of these dead guys you need to pray to instead of God. The first one is a sample prayer to Mary:

"This is the prayer to Mary, Queen of Heaven."

Remember we talked about that exact title; the Queen of Heaven? Of course, I wasn't just making that up. This is directly from their website so you can look it up too. Again, who was the original Queen of Heaven? That's the Old Testament demonic entity that Israel began to worship that is also called, "Ishtar", which is where we get "Easter." Worshiping the Queen of Heaven was and is an abomination to God, but those Israelites just wouldn't stop doing it. Here is more of what Catholic.org prescribes as prayer to this entity that they call Mary, Queen of Heaven:

"Queen of Heaven rejoice and be glad, Virgin Mary. Oh God, grant that through the intercession of Virgin Mary, we may attain the joy of eternal life."

What?! Do we go through Mary to get eternal life? No! And again, they do the same thing with the saints. Let me give a couple of examples from their website. These are from the Catholic Church to help Catholics get kick started in their communications with the dead saints. They are here to help you.

The first one, St. Anthony, is supposed to be the guy who was zealous for justice. As we'll see in a minute, they have a saint for everything, and I mean, everything! There is one for every occupation, illness, situation, and whatever else. I'm not joking. Wait until you hear some of them. And always remember to get that little trinket that reminds you of your saint. It's only $19.95. Here from their website is a sample, or model prayer to St. Anthony:

"Dear Saint Anthony, you were prompt to fulfill all justice. You gave God and His creation the service he required from you. You respected other people's rights and treated them with kindness and understanding. St. Anthony, zealous for justice, teach me the beauty of this virtue."

Wait a second. Who teaches us virtue? God does, in His word. But Catholicism says I'm supposed to get this from dead Anthony who was a Catholic? It continues:

"Teach me the beauty of this virtue. Make me prompt to fulfill all justice..."

Who gives us the ability to do what's right? It's the Spirit of God!

"Make me prompt to fulfill all justice toward God. Help me also in my pressing needs: (name them)."

It literally says there: "name them." You get to insert your personal needs because they can't make those up for you. You have to get specific on your pressing needs. But again, who is our provider and who meets our needs? Who do we go to when in prayer and supplication? It's God! This stuff is from their own examples. Does it sound like they're praying "to" this dead guy, St. Anthony? Yes, and again, they say, "Oh, we don't pray to the saints." But they do as you can tell from reading their own prayers. Listen to this Catholic sample prayer for St Jude:

"Faithful servant and friend of Jesus, the Church honors [What?] and invokes you..."

There's a weird one but having a New Age past as I do, it's understandable that they use those words. That language is used to invoke spirits, all right. But it's the Occult and you do not want to invoke this one!

"...the Church honors and invokes you universally as the patron of hopeless cases, of things despaired of. Pray for me [Pray for me, dead person.] who am so miserable;"

Well, I wonder why they're miserable? If you don't know Jesus and you're not praying to Jesus, then this isn't going to help you out.

"Pray for me who am so miserable; make use, I implore you, of this particular privilege accorded to you, to bring visible and speedy help..."

Again, where does our help come from? It's from God and not a dead person.

"Come to my assistance in this great need, that I may receive the consolations and succor of Heaven..."

Whoa! How do we get the blessings of Heaven? It's through Jesus and not some dead guy named, Jude.

"I promise you, oh blessed St. Jude, [Remember, Catholics don't pray to these saints. Yeah, right!] I will never cease to honor you as my special and powerful patron and to do all in my power to encourage devotion to you. Amen."

So, Catholicism is teaching that you should offer to never stop honoring a dead guy? Who are we supposed to honor? We honor God. And whom are we supposed to give unceasing devotion to? Am I supposed to give it to dead Jude? No, our devotion is to Jesus. Again, Catholics are really taught to pray to dead people. And it's not just Mary.

Now notice they use a particular word there: patron. You've probably heard of that. Well again, this is Catholicism's own definition of a patron from their website, Catholic.org:

"What is a patron saint? Patron saints are chosen as special protectors or guardians over areas of life."

Really?! Who is it that guards our life? It's God. And does God send angels? Yes. Hebrews talks about that. Angels, or ministering spirits, are sent to those who inherit salvation (Christians). But God does not send dead people! Oh, and by the way, as we saw before, angels are not dead people. When you die, you don't turn into an angel and you sure don't turn into a chubby baby angel with tiny wings and a harp. Angels are beings created by God just as we humans are, but angels are distinctly different. The Latin word "Angelus" means "messenger." But anyway, here is Catholic.org continuing on the subject of patron saints:

"Patron saints are chosen as special protectors or guardians over areas of life. These areas can include occupations, illnesses, churches, countries, and causes—anything that is important to us."

In a minute, we'll get more into that word I stressed: "anything." But first here is more from Catholic.org:

"Recently the popes have named patron saints, but patrons can be chosen by other individuals or groups as well."

So, if you don't have nineteen years to wait, go ahead and just make one up. The Catholic Church is fine with that.

"Patron saints are often chosen today because an interest, talent, or event in their lives overlaps with some special area. Angels can also be named as patron saints."

Whoa, whoa, whoa! What did we just see in Revelation when the angel was offered worship? The angel said, "Don't worship me." Prayer is a form of worship and the angels say not to worship them because you're supposed to worship God. Angels say not to worship them, yet, the Catholic Church says angels can become intercessing patron saints for you if you pray to them and prayer is worshiping them. All this is from Catholicism's own words.

"A patron saint can help us when we follow the example of that saint's life and when we ask for that saint's intercessory prayers to God."

Are we supposed to follow the example of a dead guys life or does the Bible say what example we should follow instead? Yes, we are to follow Jesus Christ's example. Here are some excerpts from their website of how a patron saint can supposedly help:

"Francis of Assisi loved nature so obviously he is the patron saint of ecologists. Francis de Sales was a writer so he's the patron of journalists and writers. Clare of Assisi was named patron of television because one Christmas when she was too ill to leave her bed, she saw and heard Christmas Mass even though it was taking place miles away."

So, if you're frustrated by bad reception, especially during the Super Bowl, now you know what to do about it. Of course, I'm kidding so don't you dare pray to the dead TV lady. Now again, if you think I'm embellishing some of this stuff, go on the website yourself and you notice that right underneath these particular patron saints, on their own Catholic website, CatholicShopping.com, they have to make sure you don't forget to purchase your saint's jewelry, saint's metals, and saint's pendants. There's a moneymaker. Are you starting to understand why they ripped out the second of the Ten Commandments, which says we shall have no idols? That would ruin their idol business, wouldn't it? Now here's an example of what exactly to say as you pray to your patron saint. And remember, it's perfectly acceptable, according to the Catholic Church, for you to make up your own saint if you don't have time to wait for the right saint, for your situation to be designated by the Catholic Church. Here's that prayer to your patron saint of choice:

"Oh, Heavenly patron, in whose name I glory,"

Whoa, whoa, whoa!! Who do we glorify?! We only glorify God!

"Oh, Heavenly patron, in whose name I glory, pray ever to God for me: strengthen me in my faith;"

Who strengthens us in our faith? It's Jesus.

"...establish me in virtue; guard me in the conflict; that I may vanquish the foe and attain to glory everlasting."

So, with Mary and even all these other dead people, including the ones a person can just make up, you can pray to any or all of them for everlasting life. That is crazy!!

Now as I said, the Roman Catholic Church has an almost unending list of these saints. I'm just going to rip through some of them quick because if I listed them all, you'd be reading for years. The Catholic Church isn't joking when they claim to have a saint for anything and everything. They really mean it.

According to Catholicism, you can apparently pray to St. Adrian if you're a butcher, a guard, a soldier, or an arms dealer. I am not making this up. If you're an arms dealer, you're not alone. St. Agatha is for bakers, bell making, and nurses. St. Alexander is for charcoal burners.

St. Amand is for bartenders, brewers, innkeepers, merchants, and vine growers. That's right; St. Amand is available if you're into beer and wine. St. Ambrose handles beekeepers, beggars, candle makers, wax smelters, and refiners. St. Anastasia deals with weavers, healers, martyrs, and exorcists.

By the way, you're going to see this exorcist-type stuff come up over and over again. It's no wonder those demons won't go away. You're praying to what you think is a dead person but when something shows up, it's most likely a demon and it's duping you so at that point you have demon against demon, which doesn't work well. A demon plus a demon is not good math and they don't cancel each other out. But their list of saints mentions exorcism all throughout the different descriptions of saints.

St. Andrew is for fishermen and listen to this one: St. Ann is for miners, mothers, equestrians, cabinetmakers, homemakers, stablemen, and [I'm not making this up] French Canadian voyagers. So unfortunately, if you're Swahili or from Kenya, Copenhagen, Scotland, or anywhere else but French Canada, you're on your own. But if you happen to be a French Canadian and you're on a voyage, you know what to do and who is the right dead person for that. It's crazy! St. Ann will also supposedly help gardeners, basket makers, gravediggers, butchers, swine herders, and motorists.

St. Anthony is if you've misplaced an item, lost a person, or for women seeking a husband. Both St. Antipas and St. Apollonia are for dentists, so are they competing against each other? If one doesn't work, can you switch or are you stuck with your first choice? If you can pray to both, could that cause a nasty argument between them? It wouldn't be good to argue in Heaven.

Augustine of Hippo helps printers. Saint Augustine is not just for brewers but also for theologians. Doesn't that one make a whole lot of sense in the context of this Catholic saint thing? A brewer and a theologian do not mix well as far as sound teaching so maybe it was St. Augustine who came up with this saint idol stuff since he set some of the Catholic doctrine. I don't know. But let's move on.

Again, I'm not going to go through them all, but these are just some of the different occupations. And remember, anyone is allowed to make up, pray to, and worship their own saint that would be most appropriate for whatever they're going through. St. Barbara is for military engineers, firemen, and Italian marines. Apparently, she won't help just any marine. But she will also help fireworks makers and [Seriously, I am not making this up] servicemen of the Russian Strategic Rocket Forces. She's also good for mathematicians, geoscientists, and stonemasons. St. Bartholomew is handy for tanners, trappers, and curriers. Other occupations covered by an assortment of Catholic saints are hospital administrators, Italian prison officers, nursing mothers, farmers, farm hands, bridge builders, pawnbrokers, bankers, advertisers, mountaineers, skiers, dairy workers, and unemployed gamblers. St. Cajetan covers that last one. I have a suggestion for the unemployed gamblers: how about skipping the saint thing and just stop gambling? That way you may be able to better hold a job.

Others are for a stenographer, schoolteacher, secretary, musician, psychiatrist, surfer, pilot, theater performer, goldsmith, marble worker, motorcyclist, doctor, saddle maker, undertaker, astronomer, florist, or horticulturalist.

Now luckily for them, coffee house keepers and coffee house owners have their own patron saint. You think I'm joking but that saint's name is Drogo. In fact, you may have seen some coffee houses with that name. Why? I felt like I wanted to look this one up. Here is the Catholic Church's story of the Frenchman named, St. Drogo, the coffee guy. And by the way, his feast day is April 16th so if you want a super duper triple extra-caffeinated buffet day, plan for it in mid-April. Whatever. Here's his story, according to the Catholic Church:

"His mother died when he was born, the story goes. He held himself responsible. So later in his life he went to extreme penance to perhaps relieve his guilt. At age eighteen, he rid himself of all his property and became a penitential pilgrim. He traveled to Rome about nine or ten times. [You remember, that's the penance we talked about where you crawl up and down the stairs on your bloody knees and elbows so you can prove how devout you are.] Reportedly, Drogo was able to bilocate, which refers to the ability to maintain one's actual presence in two totally different places at the same time. Witnesses claim seeing Drogo working in the field simultaneously and going to Mass every Sunday. [No, that was actually Drogo's twin brother, Lamo; for those of you wondering.] During a pilgrimage, he was stricken with an [I kid you not] unsightly bodily affliction."

So, he's not just the patron saint of coffee houses, but he's also the patron saint of:

"Those whom others find repulsive. He became so terribly deformed that he frightened the townspeople. In his twenties, a cell was built for him to protect the local citizens of the village from his appearance. [Wow] Since he was so holy, his cell was built attached to his church. St. Drogo stayed in his cell without any human contact, except for a small window in which he received the Eucharist

and obtained his food. He stayed there for the rest of his life, about forty more years, surviving only on barley, water, and the Holy Eucharist."

Which is why, and I'm not making this up, he's also the patron saint of mentally insane people. It writes itself, right? Wow! Oh, but if you're a coffee house owner and now you're feeling like the supposedly unsightly terribly-deformed Drogo may not have the right vibe for your establishment, he's not the only option to pray to if you're a coffee house owner. Let's move on.

St. Edwards is for Kings and St. Eligius for metal workers, jewelers, mechanics, and taxi drivers. Pyrotechnicians have their St. Erasmus. That same saint covers chimney sweeps and anyone who works at great heights. St Eustachius helps hunters and trappers. Other random saints are there for truss-makers, animal rights workers, radio/television workers, hand gunners, shoemakers, comedians, clowns, dancers, and boy scouts. Teutonic Knights have St. George. There are saints for linguists, lumberjacks, nurse anesthetists, bakers, confectioners, pastry chefs, laundry workers, manual laborers, computer technicians, spectacle makers, bird dealers, art dealers, teachers of youth, altar servers, editors, printers, funeral directors, air travelers, jurists, police officers, ecologists, ice skaters, schoolgirls, prostitutes, fish dealers, chemists, medical technicians, and pig keepers.

So, wait a second. If you combine that charcoal-burning dude with St. Malo for pig keepers, we just might have something. Yeah, let's not go there. Other saints are supposedly for bookkeepers, customs agents, plumbers, paratroopers, security officers, and I kid you not, lawyers in Paris bars. The latter is St. Nicholas. Others are for midwives, hospital public relations, clockmakers, bridge builders, guards, bookbinders, special forces, bombardiers, tailors, surgeons, medical record librarians, shepherdesses, tile makers, secondhand dealers, embroiders, gardeners, athletes, bricklayers, deacons, politicians, statesmen, civil servants, archers, orphans, lighthouse keepers, and photographers.

And again, I skipped over a huge number of them but whatever your occupation, don't worry; they've got a saint for you to get those prayers kicked into gear. Oh, and by the way, don't forget to buy a trinket, necklace, or jewelry in the image of your personal patron saint for only $19.95. What a racket! And that's just the occupations.

Let's take a look at the patron saints for ailments, illness, and dangers because people have jobs, but just regular life happens outside work so what are you going to do for that? By the way, this is all kind of funny but then it's really sad too because with all these issues, if they'd just turn to Jesus, He really could help them with their occupation or illness and any calamities. Instead, this organization of false teachings, that claims to be Christian, tells them to pray to these dead people as opposed to Jesus. It's crazy!

Now let me give you some of those patron saints of ailments, illness, and dangers. You can pray to different specific saints if you're a sterile woman, blind or lame, had a run in with a poisonous reptile, or if you suffer from colic, breast cancer, or headache. The latter there is St Agathius, in case you are wondering. There's a saint for bubonic plague, misfortunes, and again we see evil spirits. Now remember the name, St. Albinus, because this one could really come in handy. He has only one thing he specializes in. Some of these saints get several different tasks like one called Agrippina that is apparently spread pretty thin because he handles evil spirits, leprosy, thunderstorms, and bacterial diseases. All those duties are wrapped into just one saint. But this St. Albinus guy seems to have only one profound specialty and I'm going to share it with you to keep in your back pocket to whip out in your time of need. Albinus is your personal dedicated 24/7 saint in case of a pirate attack. What?! Are you serious?

The multitudes of Catholic saints are there for anything and everything but don't forget your powerful graven image pendants and figurine idols for only $19.95. And if you have any of the following situations, don't forget you have a patron saint if you're experiencing a fire, snakes, snake bites, against a demonic possession [There's that again] mental illness, poison, and wild beasts. You apparently pray to Saint Andrew Avellino if you're experiencing "sudden death." What?! That's a double nutty idea because at that point, St. Andy is dead, and you are dead. Dead people can't help, and you can't even ask that dead guy for anything because you're gone too! But again, the Catholic Church has a saint for anything and everything that ails you and always remember, you get a fuller effect by spending just $19.95 per saint.

You can count on other saints in the event of riots, civil disorder, missing people, lost things, epilepsy, gout, tooth ache, kidnapping, deafness, sore eyes, cattle diseases, chest problems, lung problems, gambling addictions, ailments of the throat, horse theft, sick horses, eye disease, childhood illnesses, motorcycle/bicycle accidents, and again, evil spirits. Other afflictions to be dealt with by saints are rabies, pandemics, earthquakes, the pain of women in labor, and I'm not making this up, if you suffer from procrastination! Well, if so, here's your guy for that and doesn't it sound like one of those where someone went ahead and just made it up? Procrastination is St. Expeditus. But I didn't make it up. It's right there on the Catholic Church's list. Wow!

Also, if you need it, Catholicism has a saint for venereal disease sufferers, hemorrhoids, floods, drowning, bubonic plague, knee pain, adultery, marital difficulties, loss of parents, torture victims, pregnancy, fever, rats, mice, hailstones, gout, fear of insects, epilepsy, rheumatism, bullies, immigrants, and migrant workers. Hey, what about that last one? Immigration is a hot topic today. Maybe we need to go to St. Lorenzo Ruiz. No, let's not. There is a saint for gallstones, poverty, disease of the skin, sexual temptation, alcoholics, disease of the kidneys, back pain, and school-related student's crises. Here's another saint (or possible demon), for demons: St. Patroclus.

There's a saint against criminals, for diabetics, and for cramps. How about stress relief or New Year's blues? I kid you not. That last one is almost like a pirate thing. If you're down on New Year's Eve, hey, give it up for St. Pio! Yeah, that's a pie o' falsehoods. More random saints will supposedly intervene for rape victims, coughs, sneezes, open wounds, drought, cholera, cold weather, foot troubles, angina, syphilis, panic attacks, bedbugs, and locusts. For obsessive-compulsive disorder you would apparently pray to St. Ubald. I'm not going to touch that one. This massive army of saints also has one for blight, frost, faintness, stiff neck, lightning [again], oversleeping, whooping cough, and that's right; dangers of the sea.

Now again, I skipped over a ton of them but it's apparent that the Roman Catholic Church is pointing its followers to anything and everything except God. They've got it all covered for you by any number of dead people so even if you're not into the Mary thing, there's an answer for you and it's just $19.95. I imagine it costs a whole lot more when you get special embroidered stuff. It's just crazy but this is what they do. The Catholic Church also has patron saints of places. I'm not going to go through all those because it's literally every continent and even down to the level of cities and towns. They have saints for all that stuff. It's absolutely, completely unbiblical.

In the next chapter, we're going to talk about the big questions concerning Catholicism and how to witness to Catholics. But first, while we're on the theme of what else Catholicism gets wrong, I want to show you how they are even wrong on their terms. We've already seen a ton of things they've messed up because they are following the road of a cult and their authority is not from the Bible. Again, anytime you get outside the Bible, you're going to come up with all kinds of false doctrine. Catholicism has so much false teaching that we'll have to rip quickly through the huge volume of problems with their terminology in all its corrupted instruction and practices. There's so much false teaching, it's embedded in their own terminology and it's not just a couple of issues or one here and a few there. It's pervasive in everything but here is just some of it:

" 'Absolution' is the Catholic act of releasing someone from their sin, by God, through means of a priest."

Is that Catholic term true? No. It's their own term that is imbedded in their false teachings.

" 'Assumption' is the taking of the body and soul of Mary directly into heaven."

Did that happen? No. There is zero Biblical evidence of it whatsoever.

" 'Confirmation' is a ceremony performed by a bishop that is supposed to strengthen a person and enable him to resist sin."

Who gives us the ability to resist sin? It's the Holy Spirit and not some ceremony of man.

"Confirmation is usually done at the age of twelve. The bishop dips his right thumb in holy oil, anoints the person on the forehead, making the sign of the cross, and says 'be sealed with the gift of the Holy Spirit.'"

But when are we sealed with the Holy Spirit? Ephesians 1 says it is at the moment of salvation and not by a man performing a ceremony.

" 'Consecration' is a moment during the ceremony of the mass where God allegedly, through the priest, changes bread and wine into the body and blood of Jesus."

Is that true? Absolutely not!

" 'Eucharist' is the elements of the Communion supper where the bread and wine *are* *the body and blood of Jesus Christ."*

Does the bread and wine turn into the actual body and blood of Jesus Christ? No! Again, it's not just that they have false doctrines; even their own terminology is all false teachings. It tells you how much corruption there is.

" 'Extreme Unction' is a sacrament given to a person who is ill or in danger of dying; intended to strengthen their soul and to help their love be pure so that they may enter into Heaven. It's done through prayer and anointing oil."

They believe the extreme unction sacrament has to be done by a priest and that's why, oftentimes, I'll run into an issue at hospitals because when a patient who is danger of dying and is of Catholic background, you, as a Protestant guy, can't see them. Catholicism says you have to have a priest because it's one of their sacraments and they say you better not miss this one because of this:

"Extreme unction removes infirmity and obstacles left by sin, which prevent a soul from glory. Prepares people for death by making them like the risen Christ. It prepares their soul for eternity."

No, it doesn't! If that's what you're trusting in, then extreme unction just prepared them right into Hell. But that's one of their sacraments.

" 'Holy Chrism' is the special oil used in the sacraments of Baptism, Confirmation, and Holy Orders."

" 'Holy Water' is a special water that has been blessed by a priest, bishop, etc., or a liturgical ceremony. It's used to bring a blessing to a person when applied."

What?! So, water or oil are supposed to bring me blessing? Okay, well then, I'm not recommending this but if you have a deep fryer at home, have you ever had some splash on you when cooking? Does that feel like a blessing? But that's what Catholicism says. Their person can put some oil or water on people, say prayers, and that becomes a blessing for them. No. That's baloney. It's only water or oil and it's just symbolic. There's no special power in it. That's a false teaching.

" 'Immaculate Conception' is the teaching that Mary was conceived without original sin."
But that's not true!

" 'Indulgence' is a means by which the Catholic Church takes away [Notice it's not Jesus. It's the Catholic Church] some or all the punishment due to the Christian in this life and/or purgatory because of his sin, even though that sin has been forgiven. This punishment is most often in purgatory but can be suffered in this life. Therefore, indulgences remove time needed to be spent in purgatory."

Is that Biblical? It absolutely is not!

" 'Lent' is a forty-day period between Ash Wednesday and Easter Sunday. Usually it is accompanied by some form of prayer and fasting."

Is there anything wrong with praying? No, not if you pray to God. But if you're praying to these dead people that Catholicism tells you to, that's wrong. Is there anything Biblically wrong with fasting? No. What's the problem then? In Matthew 6 Jesus says when you pray and fast, don't be like the hypocrites. He is saying not to make a big show of it so people will look at how religious you're being; Hey, look at me! And when you fast, don't disfigure your face. He said that because people of those days, in order to show their great religiosity, would put ash on their faces to make it look like they hadn't eaten in a long time. What's a similar practice with Catholics that is done on Ash Wednesday? They get a big cross of ashes on their foreheads. It's like, "Hey, look at me! I'm going to Ash Wednesday services! Aren't I spiritual?!" But again, what did Jesus say? Praying and fasting are important. Praise God that you're praying and fasting but don't make a big show of it! If that's what you do, then you just got all the reward you're going to get and it's from man, so do it in secret and keep it between you and your Father.

" 'Mass' is a re-enactment of the sacrifice of Christ on the cross in a ceremony performed by a priest. This ceremony is symbolically carried out by the priest and involves Consecration, where the bread and wine are changed into the body and blood of Jesus Christ."

Is Jesus sacrificed over and over again? Is that his real body? No!

" 'Penance' is the means, by which it all sins committed after baptism are removed."

Again, they believe Baptism removes all sin up to that point but with sins after Baptism, you're pretty much on your own. And they want your baptism to be done as a baby even though babies don't know what in the world is going on. Usually the baby's only part in the ceremony is to freak out.

"The means [of Penance] are signed by a priest and usually consist of special prayers or deeds performed by the sinner."

Is that how we get our sins forgiven? It absolutely is not. That's unbiblical.

"A 'Relic' is a part of the body of a saint, including clothing or jewelry. The relic is considered holy due to its association with the saint."

Now as we saw before, Catholicism has a long-standing practice over many centuries of making money from relics. They still do that today with people traveling around showing relics because it's a lucrative way to drum up some cash. People want to come see the stuff. And remember, that's the kind of thing they did to build the cathedrals over in Europe. It was one of the practices that caused Martin Luther and the other reforms to say, "That's it! This is nuts!" They were selling indulgences but also getting people to come check out the relics. They would claim things like that they literally had a piece of the cross or a vial filled with Mary's breast milk. I'm not making this stuff up. People would come flocking in and have extreme emotional reactions. People get passionate about that stuff.

"'The 'Rosary' is a string of beads containing five sets with ten small beads. Each set of ten is separated by another bead. It also contains a crucifix. It is used in saying special prayers, usually to Mary, where the rosary is used to count the prayers."

Oh, but they don't pray to Mary, right? Sure they do, and they admit it right there.

"A 'Saint' is a very holy person."

But who is it that makes us holy? We are not holy in and of ourselves. Jesus Christ makes us holy and it's for anyone who's belongs to God.

"A saint is usually someone who has been dead for many years and has been canonized by the Catholic Church. Saints do not have to pass through purgatory."

Uh, oh! Again, if that's a fact, what did Mother Teresa do for nineteen years after she died and before being designated as a saint by the Catholic Church? But let's just move in. Here's the final term we're going to look at:

" 'Transubstantiation' is the teaching that the bread and wine in the communion supper become the body and blood of the Lord Jesus Christ at the Consecration during the Mass."

No, again. That one is not true either, but I wanted to bring those terms to your attention because we're finishing up what else Catholicism gets wrong. Once you get off the track of the Bible, you're in trouble. And hey, flip it around and answer this question: Are you starting to understand why we as Christians should never budge from the Scriptures? And if someone comes up and says, "God told me to tell you...," you need to run! What if they say they had a vision from God about American and it made them cry alligator tears because our country is going to be blah, blah, blah? Again, you should run!

That's where all this kooky stuff with false doctrines, teachings, and practices starts from. But are just small deviations from the Bible okay? No. Once you allow even a little drift away from Scripture, then trouble is on its way. It's coming. You have to stick with the Bible. Don't let anyone dupe you with any feelings, emotions, experiences, or so-called authority that gets you away from the Bible! The good news is that if you stick with the Scriptures, no man can deceive you because you won't fall for it and you'll continue to walk in God's blessing.

I wanted to share their terminology as another aspect of what else Catholicism gets wrong, to show that they are so messed up and riddled with false teaching, that you can really see how it's even built into their verbiage. The Roman Catholic Church doesn't get it wrong on just a couple of items. It's all over the place!

In the last chapter, we're going to finish up by looking at how we can reach these people. Guess what; just like everyone else, Catholics need to be reached for Jesus. How do we best go about that? We'll take a look at some of those things in the next chapter.

Chapter Twelve

False Doctrine & Witnessing

In this last chapter, we're going to get into a couple more areas involving what else Catholicism gets wrong. Again, we could go on for a long time, but we've got to cut it somewhere. After these other aspects of what they get wrong, we'll get into how you witness to Catholics.

So, continuing in the "what else do they get wrong" category, we have what I call the "Quadruple S's," which are things I've bunched together just to give you some highlights. Those four areas of Catholicism are, Stigmata, Signs, So-Called Prophets, and Superstitious Attitudes.

Let's first look at the Stigmata. Stigmata refers to the supposed spontaneous appearances of wounds that are supposed to be the same kind Jesus had. They supposedly appear on Catholic folks and it's typically during Catholic festivals. The wounds are said to happen on Catholic's hands, feet, sides, and scalp in the same area where the crown of thorns was on Jesus. It also supposedly happens on their backs, where it is said to resemble being whipped, and on their faces as if they've been beaten.

Or frankly, maybe you just had a car accident and you're trying to make it into a Stigmata thing. A person may have one of the signs and typically you hear people saying they have the crucifixion marks in their hands. You may have seen pictures of some of that baloney. In theory, people could even have more than one or all of the Stigmata markings, according to these eyewitness accounts.

The question is whether or not it is real. The answer rhymes with wrong. That's right, the answer is: wrong. Of course it is nonsense, so what is it? Well, obviously it's demonic. It's a lie, false teaching, false occurrence, demonic manifestation, and/or some psychological issue going on with the people involved. Let's take a look at some of that evidence:

"Stigmata happens within the Roman Catholic context. I have not heard of it occurring with non-Roman Catholics."

So, it's something that is strategically within their own camp because what is it that we know is all over in their camp? That is false teaching, false teaching, false teaching, false teaching, false teaching, and more false teaching. They even listen to demonic visions from the sky, so when you have so much demonic false doctrine, what do you think this Stigmata thing is? It's a bunch of baloney! It has nothing to do with Scriptural doctrine.

"Furthermore, in the real crucifixion of Jesus Christ, the nails [near] the hands were not in the palms."

Historically, we know for a fact that the wounds from the nails to Jesus upper body were in the wrists and not in the hands. So technically, if these supposed Stigmata occurrences were even real, and they're not, why do the people always show an injury to the palms. That isn't even where he was nailed to the cross. So, if it really was from God, God's not going to lie, and he won't be inconsistent. He's holy and doesn't lie. If you're even going to try writing new Scripture about some crazy thing where people get the same wounds as Jesus, you need to have them in the wrists so the whole thing is a bunch of baloney in the first place. It's superstition and another one of their superstitious signs with supposed wonders and miracles just like the miracle springs and visions in the sky. The whole thing is just to get people sucked into their system but that's the superstition stuff.

Now when these guys say things like, "Hey, I saw a sign," "I saw a vision in the sky," "this crazy thing happened," "this trinket has magical powers," "I've got the Stigmata," or any of that kind of stuff, let's remember what Scripture says about it. John, in 1 John 4 says this:

"Dear friends, do not believe every spirit. [Okay. What should we do?] Test the spirits to see whether they're from God because many false prophets have gone out into the world."

That certainly is this case. We are told to test it. Things like stigmata is something we are to test with the Scripture. What does the Bible say? Ask whether it is consistent with Scripture. Then, if anything doesn't line up or if it feels like it is just sort of true, it needs to be rejected. It's like when people say, "So and so is the Antichrist and we have proof." They usually seem to pick on a political figure because, they say, the Bible says that the Antichrist will do this and that using world power. Well that's true but the Bible gives about forty different descriptions of the Antichrist. We can point out Biblically that he does sort of look like he'll be a political person, so I'll give you that. But if he's not like or doing other aspects talked about in Revelation, we should reply with something like, "It fulfills most of them. But that's not how God works! If it's the real Antichrist, he'll fulfill every single one of them."

That's the same lesson to learn with all this stuff like stigmata, signs, superstitious attitudes, and so-called prophets. People see things and think it's part of events lining up Biblically. They think, well, it's kind of, sort of like what the Bible says. But, no! If they even get one thing wrong, it cannot be from God! Test it all by going to the word of God. Unfortunately, that is not something these people do with their superstition, stigmata, signs, and so-called prophets. In fact, let me give you another one of their supposed signs that they're big on. I want to go back a few chapters where we saw the people who were worshiping these statues of Mary. One was supposedly crying with oil coming out of her eyeball. And one Mary statue had the supposed blood coming out of the temple. Do you remember that I commented about how it looked like pigeon droppings? Well, I had to mention this further information: I received a text from a former intern at my church who moved back to Louisiana. After watching the study of that material on our website, he sent me a text. Listen to what he said about the supposed blood running down the statue of Mary's head that I said looked like pigeon poop:

"Pastor Billy, hope all's well with the family in the church and I saw the service from last night and you probably don't remember, but that bleeding Mary statue is in Louisiana and is right across the street from my house. Ha, ha. You said that the blood was from a pigeon. Listen, I was there during that TV broadcast. A reporter asked me while it was going on what I thought about it and I said, 'Well,

I don't know but we have twelve tomato plants in the back yard, so you tell me what's more likely, that concrete is bleeding or maybe a bird had too much tomato.' It didn't make the news though. Ha, ha. Anyway, tell everyone I said hello."

Can you believe that?! What are the odds? He lives right next door. This Mary statue stuff is all a bunch of baloney. Get back to testing everything with the word of God. All of this superstitious nonsense sucks people in. And that's not Mary in a piece of bark. It's just a piece of a tree. You just want it to be more.

Here's another one, which is the latest. Did you know, according to Catholic superstition, 2017 was the year for a bad omen and one of the most famous reoccurring Catholic miracles is supposedly the liquefaction of the dried blood of Saint Gennaro; a bishop of Naples, martyred around 305 A.D.? He's also the city's patron saint. So, this dead guy is supposed to be looking after the city. Would you say that city is in a heap of trouble? Anyway, here's how the story goes:

"Starting in 1389 the vial of Saint Gennaro's blood typically turns liquid three times a year, with the first time on the Saturday before the first Sunday of May, on his saint's feast day."

So, if it's a Thursday and you're on a southbound train and you see a basket of oranges going north and it's humid on the third day of the fourth leg of a chicken sandwich... Whatever. Anyway, these things always get confusing. The other two times it supposedly happens each year are September 19th and then again, on December 16th. By the way, they say one of these days was when Mount Vesuvius erupted in 1631. Are you getting all this? It's serious stuff, right? No, not really. Now listen to this about a recent year:

"The blood liquefied, they said, on September 19th but it did not on December 16th. The failure of the blood to liquefy, signals war, famine, and disease."

Yeah, I'm not too worried about that, but listen to their supposed proof and remember, if any part of it is incompatible with the Scripture, it can't be from God. Of course, we know it's a bunch of baloney but listen to their supposed proof and it's about the fact that this non-liquefaction has happened before, and all kinds of bad stuff followed:

"The relic failed to liquefy in September 1939 when World War II broke out."

Oops! Notice they said it was in September but remember they also said the dates it has to happen are specifically, September 19th and December 16th? Do you know why they left the 19th out of their description of how it supposedly happened in September? Because the 19th was not when World War II broke out. It was September 1st. So, it appears they are doing some stretching there. And that should have been an easy catch for them since it was in the same article and the very next paragraph, they say there was also a cholera outbreak around Naples in 1973 and 1980 saw a deadly earthquake. Yeah, that is along with 5000 other earthquakes. Are you kidding me?! Get back to the word of God!

There's another popular story out there that people are getting duped on but with all this stuff it's hard to believe the Catholic Church is even serious with much of these signs and superstitions. I wouldn't listen to any supposed truth from the Roman Catholic Church because they don't test things with the Bible. They don't stick to the word of God. Instead, their faith is all these visions, dreams, experiences, supposed miracles, all kinds of craziness, and even the head of a statue being bird boomed with tomato droppings. But here's one I need to hammer on a bit because it's not only getting popular, but that's true even in the Protestant Church. It's the old "Saint Malachy's Prophecy." Some of you who study prophecy may have heard of this guy but let me expose this for what it is:

"Saint Malachy was a Catholic priest."

So, there's huge problem number one. Does Catholicism follow and teach Scripture? No. Is Catholicism Biblical? It absolutely is not.

"Later, Malachy was an archbishop. Several miracles were attributed to him, according to the Roman Catholic Church. [Maybe pigeons landed on him too. We don't know] He was also the first Irishman to be canonized by the Roman Catholic Church."

So, he's not only Malachy, he's Saint Malachy. The whole thing is surrounding Roman Catholic false teaching. Should we listen to anything that comes from this guy? No! You might as well listen to Nose-Hair Domus; I mean, Nostradamus, or any of those other guys who supposedly get visions, or whatever.

"Malachy is known today for a set of prophecies purportedly written by him, in 1139, concerning the future line of popes. His list started out with his contemporary, Pope Celestine III and continued through the next 112 popes. The last pope, according to him, was going to be a guy named Petrus Romanus, or Peter the Roman, whose reign would end with judgment day. Malachy's vision of the future included a brief cryptic description of each pope."

Now this is a Catholic saint guy who supposedly did Catholic miracles, so right there just from those aspects, it should already be considered wrong, wrong, wrong, and wrong, so I'm not going to put any stock in the rest of this. But here's what is buzzing around the Internet with what Malachy said about the last five popes to come before judgment day: "Flower Of Flowers," is supposed to be Pope Paul VI; "Of The Half Moon," is supposed to be Pope Juan Pablo I; "From The Toil Of The Sun," is supposed to be Pope John Paul II; "The Glory Of The Olive," is supposed to be Pope Benedict XVI; and then Peter The Roman is supposed to be the present pope, Pope Francis. Also, in Malachy's writings there is supposed to be a sort of black pope.

But here's the whole point: Should we listen to this guy? Is he going to tell us how the end times will unfold, and should we give credence to anything he says? Are you kidding me?! I can't believe Christians are getting caught up in this crazy stuff. I don't care if it's Saint Malachy, Saint Catch-a-Fly, or whatever. And Catholicism can make their sign-of-cross hand motions with the wax-on, wax-off stuff or whatever. I don't care. Your whole system is outside the Scripture and you're supposedly doing these supernatural miracles from God but instead, your organization listens to demonic teachings and teaches a false Gospel. For that reason, I'm not going to listen to anything you say to determine my future or anything else. But still, people are getting into this type stuff, even in the Christian Church. Now listen to this:

"Malachy was immersed in the teaching and the dogmas of the Catholic Church. His so-called prophetic utterances and dreams are questionable at best. His prophecy is extra-biblical."

It's not found in the Bible! That's his number one mistake. So, what are we supposed to do? Again, you test it according to Scripture. Is Malachy Biblically based? No! And secondly, the whole concept of his prophecies is based on popes and the office of the pope, which is totally unbiblical. Here's another issue:

"None of it lines up with the word of God. Rather than interpret the end times according to the dreams of a false teaching Catholic mystic, shouldn't we trust the word of God?"

And isn't that especially true for us Protestants? If you want to know the end times, the Bible is your book for that. Nearly one third of the Bible deals with Bible prophecy. And I'm now talking to Protestants instead of Catholics: Is the Bible not good enough for you anymore? Is Revelation too boring for you? What about Daniel? Protestants says things like, "Oh, I can't listen to Daniel one more time or that dull Zechariah either. I need to find something more exciting. Hey, how about the dreams of a false-teaching Catholic mystic dead guy who I can't verify?"

No! What in the world are we doing? We sit here on the one hand and say we only follow the Bible but even we get sucked into this baloney like the rest of them. Again, what does God say? He tells us to test it! And if it's not Biblical, you need to run! If it is from God, it will be 100% correct all the time. It's not sort of, maybe, or kind of right. It must be completely Biblical so stick to Scripture because we're getting duped. I love this:

"The Bible warns though about false prophets who speak as though their oracles were given by God. And yet God says to these people in Jeremiah 23:32: 'Indeed, I am against those who prophesy false dreams.' Declares the Lord, 'They tell [the dreams] and lead my people astray with their reckless lies; yet I did not appoint them.'"

Is there any Biblical evidence that God would ever appoint a false-teaching Catholic mystic in a false organization that has a false Gospel? No, there is zero chance of that. Why would you expect to get truth out of that source? So, all that was the "Quadruple S's", now I want to get into a couple more false doctrines from the Catholic Church, and then we'll answer the question about how to witness to these folks.

Continuing in our efforts to figure out what else they get wrong, I want to point you to 1 Timothy 4. What is interesting in 1 Timothy is along the lines of what we just talked about as far as the events and characteristics of the last days. Here's what God says and guess what religion this sounds like with both of the characteristics of those days? It rhymes with Roman Catholic so it's kind of ironic and also very interesting. Here's what Paul says in, 1 Timothy 4:

"The Spirit clearly says that in the latter times some are going to abandon the faith, get away from the Bible [Unfortunately, that is happening], and follow deceiving spirits."

Doesn't that sound like these modern days when we see frantic people who think they are looking at tears or blood running down an idol's face but it's most likely only tomatoes that were processed through a pigeon? Paul continues:

"...deceiving spirits, things taught by demons."

And that sounds like the demonic apparitions and how they say things like this: "Hey, I am appearing to you as the Virgin Mary. You must now worship me and build shrines for idols of me. I'm the mediatrix so you have to go through me to be saved. I'm the one to worship." That's demonic! In fact, much of what we've been studying is exactly what the Scripture is mentioning. Now I'm not saying it's all just about Catholics, but their doctrine and practices seem to follow right down this list. Paul continues:

"Such teachings come through hypocritical liars whose consciences have been served with a hot iron. They forbid people to marry and they order them to abstain from certain foods."

What that verse is talking about is when you are told you are not allowed to eat something. First Timothy is saying that these hypocritical liars will tell you to abstain from certain foods and forbid you to marry. Now about that food decree, even to this day, what food practice is there with Catholics because of these type teachings? It's about Fridays, right? Catholics are taught not to eat meat, but they say it's okay to eat a fish. First of all, last time I checked, fish is meat so that sounds like it's coming from a hypocritical liar. Let's take a look at that. Why don't Catholics eat meat on Friday? Here is the technical rule: to abstain from warm-blooded flesh meat on Friday. The whole idea is from Catholic penance, which again is a work "you" do to supposedly get rid of "your" punishment for your sins. Is that Biblical? It absolutely is not. So, it's a Catholic penance and the reason why it's Fridays is because, according to what Catholicism says, that's the day our Lord Jesus, the real Jesus, was crucified. But here's the issue. They keep changing it. Centuries ago, this is how the practice began:

"It started as a law that forbid consuming meat, including fish, on all Wednesdays, Fridays, and Saturdays."

That's how it started.

"Then later this rule was relaxed to remove meat from the diet on Ash Wednesday and all Fridays. Then in 1966, Catholic bishops here in America, with the blessing of Pope Paul VI, further relaxed the rule."

Hey, wait a second. Now you've got an oxymoron, and talk about hypocritical liars; on the one hand you say the rulings of the church councils and the decisions and decrees from the Pope and the Vatican are "ex cathedra", which means they are supposedly on par with the Scripture and <u>infallible</u>. But if they're infallible, why do you keep changing it? The Bible knows what that is called and it's "hypocritical liars." But of course, when you try to point that out, their consciences are seared so we can't even talk about it with them. Again, that's exactly what the Bible says they will be like.

"Nowadays meat is only prohibited on Ash Wednesday, Good Friday, and the Fridays during Lent season. Catholics are obligated to observe this fast as a minimum, but they can make up stricter requirements for themselves if they so desire. The stated reason for abstaining from meat on Fridays during Lent is to remind the faithful that Jesus died on Friday. Jesus gave up his body, his flesh. Catholics, in an effort to attain greater communion with Christ, refrain from consuming flesh."

Again, wait a second! There is more of that same hypocritical lying. Here Catholicism has a practice, right now today, where they are still enforcing the rule that in order to attain a greater communion with Christ, I need to refrain from consuming flesh. Yet they promote this thing called the Eucharist in their mass, which they say turns into the actual flesh, or body and blood of Jesus Christ, before followers consume it, which Catholicism also prescribes that their followers must do. But they have another practice that says Catholics will grow closer to Christ if they refrain from flesh. So, which is it?! And what do you do if this lands on the same day Catholics are told they must attend mass? What are you doing with those competing, supposedly infallible teachings?

With all that said, the whole question is, what about the fish? Fish is meat so what's going on with that? Well, listen to this:

"The United States Conference of Catholic Bishops states that 'fish is a different category of animal.'"

Wow! There it is again: the hypocritical liars. What you see there is just them getting caught in a lie so they make up more stuff to cover their tracks, and by the way, even though other foods also come from animals, you can apparently still eat eggs, butter, and milk, so again, if it rains on a Saturday and you're on a train, and hopping on one leg as you go southbound, then you're maybe allowed to do certain things but only if it's a misting rain and you forgot your wallet. I don't know. Let's move on with this analysis:

"Abstaining from meat is a handmade ritual from the Catholic Church. It has no inherent spiritual value. It cannot and does not draw a person closer to Christ."

Yes, give me a break! But again, it's supposed to be a penance where you do it because Catholicism has these actions they've prescribed for you to take care of your sin, instead of Jesus doing it. They have a lot of them to supposedly work off your punishment. However, it's total blasphemy!

I came across something else interesting about Catholicism's anti-biblical proclamations to abstain from certain foods. This is an answer to one of those questions you may have about why this restaurant chain even still has this item on their menu:

"The Catholic practice of abstaining from meat on Friday was the reason for the creation of McDonald's Fillet O' Fish sandwich. It was because the hamburger sales dropped off noticeably on Fridays, so the owner of the franchise in Cincinnati introduced the new offering, the Fillet O' Fish sandwich and sales picked up again."

They took advantage of this crazy Catholic practice. Can you believe that? So, there's your reason why McDonald's won't take it off their menu. It's a guaranteed sale as long as people are falling for this baloney. However, the Catholic Church is having a bit of an issue with their practice:

"Many Catholics though are not aware that the Friday abstinence rule is still in effect. The post-Vatican II modification of the church law only allowed the consumption of meat IF some other sacrifice or good work was substituted in its place."

So, if you're sick and tired of that McDonald's Fillet O' Fish, you still have to do something else and your only other option is to remember the three subsections given by the Catholic Church that will allow you to stop eating that fish sandwich on Friday. Here are your other options:

"You could pray to the Stations of the Cross, say extra Rosaries [whip out those beads], or do some other additional similar offering."

And that is all to supposedly work off your punishment for your sins.

Now while it might not be a good thing, believe it or not, many Roman Catholics have come up with all types of liquors. You've probably heard of Dom Pergnon champagne. A Catholic monk invented it. It was introduced from Benedict Abbey in the Champagne region of France. Here's more on that:

"The story goes that when he was experimenting, he tasted the first product of the new method, called his fellow monks, and said, 'brothers, come quickly! I'm drinking the stars!'"

"Catholics have also created all kinds of wines, brandies, different liquors, and even beers. [A lot of beers come from the Catholics, in case you're wondering.] In fact, one [liquor] called Jagermeister has a picture of a stag with a cross between the antlers. [Is it because that's cool and manly so men will buy it? No.] It's an allusion to the conversion of Saint Hubert who is the patron saint of hunters."

And we all know getting drunk while hunting is a good thing, right? Wrong. Wow. Also, believe it or not, Catholics are behind cappuccinos. Listen to this:

"A Capuchin friar named Marco found sacks of coffee beans left behind by the Turks and after he brewed himself a cup, he found it bitter for his taste. So, he added milk and honey, thus creating the first cup of the tasty beverage. The Viennese named it the 'little capuchin,' or 'cappuccino,' which was also after the Friar, Marco, whose habit [robe] was the same color as the drink."

Well okay, it's must be from God then, right?

Now returning to 1 Timothy 4, again, what were Paul's warnings? He cautions the Church that these people are going to turn away from the truth, get into all the superstitious nonsense, practice demonic teachings, they're hypocrites, they're liars, they are even hypocritical liars, they'll forbid people from eating certain food, and also forbid them, of all things, to marry.

How about that last one? It's very specific, and interesting considering our subject matter here. Does Catholicism do that? Yup! It's called the celibacy of the priests. First of all, the whole Catholic priesthood itself is not even Biblical because we don't have a priesthood as our leadership here in modern times. That was in the Old Testament with the Jewish folks. Instead, in the Christian Church, we have pastors who are elders and other elders, as well as deacons and positions of that nature but we don't have the official priest.

Secondly, in 1 Corinthians 7:32, Paul says this in regards to celibacy:

"An unmarried man is concerned about the Lord's affairs, but a married man is concerned about the affairs of this world, how he can please his wife, so the interests are divided."

There we see the Bible does talk about the fact that there are people who are celibate and that's okay if that's what you want to do. The Bible says it's allowed but it's not commanded. It's not like you have to be celibate or you're doomed or excluded from leadership. The only thing Paul is saying is about how it's a practical thing. If you don't get married, you can devote one hundred percent of your time for Jesus. However, when you get married, what happens? You have someone else to take care of. Then along comes the crumb snatchers pulling at your pant leg, looking up at you, and saying, "food, food!" Right? After that comes a pet, a house, a lawn to mow, and you lose a bunch of your free time when you get married. There is nothing wrong with marriage and in fact, it's a gift from God, as are children.

So, if you're single, praise God! You get more time to serve God. But at the same time, I'm not against marriage. In fact, do you know that when the Bible addresses leadership, frankly, it assumes all leadership is married; not celibate. Let me give you a couple of those examples:

In 1 Timothy 3 and Titus 1, Paul assumes that elders, bishops, overseers, and deacons [Notice that none there are priests] will be married. Here are those phrases:

"The husband of one wife, he must manage his own family well. His children must obey him with proper respect."

So therefore, the point is that it is unbiblical to require celibacy for leadership. Even if Catholicism had true Biblical leadership, which it does not, it's still an unbiblical practice to say you have to be celibate. If it's not Biblical, do you think God is going to bless it? No. Eventually, what happens to anything that is unbiblical? Well, it's a lie and lies hurt things so there are going to be consequences. The enemy is out to kill, steal, and destroy. Sin hurts, harms, and destroys. So eventually it's going to cause destruction. That's just what lies do and this lie of celibacy for Catholic leaders is no different. Listen to this:

"The Roman Catholic Church requirement of celibacy is a sad example of taking something the Bible encourages, but does not demand, and transforming it into something absolutely harmful. The result is failures in the areas of adultery, fornication, and sexual abuse of children."

Folks, I think we all know about that because it's unfortunately been part of our news for decades. It doesn't stop. In a minute, we'll get to why it continues. Just from the victims who have gone public and not including the enormous number who haven't, thousands and thousands and thousands of individual victims have come out and what?

"...claimed and proved and shown sexual abuse from the priests of the Roman Catholic Church."

Well, why do you think they're having sexual problems? What is Catholicism's false teaching that the Bible specifically said would show up in last days? They are saying these guys can't marry. And the results are not just adultery. These pedophile priests are going after children. This is pedophilia! All sins are bad, including all sexual sin like fornication and sex outside of marriage so I'm not trying to categorize sin, but this is pedophilia and it goes on and on and on. Here is more about that:

"But rather than defrocking the priest, the Catholic Church, in most instances, attempts to cover up the sex abuse and then they simply transfer him to a new parish."

Where, of course, the guy keeps doing it again and again.

"This scandal and the attempted cover up, continues to expand, reaching all the way to the papacy itself. Also, the structure of celibacy is appealing to some men with abnormal sexual tendencies who view the priesthood as a means of keeping their desires under control."

So, many of these guys already have problems with temptation and then they're lured into this system of works where they think if they become a Catholic priest, even though they are not saved, they can just follow their rituals and maybe that way it will help clean up their act. But what do we know is the only thing that keeps us from sin? It's the Spirit of God. When do you get that? It only happens at the moment you become a born-again Christian. You won't be led to Christianity under the false doctrines of Catholicism. But these guys are lured in, thinking it will help their sexual sin issues. Then they find out, sure enough, that when they start doing the works, the temptations don't go away. Unfortunately, they're already in the Catholic priesthood at that point, so they're stuck.

"Rules do not change the heart. Then they give into sexual temptations. The result is unnatural sexual acts such as homosexuality and pedophilia."

Of course, homosexuality is a whole other issue that is also rampant in the priesthood. Now what we talked about is just the guys who recognize they have a problem and think the Catholic works-based system is going to help them get rid of those unfortunate sexual sinful desires. Besides them, there are those who know they're doing this stuff and they want to do it. Those guys specifically go into the Catholic Church because they know they can get away with it.

"The lax rule enforcement and cover ups have encouraged the application of pedophiles, specifically to go into the priesthood because many pedophiles see the priesthood as a means of easy unsupervised access to kids."

And even if they get caught, what's the consequence from the Catholic Church? They just pay somebody off, cover it up, and send them to a new location where he gets to keep doing the same horrible acts to other children.

"Pedophile priests should be arrested and punished just as any other pedophile should be and would be. Anyone covering up and/or, by negligence, enabling pedophilia anywhere, should be prosecuted. [That includes the Catholic Church] A priest, who has sexually abused anyone, should never be allowed back into any

kind of leadership. The pedophile priest scandal in the Roman Catholic Church is absolutely horrid. There is nothing more antithetical to the message of Christ than priests sexually abusing kids."

Now I want to read some excerpts from an article by Jack and Diane Ruhl with the National Catholic Reporter. The Ruhl's did a three-month investigation. Of course, they could have invested more time in this but at least there are three months here where they investigated the facts. Also, we need to keep in mind that those facts came from the U.S. Conference of Catholic Bishops. So, first of all, do you think the bishops gave them everything? Catholicism has a history of covering things up. And secondly, is there a way to even get what you need for an in-depth study on this? But anyway, just based on three months and just what was given to them, they have calculated this: since 1950, the amount that the Roman Catholic Church has paid out to sex abuse scandal victims is four billion dollars. Folks, that's not millions. We are talking about billions!

Again, that is only a three-month investigation and just relying on what these Catholic bishops were willing to say to people who would be printing a public story on it. So, what do you imagine is the real number? Now you might be thinking, man, Catholicism must be going bankrupt with all that expense, but no. What did we see in a previous chapter about how much wealth these people have all over the planet? They've got money in warehouses, at the Vatican, cathedrals, and even monasteries stacked from floor to ceiling with golden trinkets and all kinds of other treasures. They've got more wealth than they know what to do with. This amount of hush money and court settlements is a pittance compared to the Catholic Church's net worth, which the public is not allowed to know. But as crazy as the surely underestimated total of four billion is, and remember, this is from the National Catholic Reporter, listen to this:

"[The Ruhl's say], and yet there are still people who happily hand over their money to the Roman Catholic Church, enroll their children in Catholic schools, and continue to go back to celebrate life events like weddings and baptism. [These are their words and not mine.] It's appalling that anyone would look at the Catholic Church and its leadership, including Pope Francis, as figures of moral authority."

Wow! Even with widespread sexual abuse to this degree, people still keep going back. This is how much of a seductive tie there is. And you may know about that if you've ever tried witnessing to a Catholic. That Catholic doctrine gets deeply engrained in them. Remember, it starts when the Catholic Church gets you as a baby when you don't even know what's going on. They have your parents already warped. It starts off with that sprinkling of water on your tiny head and from then on, it's works, works, works. But don't you dare leave the Catholic Church or you're doomed. Catholicism even prepares their followers with the idea that Protestants are out to get them. So, if that's all they've ever known and along comes a Protestant who wants to tell them about Jesus, but they've got all this pre-programming, it's very hard to bust through.

So, there's the question: how do you witness to Catholics? I like to focus on two important aspects. The first one I call, "New Thoughts." They're not going to hear these points from their own camp, so you just want to give them new thoughts. You can just drop a new thought in their head that is maybe something they've never considered. What it does is get them to start thinking, "What am I believing in and is it right?" So again, just give them a new thought, or a few new thoughts.

The second thing and the most important is to follow that up with the Bible. Get them back to the Bible because there's something about reading it with your own eyes. The word of God, the Spirit of God, will begin to draw them out. So those are the two areas to focus on.

Now let me give you some of those new thoughts, which are just ideas for Catholics to ponder when you come across them. Let's look at some of the things they believe, starting with the Eucharist. We know communion, or what they call the Eucharist, is symbolic. Catholics believe it is the literal body and blood of Christ. Here's a good question for Catholics that will bring up a new thought:

"When Jesus instituted the supper, he had not yet been crucified. How then was the Eucharist his crucified body and blood?"

Jesus is sitting right there next to them handing out the supper, so it has to be symbolic. Again, that's just a new thought. You can ask if they've ever considered that?

"If, as the Roman Catholic Church teaches, the Eucharist wine literally becomes the blood of Jesus Christ, then how is that not violating the old testament law that prohibits us from drinking the blood of any flesh (Leviticus 17)?"

Again, that's just a new thought, or just a question to give them something to think about.

What about interpreting Scripture?

"The Roman Catholic Church says individuals are not allowed to interpret the Bible, but they must submit to the teaching and the authority of the Catholic Church. Well, how can you know if the Catholic Church is correct if we can't check it against Scripture?"

That's just a new thought for them. And what did Paul say to the Bereans that is in stark contrast to Catholic teachings? In Acts 17, he praised the Bereans for checking everything he taught to see if it lines up with the Bible.

Here's a third new thought that ties into how Catholics will say, "Oh yeah, we believe in Jesus. It's only Jesus." With that in mind then, here's a new thought for them:

"Can you, as a Catholic, pray directly to Jesus, not going through Mary, and ask Jesus to forgive you of all of your sins?" Then you ask, "Well if you did, would you be forgiven of all your sins? And if you were forgiven by Jesus of all of your sins, then do you need all the rituals and sacraments of the Roman Catholic Church in order to be forgiven?"

You are slowly dismantling their deeply engrained thought process.

"If you're not forgiven by Jesus when you pray to him and ask him to forgive you, then tell me why Jesus is not enough to save us?"

There's another new thought; just something to think about as far as the ramifications of what they have been taught and believe.

Now with a new thought about Mary, we flip it around because that goes hand in hand with the previous Jesus thought. Even though Catholics will say they are not attributing God-like abilities to Mary, they certainly do. Here's a thought to get through to them about that:

"Do you really believe Mary is able to hear and understand the prayers of millions of people all over the world simultaneously in different languages both spoken and thought? If you do believe all those abilities, how are you not attributing God-like abilities to her?"

Again, it's just a new thought. Oh, and by the way,

"Why pray to Mary when Jesus specifically said to pray to him. Matthew 11; 'ask Him anything,' John 14; 'He has all authority in Heaven and on Earth,' Matthew 28; 'is not Jesus capable enough to take care of you?'

That is, without Mary? There's just one more new thought. Now here's another new thought about prayer:

"Is a Protestant wrong for praying to Jesus alone and asking Jesus to forgive them of all their sins?"

Of course, the answer is, no. If a Catholic confirms that it is, no, then again, hand them a new thought:

"Then why do you keep praying to the saints and continue praying to Mary?"

That's a helpful new thought to float around in their head.
How about salvation? Ask them this:

"What is the saving Gospel?"
"How do you get to Heaven?"

Try to get them to voice that because you can get all kinds of things wrong, but you must not get this wrong. And to flip it around again:

"Are you doing what is necessary to be saved? According to the Catholic Church, this is what is necessary to be saved and it's from the Catholic Catechism, numbers 846, 1257, 980, 1129, 1816, 2036, 2070, and 2556: According to the Catholic Church, are you doing these, in order to be saved: baptism, penance, sacraments, service to the witness to the Catholic faith,

keeping the Ten Commandments, and detachment from riches? And if you are keeping the Ten Commandments of God, do you go to confession?"

Confession is something they tell you that you have to do. But wait a second. If you think you're keeping the commandments, then why are you going to confession? Again, it's just another new thought. Here's another on salvation, which they don't have in the first place if they follow their Catholic teachings:

Now, here's the big question: *"Since it is possible, according to the Catholic Church, to lose your salvation, are you doing enough good works to keep yourself saved?"*

If there is no assurance, how do you know whether enough is enough? How do you know if you've done enough to get to Heaven? Right? Here is another Scripture question that pertains to the fact that Catholics say they believe in the Bible:

"According to the Scripture, is it okay to exceed what is written in the Scripture and to teach things that are not taught in the Scripture as though they were doctrinally true?"

Well, then would it be right for somebody to appear on the scene and teach something outside the Bible that doesn't agree with the Bible? The answer you should hear is, "absolutely not!" Our response: "Then why do you listen to the popes? Why do you pray to Mary? Why do you pray to saints? Why is it that when the Bible says salvation is not of works lest anyone should boast and only Christ can forgive our sin, why are you trying to do works for your salvation? There's another new thought for them.

Are Catholics even saved?
Let's take a look at it:

"That's the most crucial question, obviously. Is belief alone, in Christ, sufficient for salvation?"

Well, do Catholics themselves believe that? Unfortunately, the answer is, "no."

The Bible clearly and consistently states that receiving Jesus Christ as Savior by grace through faith, is how you get saved. But the Roman Catholic

Church rejects this. The official position of the Roman Catholic Church is that a person must believe in Jesus Christ and be baptized and receive the Eucharist, along with all the other sacraments, and obey the decrees of the Roman Catholic Church, and perform meritorious works, and not die with any mortal sins, and etc., etc., etc. So, the Catholic divergence from the Bible on this critical issue of salvation means 'yes,' Catholicism is a false Gospel. Therefore, if a person believes what the Catholic Church officially teaches, he or she *cannot and will not ever be saved*. Any claim that works or rituals must be added to faith in order for salvation to be achieved, is a claim that Jesus' death was not sufficient to fully purchase our salvation.

I've said it before: I don't care who they are, if anyone says to you that salvation is from "Jesus and..., Jesus or..., or Jesus but...," that's not the Gospel. That is what the Catholic Church does and from there they even keep going on and on; over and over again. It's not the Gospel.

What about the person that says, "Well, I know of a guy who's in the Catholic Church and I know he's a born-again Christian." Let's examine that with a first point:

"It's impossible to give a universal statement on the salvation of all members of any denomination."

Are all Baptists saved? If you believe that, I've got some swampland to sell you. Give me a break. No, we don't know that all Baptists are saved, right? You can't say everyone who goes to a Baptist Church is saved. Are all Presbyterian or Lutherans saved? No, of course not.

"Salvation is determined by a personal faith in Jesus Christ alone for salvation, not by titles and not by denomination affiliation, despite the unbiblical beliefs and practices of the Roman Catholic Church..,"

Of course, there is the possibility that someone in their midst is a born-gain Christian. But listen:

"However, they have to be and must be believers despite what the Catholic Church teaches..."

So, it won't be because of what Catholicism teaches. They had to have gotten it from somewhere else. But again, you can't take something that has a small possibility of happening like a Catholic finding salvation, despite the doctrine they follow, and then say you'll accept that the whole Catholic following is saved. It's ridiculous. We don't even claim that in Protestant denominations. But here's more to that point:

"However, they have to be and must be believers despite what the Catholic Church teaches, and they remain in the Catholic Church out of ignorance of what the Catholic Church truly stands for or [Here's a big one] out of family tradition, family and peer pressure, or they have a desire to reach other Catholics for Christ."

And some of those type people are in the Catholic Church. I've run into Catholics who I really think are born again. They'll say things like, "I know it's wrong and I don't believe all this stuff and it's a bunch of baloney, but I'm staying behind because I'm going to help them out. I'm going to reform them."

But you're never going to change the Roman Catholic Church. And eventually, just like what happened with some folks who are now at my church, when the Catholic Church finds out you're teaching the Bible, they're going to kick you out. They won't wait for you to leave. Just look back at what we saw in an earlier chapter. Catholicism teaches that everything we Christians believe about the Gospel is an anathema. They say we are the cursed ones. So, if Catholicism finds the very unlikely person in their midst that somehow got saved outside the Catholic Church, and if that saved person actually starts to teach the Bible, that Christian is going to be kicked out. It's the reality of what goes on there.

"At the same time, the Catholic Church obviously leads people astray, away from the genuine faith."

Again, Catholicism says we Christians are the cursed ones because of what we believe.

"Jesus' words in Mark 7:9, directed toward the Pharisees, describes the Roman Catholic Church: 'you have a fine way of setting aside the commands of God in order to observe your own traditions.'"

So again, how do we witness to these guys? Well, first of all, they have been brainwashed from wee-high and that includes expecting resistance from the Protestants. Because of that, when they come across you, they already have a negative mind-set about Protestant witnessing. If they are just waiting for Protestants to start saying the Pope is wrong and the Mary stuff is an abomination, what then is the best way to reach them because they may be ready to just shut you off? I'm not saying you shouldn't ever talk about those things. If God leads you, then more power to you! But typically, a better approach is to not necessarily go down that route at that time. If they truly get saved, God is going to start cleaning them up as they get into the Bible. He'll take care of that stuff.

The goal is to get them to ponder the new thoughts: "Have you ever thought about…?" Just try to place some new thoughts in their mind. Bring out some of those inconsistencies about Catholicism and do it in love. Don't overwhelm them by throwing up your information on them all at once, but just reach it out, then get them a Bible, and get them to read the Bible. When you're making points, point out passages. Be able to defend it Biblically. There's something about reading the Bible. With one lady I witnessed to in my California office at that time, we were going back and forth and I was getting nowhere. It was like talking to a concrete wall until we got to the issue of works. I obviously had my Bible with me, so I flipped through to the right verses as she scooted up to my desk. I said, "Could you read this for me? This is in the Bible." She obviously respected the Bible so I asked if she would read Ephesians 2:8-9.

She read that and then started her attempt to disagree but then stopped. I saw her countenance literally change right before my eyes after reading just these two verses from the Bible: *"For by Grace you have been saved through faith; and that not of yourselves, it is the gift of God; not as a result of works, so that no one may boast."* She stopped with her mouth open. She said, nobody ever told me. It was the first time she'd ever seen that. Catholics are not encouraged to read the Bible.

So, there is the power of the Spirit of God from the Word of God and you combine it with new thoughts. Just draw them out and build that relationship so that they will be more open to what you share. Ask if they can read certain Bible verses for you. There's something about the Word of God that will begin to have a strong influence on them.

I have many testimonies from former Catholics and most all of them say the same thing when asked what it was that drew them out. It was that they began to read the Bible for themselves. Over and over again, that was the case. We don't have space here for me to share all of them but understand that these Christians are in the mission field witnessing even to the Catholic priesthood and monks. It doesn't matter the level in the Catholic Church, it's usually the same thing: they got acquainted with the Bible and began to see, from the Bible, that what they were being taught was completely wrong. Listen to what this ex-Catholic said who was with the Order of the Hermits of St. Augustine:

"Ignorance and superstition and idolatry are everywhere in the Catholic Church, and little effort, if any, is made to change the situation. Instead of following Christianity taught in the Bible, the people concentrate on the worship of statues and their local patrons as saints. [Listen to this.] When I was in Cuba, I met a genuine pagan who worshiped idols (a religion transplanted from Africa by his ancestors). I asked him (as I was Catholic at that time), how he could believe that a plaster idol could help him. The pagan replied that 'the idol was not expected to help him; it only represented the power in Heaven which could.' What horrified me about his reply was that it was almost word for word the explanation Roman Catholics give for rendering honor to the statues of saints." It's just pagan worship. Another guy said this about the time when he started reading the Bible:

"I gradually observed a wonderful change. With subjects such as the primacy of Peter, papal infallibility, the priesthood, infant baptism, confession, the mass, purgatory, the immaculate conception of Mary, and the bodily assumption of Mary, in time I realized that not only are these beliefs not in the Bible, they are actually contrary to the clear teaching of Scripture."

Did anybody have to give him a sermon on this? No. What did he get acquainted with? He started reading the Bible; the Word of God. So, drop new thoughts and get them into the Bible. There's something about that combination. At this point, they don't necessarily need to realize that Saint Malachy catch-a-fly, or whatever his name was, is wrong. Now again, I'm not saying you can't ever talk about those things, but Catholics need to get into the Word of God. Also, remember to stick to salvation. The big issue is salvation, which of course is how you get saved. If they become a born-again Christian, God will clean up the rest of it.

You may have heard this example before about when I got saved but believe it or not, you're looking at a guy who believed abortion was perfectly fine. I thought people had no right to tell me, or any woman, what to do. That was my mindset. Then literally the moment I got saved as a brand new creature and indwelt with the Holy Spirit of God, instantly I knew I was wrong. And I hadn't heard even one sermon on it, read even one passage in the Bible about it, had someone give me a tract on it, listen to a study about it, and I didn't read one article or book on it, before even seeing the reasoning for why it is wrong with the Biblical basis for why it's murder, with the Holy Spirit's help, instantly, I knew it is murder. No one had to tell me.

I'm not saying we can't deal with superficial issues, but when you're witnessing to a Catholic or some of these other folks, the main thing you need to keep coming back around to is how you get saved, how do you get saved, and how do you get saved. Again, it's because if a person becomes born-again, guess what the Spirit of God is going to do? He'll lead that new Christian into the truth. Once they start reading the word of God, Catholic doctrines like papal infallibility, succession from Peter, and all those other things start to go out the window for them, because praying to Mary is not Biblical, as they get into the Bible, it becomes apparent to them, so don't get off on rabbit trails.

Now, believe it or not, we're close to finishing our study of Catholicism. But again, what was the big question we just looked at? It is whether someone from the Roman Catholic Church can be saved. The answer is yes, but it's only in spite of the Catholic Church because:

"They are not saved through their gospel. That's a false gospel. The Roman Catholic gospel is a false gospel. A Catholic can be saved through the true Gospel, at which time they are no longer Roman Catholic because they've accepted the Gospel that the Roman Catholic Church condemns."

So, at the point where you accept the Bible's Gospel and become a Christian, you really shouldn't even call yourself a Roman Catholic because their teaching condemns what a born-again Christian believes.

Once saved, can a Christian stay in a Catholic Church? Yes, but again, it doesn't make sense to do so. We looked at many areas that there is a false Gospel. There is a multitude of unbiblical teachings; Mary, praying to saints, praying for the dead, purgatory, etc. If a person claims to be a true Christian, yet stays in the Roman Catholic Church, [Here comes the key words] supporting it's doctrines, then that would seem to indicate that they still have accepted the Roman Catholic Church's false Gospel.

They may say they are saved, but if so, eventually you're going to come out of Catholicism. You're either going to leave them or they're going to kick you out. You're not going to stay with them forever. Unfortunately, you're not going to change the Catholic Church because they're not going to budge. But if you sit there and support what they're doing, then it becomes suspect as to whether you really believed the true Gospel.

Other aspects that are also important when witnessing to any lost souls, is for you to:

Sanctify your heart, be ready to give a defense [which is why you are reading this book], pray [It's a spiritual battle. Pray that God would open their hearts and minds], be ready with a good understanding of the Scriptures, don't argue, don't attack them, define your words, and don't get off on tangents. Stick to the important points: authority [the Bible], the nature of God, the personal work of Jesus, the nature of man, and the means of salvation. Avoid the Christian jargon and share your testimony as an assurance of eternal life.

Why is that last one important? It's because of what they lack, compared to a Christian. And if you know about Islam because you've done the research yourself this won't sound off base. If not, then I'll explain but here's what I'd say: The Catholic experience isn't much different from what the Muslim must feel like. A Muslim does not have what we Christians have because they're not taught the whole Bible. They don't have an intimate "Abba Father" personal relationship with God. The Muslim god is not the God of the Bible. Allah is a mean ogre of a guy and there is no intimacy there at all, so what we oftentimes take for granted, which is a personal loving relationship with God and having the Holy Spirit living inside of us, Muslims don't have. Can I tell you something else? The Catholics don't have that relationship either because they're always afraid they are going to Purgatory, so they are always doing this, that, confession, and the other things to hopefully shorten their coming Purgatory sentence while they continue sinning and by that, also making their supposed Purgatory stay, longer.

That leads us to the second thing Catholics don't have and neither do the Muslims. That is Eternal Security. They don't even know if they're going to get there. We Christians don't have to sweat bullets. Through Jesus Christ, we have peace with God right now. We know for sure right now that we're headed to Heaven. Neither Catholics nor Muslims have that so when you share your personal testimony about your direct relationship with God, who is the Creator of the universe, and how through the Word of God of the Bible, you know you're headed to Heaven, it speaks volumes because they don't have that or anything close to it.

Now let's wrap it up with one more piece of advice when witnessing to Catholics:

"Avoid getting bogged down with secondary issues like Mary, transubstantiation, icons, etc., that are not central. Focus on sin and the inability to save yourself through good works and give them..."

Again, what should we give them? The most important is a New Testament, which is in the Bible. If you can only give them a part of the Bible, make sure they have the New Testament, and in that way, you are presenting them with the true Gospel.

So those are the aspects to consider, and keep in mind when witnessing to Catholics. Again, if we didn't know it already, we sure know it now; we don't do works to pay for our sins, Jesus Christ took care of that, praise God!

How to Receive Jesus Christ:

1. Admit your need (I am a sinner).

2. Be willing to turn from your sins (repent).

3. Believe that Jesus Christ died for you on the Cross and rose from the grave.

4. Through prayer, invite Jesus Christ to come in and control your life through the Holy Spirit. (Receive Him as Lord and Savior.)

What to pray:

Dear Lord Jesus,

I know that I am a sinner and need Your forgiveness. I believe that You died for my sins. I want to turn from my sins. I now invite You to come into my heart and life. I want to trust and follow You as Lord and Savior.

In Jesus' name. Amen.

Notes

Billy Crone, *The Final Countdown Vol.3*,
(Las Vegas: Get A Life Ministries Inc., 2018, Pgs. 99-124,230-242)
https://www.valleybible.net/AdultEducation/ClassNotes/WorldReligions/Lesson%205%20-%20Catholicism.pdf
https://.org/catholic-mary-summary
https://www.gotquestions.net/Printer/Queen-of-Heaven-PF.html?_ga=1.12655671.123911806.1483478577
https://carm.org/roman-catholicism-mary-idolatry
https://carm.org/cut-catholic
https://cruxnow.com/Vatican/2016/12/08/today-popes-love-affair-mary-display/
https://www.gotquestions.net/Printer/perpetual-virginity-Mary-PF.html?_ga=1.185693481.123911806.1483478577
https://carm.org/what-are-the-four-marian-dogmas
http://carm/org/cut-catholic
https://www.irreligion.org/2008/03/10/50-people-go-blind-after-staring-at-the-sun-trying-to-see-the-virgin-mary/
https://carm.org/what-are-the-approved-mary-apparitions-of-the-roman-catholic-church
https://www.gotquestions.net/Printer/familiar-spirits-PF.html?_ga=1.176821669.123911806.1483478577
http://en.radiovaticana.va/news/2017/02/22/pope_francis_remembers_centenary_of_fatima/1294236
http://www.biblestudytools.com/search/?s=bibles&q=saint&t=kjv&c=all
http://www.biblestudytools.com/lexicons/Hebrew/kjv/qadowsh.html
http://www.biblestudytools.com/lexicons/Greek/kjv/hagios.html
https://www.gotquestions.net/Printer/prayer-saints-Mary-PF.html?_ga=1.176838309.123911806.1483478577
https://carm.org/praying-saints-biblical
http://biblereasons.com/praying-to-saints/
http://www.catholic.org/prayers/prayer.php?p=314http://www.catholic.org/prayers/prayer.php?p=154
http://www.cathlic.org/prayers/prayer.php?p=187
http://www.catholc.org/saints/patron.php
http://www.catholic.org/prayers/prayer.php?p=1690

https://en.wikipedia.org/wiki/List_of_saints
https://en.wikipedia.org/wiki/List_of_patron_saints_by_occupation_and_activity
https://en.wikipedia.org/wiki/Patron_saints_of_ailments,_illness,_and_dangers
https://en.wikipedia.org/wiki/Patron_saints_of_places
https://carm.org/stigmata
https://theweek.com/speedreads/668384/ancient-vial-miracle-blood-failed-liquefy-thats-bad-omen-2017
https://gotquestions.net/Printer?malachy-prophecy-PF.html?_ga=1.58540906.1988321667.1470080683
http://Catholicism.org/why-do-catholics-eat-fish-on-Friday-2.html
https://gotquestions.net/Printer/meat-on-Fridays-PF.html?_ga=1.124609226.1988321667.1470080683
http://catholicismorg/why-do-catholics-eat-fish-on Friday-2.html
https://gotquestions.net/Printer/celibacy-priests-PF.html?_ga=1.225019706.1988321667.1470080683
https://gotquestions.net/Printer/Catholic-abuse-PF.html?_ga=1.58656490.1988321667.1470080683
http://www.patheos.com/blogs/friendlyatheist/2015/11/04/the-catholic-church-has-paid-out-3994797060-10-as-a-result-of-the-sex-abuse-scandals/
https://carm.org/questions-for-roman-catholics
https://gotquestions.net/Printer/witnessing-Catholics-PF.html?_ga=1.19745656.1988321667.1470080683
https://carm.org/testamonies-ex-roman-catholic-priests
https://en.wikipedia.org/wiki/indulgence
http://www.catholic.com/tracts/the-rosary
http://www/rosary-center.org/howto.htm#loaded
http://www.fordham.edu/info/26119/interfaith_ministry
http://www.fordham.edu/info/20100/programs_and_ministries/130/Jesuit_vocation_group
https://en.wikipedia.org/wiki/Our_Lady_of_Lourdes
http://www.historylearningsite.co.uk/the-reformation/roman-catholic-church-in-1500/
http://www.calverychapel.org/library/foxe-john/text/bom.htm#08
http://www.greatsite.com/timeline-english-bible-history/john-hus.html
http://logoresourcespages.org/History/huss_b.htm
https://gotquestions.net/Printer/Roman-Catholicism-PF.html?_ga=1.212101460.1988321667.1470080683
https://carm.org/catholic-terminology
https://carm.org/comparison-grid

https://gotquestions.net/Printer/origin0Catholic-Church-PF.html?_ga=1.212101460.1988321667.1470080683
https://en.wikipedia.org/wiki/Constantine_the_Great_and_Christianity
https://gotquestions.net/Printer/origin-Catholic-church-PF.html?_ga=1.254747208.1988321667.1470080683
https://gotquestions.net/Printer/origin-Catholic-church-PF.html?_ga=1.254747208.1988321667.1470080683
https://gotquestions.net/Printer/Holy-Roman-Empire-PF.html?_ga=1.250374470.1988321667.1470080683
https://gotquestions.net/Printer/inquisitions-PF.html?_ga=1.112665156.1988321667.1470080683
https://www.gotquestions.net/Printer/inquisitions-PF.html?_ga=1.15147510.1988321667.1470080683
https://www.gotquestions.net/net/Printer/middle-ages-PF.html?_ga=1.255223240.1988321667.1470080683
https://gotquestios.net/Printer/middle-ages-PF.html?_ga=1.255223240.1988321667.1470080683
https://gotquestions.net/Printer/Counter-Reformation-PF.html?_ga=1.11928436.1988321667.1470080683
https://www.gotquestions.net/Printer/Inquisitions-PF.html?_ga=1.15147510.1988321667.1470080683
https://www.en.wikipedia.org/wiki/Congregation_for-The-Doctrine_of_the_Faith
https://www.gotquestions.net/Printer/book-Enoch-PF.html?_ga=1.44002149.1988321667.1470080683
https://carm.org/is-catholicism-christian
https://www.catholiccompany.com/getfedtrue-devotion-mary-pope-john-paul-ii/
https://cruxnow.com/Vatican/2016/12/08/today-popes-love-affair-mary-display/